The Fatal Hero

Writing About Women
Feminist Literary Studies

General Editor

Esther Labovitz
Pace University

Advisory Board

Marie Collins
Rutgers–Newark University

Doris Guilloton
New York University

Lila Hanft
Case Western Reserve University

Mark Hussey
Pace University

Helane Levine-Keating
Pace University

Vol. 21

PETER LANG
New York • Washington, D.C./Baltimore • San Francisco
Bern • Frankfurt am Main • Berlin • Vienna • Paris

Gil Haroian-Guerin

The Fatal Hero

Diana, Deity of the Moon, as an Archetype of the Modern Hero in English Literature

PETER LANG
New York • Washington, D.C./Baltimore • San Francisco
Bern • Frankfurt am Main • Berlin • Vienna • Paris

Library of Congress Cataloging-in-Publication Data

Haroian-Guerin, Gil.
The fatal hero: Diana, deity of the moon, as an archetype of
the modern hero in English literature/Gil Haroian-Guerin.
p. cm. — (Writing about women; vol. 21)
Includes bibliographical references and index.
1. English fiction—History and criticism. 2. Heroines in literature.
3. Femininity (Psychology) in literature. 4. Archetype (Psychology) in
literature. 5. American fiction—History and criticism. 6. Diana (Roman deity)
in literature. 7. Fate and fatalism in literature. 8. Goddesses, Roman, in
literature. 9. Fiction—Classical influences. 10. Feminism and literature.
11. Women in literature. 12. Moon in literature. I. Title. II. Series.
PR830.H4H37   823.009'353—dc20   95-25088
ISBN 0-8204-3025-0
ISSN 1053-7937

Die Deutsche Bibliothek-CIP-Einheitsaufnahme

Haroian-Guerin, Gil:
The fatal hero: Diana, deity of the moon, as an archetype of the modern
hero in English literature/Gil Haroian-Guerin.–New York;
Washington, D.C./Baltimore; San Francisco; Bern; Frankfurt am Main;
Berlin; Vienna; Paris: Lang.
(Writing about women; Vol. 21)
ISBN 0-8204-3025-0
NE: GT

PR
830
·H4
H37
1996

To
Rose, Felicia, and Sarkis

℘ CONTENTS

❧ INTRODUCTION

As when faire *Cynthia*, in darkesome night,
  Is in a noyous cloud enueloped,
  Where she may find the substaunce thin and light,
  Breakes forthe her siluer beames, and her bright
  Discouers to the world discomfited;
  Of the poore traueller, that went astray,
  With thousand blessings she is heried;
        —*The Fairie Qveene*, Edmund Spenser (III, i, 43)

With the birth of the modern world came the birth of a dynamic, new female hero. Her genesis was the result of the revolutionary mythmaking of modern authors, of those poets, male and female, who sought to tell the "other side" of the story of traditional myths, ones that had been the products of centuries of androcentric thought. With the revolutions in politics, technology, and religion that convulsed the Western world from the 18th century onwards, fresh images of men—and, critically, of women—were needed for the new worlds waiting to be born in our fiction. Only by re-visioning past ideas of male and female protagonists could modern poets successfully shape the future's protagonists. This New Woman had to have powers equal to achieving victory in the struggle for apocalypse. She would herald the destruction of stale ideologies, ones become conceptual prisons, to make way for actualizing fresh modes of thought and action.

Novelists, specially, are engaged in the business of creating entire worlds in their panoramic texts, and by the dawn of the 19th century, they were searching for and shaping a hero of regeneration to realize their visions of a new domain. Charlotte Bronte, Nathaniel Hawthorne, George Eliot, James Joyce, Edith Wharton, Henry James, and many others undertook the radical act of re-evaluating traditional representations of women in our culture. Many turned to the enduring myths—of Diana, Venus, Juno, Ariadne, Athena—that had served as emblems of powerful women. The original interpretations that novelists now offered of these goddesses revolutionized the shape of the female hero in modern texts.

One of the most potent models for this new heroic type was the goddess Diana, and my goal for this study is to explore the richly subversive "re-vision" of Diana's figure as an ideal one for modern female heroes. This new type, titled the Diana-hero, exists in the works of many major writers as well as several minor ones, from the literature of the

Romantic era to our day. Intriguing is both the unique line of metaphoric development that each author took with her, or his, Diana-hero, and the resulting symphony of Diana-heroes throughout Western literature. These Diana-heroes exist in a kaleidoscopic *Gestalt* in our fiction.

By identifying and analyzing the Diana-hero, I hope to offer an entirely new, and slightly subversive, way of reading modern texts, and by modern I mean the literature of the last two centuries. The analysis of the subtly radical manner in which authors re-imaged and re-shaped the traditional figure of the goddess Diana for their heroes can change how we see modern literature, its characters and structures, its themes and generic forms, its language and images.

The phenomenal appeal of the Diana-hero springs partly from the revolutions in gender ideology in the 19th and 20th centuries, for of the revived and re-interpreted figures of mythical deities, Diana was one of the most free-spirited and independent females. There was a singleness of being to her. She was a maverick, the huntress free in the green chase, and this energetic Diana was an excellent choice to be the pattern for a female hero who could rebel against and revitalize a troubled, old world. Such apocalyptic powers had, traditionally, been assigned to male protagonists, and the Diana-hero's assuming these for herself was a sign of a major shift in the ideational structure of English literature. Her figure is highly significant of the revolutionary myth-making of modern authors, a field that is just beginning to be explored.

I also strive to show the profound connection between a social revolution in gender politics, the Western world's search for the New Woman, and the literature of its day, which reflected that quest in its re-visioning of a new female hero. Through this, I can demonstrate the hitherto unidentified but powerful nexus between women's studies and modern literature. Her figure was important to those modern authors ready to stir up our conceptions of the world and the role of the female hero in it.

Novelists conceived of a subversive experiment. They shaped a female hero derived from the goddess who was queen of the moon, whose spirit shines, and they transplanted her into the sublunar realm, full of social disturbance and material corruption. In her quest, she often struggles to find a sacred space for herself. She many times discovers a prison for herself, one devised by intriguing males and females, and one sanctioned by the larger society in which she has been immersed.

From her imprisonment, she must, somehow, break free. She may do so by abandoning her confining situation and commencing an arduous physical journey, or she may do so by striving, with strenuous effort, to transcend her situation spiritually. In either case, her breaking free of her entrapment is necessary not only for her own salvation, but frequently for the salvation of other women—and men. Her success is always costly and qualified, and sometimes she is even left amid her on-going struggles at the end of the text. The future of the heroic woman is left open to question. The degree to which each author leaves the Diana-hero in this condition is revealing of that individual author's ideas on social progress and the New Woman's place in our troubled modern world.

By the dawn of the 19th century, various Romantic poets had begun to employ the figure of Diana in their works. Keats's "charmed" Dian in *Endymion* is typical of the initial image of the Romantic Diana.[1] He needed a goddess glorious and illuminating to inspire the transformation of a male questor and worshipper, and Diana, goddess of the moon, was well-suited to the role. For Keats, Diana was a heavenly being untouched by worldly corruption, a goddess who was the embodiment of light, chastity, and rhythmic renewal. She still existed, in the main, in her traditional shape as a radiant vessel for the male hero's transformation, but her new proliferation in Romantic poetry was significant, for the Romantics, as the immediate precursors of modern literature, wielded a strong influence on it.

Keats turned to the image of Diana for another reason, too. The Romantic poets were the first to experience the dire need to create a new world. Already, their society was in the grips of scientific, political, and religious revolutions, ones turning upside down the traditional beliefs of the Western realm. There were crises on every front. England's ministers decried from their pulpits the growing evil of modern schools of thought, from Darwinian evolution to the new psychology and atheism. Even England's centuries-old monarchy was threatened with the spectacle of the bloody French Revolution.

For Romantic poets, the urban, war-filled, and industrial world threatened to disintegrate the human spirit, and in particular its poetry. Edgar Allan Poe cried in "Sonnet—to Science":

Hast thou not dragged Diana from her car?

And driven the Hamadryad from the wood
To seek a shelter in some happier star?

In the midst of this awful fate, the Romantics sought to reclaim Diana's image.

Romantic poets proclaimed that the new world was to be shaped and "made" by poets because the poet is, as Shelley said well, the "unacknowledged legislator" of the world. In their task of legislating the new world, Romantic poets focused on recovering their mythopoeic powers. More and more, they began to turn to and reclaim for their own uses myths, the grand models and enduring structures of once-living religions and cultures. The myth of Diana was one of these, and for those such as Keats, she became the enlightening vessel for the poet-hero's transfiguration. She enabled him, once he was born afresh in her celestial love, to transfigure, to "make" anew, his own society.[2]

The beauty of the Romantic Diana spilled over into the modern novel. Critics immediately recognized Sir Walter Scott's Diana Vernon as a "prototype" of a new class of heroines (p. xi). A parade of praise followed her advent:

> Diana...is altogether glorious and resplendent, full of truth and ingenuousness and genius; and whether she is shining like the morning star of Spenser's Belphoebe amidst the animation of the chase or is seen gliding like a spirit in the dusk of evening...we always find her the same lively powerful being, penetrating into the hearts of men with a glance of her practiced eye and fearless in giving, with all the play and keenness of her wit, the full expression and name to her discoveries (pp. ix–xiv).

Some readers may argue that Die Vernon has now changed from Keats's muse into Scott's modern hero, for she is a free-spirited and brave woman. However, the authorial pen of *Rob Roy* is still firmly in the hands of the male hero and poet, Frank Osbaldistone. The act of poesis is still his. Diana inspires him. Not until the advent of Charlotte Bronte's *Jane Eyre* does a Diana-hero grasp the authorial pen. The power of poesis becomes hers.

The transplanting by modern noveslists of a Romantic heroine into modern literature was itself one sign, among many, that these authors perceived themselves as charged with the same enormous task of legislating a new culture. Both Helen Moglene and Irene Tayler have noted in *Charlotte Bronte: The Self Conceived* and *Holy Ghosts: The Male Muses of Emily and Charlotte Bronte* respectively that 19th century novelists were profoundly influenced by Romanticism and by Romantic modes of thought, and they began to do in their novels what had been before the province of poetry. Importantly, Felicia Bonaparte demonstrates in *The Triptych and the Cross* that 19th century fiction began to assume a serious symbolic dimension inherited from the Romantics, and in *"Middlemarch:* The Genesis of Myth in the English Novel: The Relationship Between Literary Form and the Modern Predicament," Bonaparte further confirms her theory that Victorian authors saw themselves no less than Romantic poets as charged with the task of remaking the world. With this task before them, modern novelists desired increasingly to explore the limits and potential of the powerful Diana-hero.

This desire signalled a major ideational shift in our literature in another way, too. As a specialist in 18th century British literature, Shelly Ekhtiar, has commented on this study, the novel's early female protagonists, such as Moll Flanders, "grow right out of the journalistic tradition." By the dawn of the nineteenth century, however, novelists had begun searching for new "sources of power or energy...needed to go beyond" the early limits of those female protagonists. When various and many authors, such as Charlotte Bronte, turned to "powerful female mythic figures," they succeeded in plugging their female protagonists "into a power source that facilitates psychological and spiritual growth and even radical change that ironically turns them into *heroes* instead of *heroines.*"

One strong final attraction for an author shaping a Diana-hero arises from the variety of her configurations throughout myriad lands and ages. She was Diana to the Romans, Artemis to the Greeks, Isis to the Egyptians, and much more. With each change in name came interesting alterations in her shape. The main, and greatest, configuration through the ages has been the Triple Goddess, she who rules heaven, earth, and hell. To this powerful Triformis many poets have paid homage. She was Keats's "Queen Moon," honored as "Queen of Earth, and Heaven, and Hell" in "To Homer." In *Orlando Furioso*, the poet Ariosto sings to this Diana:

O sacred goddess, who in times gone by
Hast rightly worshipped been as three in one,
Who on the earth, in hell and in the sky
In triple loveliness thyself hast shown.... (I, XVIII, 184)

Or, Michael Drayton praises the Triple Diana in "The man in the Moone":

So the great three most powerful of the rest,
Phoebe, Diana, Hecate, do tell,
Her domination in heaven, in earth and hell (p. 118)

Drayton's praise to "Phoebe, Diana, Hecate..." is typical of the different titles born by the Triple Goddess in her three different phases. From ancient times, the Queen Moon has been titled the "Myriad-Named." Of crucial importance is the underlying similitude among the differently-titled aspects of the Triple Goddess, and that is, always, her power of apocalypse.

When the Queen Moon glowed inspirationally in the heavens, she could be titled Phoebe, and she represented the phase of the bright full moon. When she roamed the green woods of earth, she was titled Diana, by the Romans, or Artemis, by the Greeks, and she represented the phase of the waxing crescent. When she ruled black Hades, she was most often titled Hekate, and she represented the phase of the waning moon. But in all three configurations, she was one and the same—*a fatal goddess*. The rays of the shimmering Phoebe, the silver shaft of the huntress Diana, or the black magic of Hekate—all three could translate a human being into the otherworld realm.

Thus, Diana's fundamental act, in any aspect, is to transfigure the mortal into the immortal state. To Endymion she gave love and eternity, to Acteon elation, then death, and to Iphigenia salvation and ascension. To any mortal she looked upon came transformation, a death literal or symbolic that presaged rebirth into another state. Herein lies the "fatal" heroism she brings to the modern world.

I term this function "apocalyptic" for I use the word as it is used in The Book of Revelation. That is the definitive work in Western literature on the coming of the apocalypse, on the advent of the New Jerusalem. In The Book of Revelation, the "apocalypse" signifies a destruction which precedes a rebirth, one that is no less than the realization, the creation, of heaven on earth. It means that moment in which the worthy are glorified and this world is translated into the next. It means, in short, transfiguration.

The idea of "apocalypse" is as multi-faceted in its meaning as any other idea is in The Bible. It can refer to the internal revolution within a believer, the Christian who is born again in the New Testament, for to be reborn in spirit is to reach the New Jerusalem. One's state in this world determines one's destination in the next. Milton expressed this so beautifully in *Paradise Lost*. Satan loses heaven forever and ends up in hell precisely because his spirit corresponds to the Christian idea of hell, the loss of God's knowledge. This entails a death of the soul and with it any hope of reaching the New Jerusalem. Satan realizes a false kingdom that parallels his false nature:

> The mind is its own place, and in itself
> Can make a Heaven of Hell, a Hell of Heaven. (I, ll. 254–55)

Similarly, the Angel who has been sent to expulse Adam and Eve from Eden instructs them that if they realize a personal apocalypse, if they reach an Edenic state internally, they shall discover another paradise, one equally blessed:

> ...then wilt thou not be loath
> To leave this Paradise, but shalt possess
> A Paradise within thee, happier far. (XII, ll. 585–87)

In this manner, oftentimes in Western literature a hero's internal regeneration prefigures the hero's arrival in the New Jerusalem. Diana–heroes are no exception to this idea; many achieve a personal apocalypse that presages their entry into the New World envisioned by St. John the Divine.

In fact, the transformative Diana is manifest in The Book of Revelation. One herald of the apocalypse is the appearance of the woman with the moon beneath her feet. In the majority, though not all, of the body of interpretation on The Book of Revelation, from Catholic to secular, St. John is taken to be referring to Mary. Marina Warner in *Alone of All Her Sex: The Myth and the Cult of the Virgin Mary*, M. Esther Harding in *Woman's Mysteries*, Robert Graves in *The White Goddess*, and

Robert Briffault in *The Mothers: A Study of the Origins of Sentiments and Institutions*, have all clarified that Mary is, at least in one sense, a devolved configuration of the archetypal moon goddess. And it is the image of the apocalyptic Queen Moon, whether in her pre-Homeric, Homeric, or Christian configuration, that modern fiction invokes in the creation of new heroes and new worlds.

ONE

JANE EYRE: THE CREATIVE QUEST OF THE MODERN HERO

"...the soul made of fire"

The birth of Diana-hero occurred at that moment when she ceased to serve largely as the inspiration for male heroes to achieve their act of poesis, and she began instead to appropriate for her own the heroic role of engendering poesis. Whereas the Diana of Keats's *Endymion* exists in the main to achieve the heroic apotheosis of the male poet Endymion, in Charlotte Bronte's *Jane Eyre*, the Diana-hero exists to achieve her own heroic aims. Bronte re-visions and re-writes the myth of Diana so that Jane Eyre, modelled on the goddess, can realize her own heroic goals and life. Eyre, the poet of her own life, embarks to forge her own identity and discover a new world. She embarks on a quest for her own creative generation.

It is Jane herself, not Rochester, who is the shaper and the author of the novel. In the pre-modern, and romantic novels, of Sir Walter Scott, the glorious Diana Vernon is splendid, and she, like Keats's Dian, is a radiant woman typed after the glowing Queen Moon, as both names of the characters indicate. However, it is Frank Osbaldistone who writes the story, of himself and his lover, who envisions and records both of their lives.

But Eyre is writing her own "autobiography." Her hands grasp the authorial pen. Eyre is also the novel's "artist," both literally and figuratively, for like Charlotte Bronte herself, she is a graphic artist who sketches the world and other characters. She is often identified as the most skilled "artist" in the novel:

> [The Rivers] discovered I could draw: their pencils and colour-boxes were immediately at my service. My skill, greater in this one point than theirs, surprised and charmed them (p. 308).[1]

Eyre's being an artist, as well as a biographer, will prove to be a critical hint to the symbolic import of her role as a poetic shaper and hero.

The "Type" of Diana

Eyre's poetic nature derives from the powers of the ancient moon goddess that she has subsumed back into herself. These powers are many and opalescent, and this is one key factor relating to the archetype of Diana, for the ancients had bestowed the epithet of "Myriad-Named" upon the Queen Moon. As the cyclical moon goddess, she is "heterogeneous many-hued, and subject to all changes" (Plutarch, *DIO*, p. 191). Her powers are kaleidoscopic. And, "heterogeneous" is exactly what Jane Eyre declares herself to be— "... a heterogeneous thing"—from the opening pages (p. 12). Such allusions, along with myriad references and images, continue to identify and to anchor Eyre's figure neatly, and profoundly, as a type of a powerful Diana to the final pages, where she discovers the New World for herself.[2]

Eyre's name is another significant hint to her identity, for within the text, it is associated with the moon's ethereal regions. Right after meeting Eyre, Rochester tells Adele Varens that he wants to go live in one of the "white valleys" filled with "manna" on the moon, and he explains that "Fire rises out of the lunar mountains" (p. 234). Adele objects that it is impossible for Rochester and Eyre to reach this celestial paradise because there is no road to the moon, one has to go through air. But "Eyre" is precisely Jane's name, and precisely how Adele mispronounces it when the two meet: "Aire?" (p. 89). Rochester reinforces the connection between Eyre and air when he proclaims she is "just after the desire of my heart,—delicate and aerial" (p. 227).

Studying the aerial sphere of the moon reveals another relevant aspect of the deity. Plutarch, in his lengthy treatise on the moon, wrote of her airy, paradisiacal, and fiery nature. He claimed that the airs of the moon, so smooth and harmonious, make her no less than a "celestial earth" for the moon garners the pure light and warmth of the heavens, to create gleaming fires of beauty:

> ...regions of marvellous beauty and mountains flaming bright and...zones of royal purple with gold and silver not scattered in her depths but bursting forth in abundance on the plains or openly visible on the smooth heights (*Moralia*, XII, p. 141).

Fiery imagery is traditional in literary descriptions of the moon and her goddess. In *The Golden Ass*, Apuleius describes his vision of Isis, the ancient Egyptian goddess of the moon, "...and in the middle of [the stars] was placed the moon in mid-month, which shone like a flame of fire" (p. 545).

Rochester's descriptions of "fire" rising out of lunar mountains parallels this traditional imagery of the moon and her goddess, as does his declaration on that moonlit night when he and Eyre first reveal their love for one another:

I have seen what a fire-spirit you can be when you are indignant. You glowed in the cool moonlight last night, when you mutinied against fate, and claimed your rank as my equal (p. 230).

Repeatedly, he uses such allusions. He claims that he loves her for she is "the soul made of fire" (p. 229).

Charlotte Bronte's early poetry indicates that she knew many of these traditional literary images of the moon. As a typical instance, she ties Eyre, and her quest, to the idea of harmony. That is an idea fundamental to the mytheme of the moon goddess, queen of the harmonious, ethereal airs above this troubled earth. This idea Bronte writes about as early as the age of 14. She hymns to the moon in "Morning":

Peerless Queen of Harmony,
How I love thy melody!

In this context should Bronte's description of Eyre's journey as a quest for harmony be taken. Eyre declares, "I was in discord at Gateshead Hall .... I had nothing in harmony with Mrs. Reed or her children, or her chosen vassalage" (p. 12). Eyre constantly seeks for sweet communion with a mind that is "bright and energetic, and high" (p. 222). That mind will be Rochester's, and their harmonious unions will be soaked in moon imagery: "He saw me for the moon had opened a blue field in the sky, and rode in it watery bright" (p. 244).

Jane Eyre's lofty spirit even experiences direct communion with the moon. On a walk one night, she pauses before she re-enters the house it is opposite image to the glowing moon, for it is a "grey hollow filled with rayless cells" (p. 102). She turns to the night skies:

... the moon ascending it in solemn march; her orb seeming to look up as she left the hilltops, from behind which she had come, far and farther below her, and aspired to the zenith, midnight-dark in its fathomless depth and measureless distance: and for those trembling stars that followed her course; they made my heart tremble, my veins glow when I viewed them (p. 102).

The novel will end when Jane Eyre has fulfilled her quest to attain harmony. She has achieved "perfect concord" in marriage with Rochester (p. 397).

The Signs of the Quest

In all stages of Jane Eyre's quest, the imagery of the text forms parallels between the state of her mind and the state of the moon. The first time we meet Jane Eyre, she is trapped in Gateshead. Fittingly, she sits forlorn and reads of the "death-white" Arctic Zone and its "... cold and ghastly moon glancing through bars of cloud at a wreck just sinking" (p. 2).

Opposed to the "ghastly moon" in the pages Eyre reads during her captivity in Gateshead, however, is another moon, the "newly-risen crescent" outside of Gateshead (p. 2). Beyond Gateshead is this image of freedom and growth, and the image is appropriate, for this is the day on which Eyre's inner fires will first ignite in rebellion. Thus, the movement of the text's images, from the ghastly moon imprisoned in the book's pages to the newly risen crescent on the outside horizon, reflects the coming movement of Eyre's spirit.

Future changes and moments of crisis concerning Eyre are also heralded by the moon. Eyre and Rochester meet beneath a "rising moon" that is "waxing bright" (pp. 97–99), and at the end of the novel, the forlorn, blind, and maimed Rochester stands in the "luminous haze" of the moon and cries out to Eyre for help (pp. 393–94). His call reaches her in a room flooded with moonlight (p. 369). During Eyre's troubled turning point at Thornfield, the "white spirit" of the moon guides her onto the correct path she must travel:

The light that long ago had struck me into syncope, recalled in this vision, seemed glidingly to mount the wall, and tremblingly to pause in the centre of the obscured ceiling. I lifted up my head to look: the roof resolved to clouds, high and dim; the gleam was such as the moon imparts to vapours she is about to sever. I watched her come—watched with the strangest anticipation; as though some word of doom were to be written on her disc. She broke forth as never moon yet burst from cloud: a hand first penetrated the sable folds and waved them away; then, not a moon, but a white human form shone in the azure, inclining a glorious brow earthward. It gazed and gazed and gazed on me. It spoke to my spirit: immeasurably distant was the tone, yet so near, it whispered in my heart — "My daughter, flee temptation!" (p. 281)

The moon is so much the sign of Eyre's quest that its absence is as telling as its presence. Jane Eyre's worst moments, of dark confusion and loss, are echoed by missing moonlight. On the eve before Eyre and Rochester's ill-fated attempt at marriage, Eyre runs to meet Rochester at the gates. Over the open road, the moon looks out momently: "I lingered the moon shut herself wholly within her chamber, and drew close her curtain of dense cloud the night grew dark" (p. 244). The next day, Rochester's mad wife is exposed and Jane finds herself in despair, with a depressed "rayless mind," as rayless, one takes it, as the previous night's shut-up moon.

Moreover, not only the moon itself but its triple colors are signs of Eyre's trials during her quest. The text's images of a "red" moon serve as typical illustration. In *The White Goddess*, Robert Graves reiterates the traditional symbolic meanings of the moon's triple colors: white for the new moon of birth and growth, blood red [or golden red] for the full moon of passion, conflagration, and apocalypse, and black for the waning moon of death and divination.

Bronte employs images of a red moon as an emblem of emotional passions and conflagrations.[3] On the night before the false marriage ceremony, Eyre runs through a landscape of rain, wind, and broken trees:

As I looked up at them, the moon appeared momentarily in that part of the sky which filled their fissure; her disc was blood-red and half overcast; she seemed to throw on me one bewildered, dreary glance, and buried herself again instantly in the deep drift of cloud" (p. 243).

Or, Rochester describes the night on which he was tempted by an infernal vision of regeneration that consisted of flight from the burning tropics and his "lunatic" wife:

the moon was setting in the waves, broad and red, like a hot cannon-ball—she threw her last bloody glance over a world quivering with the ferment of tempest. I was physically influenced by the atmosphere and scene, and my ears were filled with the curses the maniac still shrieked out (p. 271).

This traditional context of the "red" moon increases the significance of Jane Eyre and her "madness" in the "red" room, too, for there she discovers, and indeed is terrified by, her own fiery nature as a Diana-type.

An analysis of that scene also provides a key to grasping the meaning of the other moon imagery—gleams of light, white thrones, and bewitching spirits—which flood the "red" room. Ten-year-old Eyre turns to the "dimly gleaming mirror" in the red room, and there her mind is first troubled:

my fascinated glance involuntarily explored the depth it revealed. All looked colder and darker in that visionary hollow than in reality: and the strange little figure there gazing at me, with a white face and arms specking the gloom, and glittering eyes of fear moving where all else was still, had the effect of a real spirit (pp. 9–11).

The moon, and her goddess, have traditionally and extensively been associated with mirrors. Lunar goddesses hold or wear mirrors in myth, art, and literature because the moon's uniformity and lustre had from the beginning led many to consider her to be, as Plutarch declares, the "finest and clearest of all mirrors." The shadows of her face were even thought to be reflections of the earth's great oceans:

Or swell of ocean surging opposite
Be mirrored in that looking-glass of flame.
          (Agesionax qtd. in Plutarch, *Moralia*, XII, p. 43)

Apuleius writes of his vision of the moon goddess in *The Golden Ass*, "...in the middle of her forehead was a plain circlet in fashion of a mirror, or rather resembling the moon by the light that it gave forth" (p. 543). In the "pomps and processions" of her festivities, "Others carried shining mirrors behind them which were turned towards the goddess as she came, to shew to her those which came after as though they would meet her" (p. 555).

Importantly, Susan Finkel Smith has explored the manner in which the moon goddess functioned as a type of Luna-Ecclesia in medieval and Renaissance literature. As Luna-Ecclesia, her link with mirrors became significant because she was reflector of the Light and Truth of her brother Apollo to her worshippers and poets below. We see this in Dante's *Divine Comedy* with its moony Beatrice, "To see with the light which Beatrice represents in the allegory is to see by reflection, hence the stress on mirrors and mirror images throughout that part of the journey for which she is guide" (p. 221).

Charlotte Bronte commits a revolution in literature, then, when Jane Eyre looks into a mirror to see her own image. Her "mirror" no longer serves its former purpose to reflect visions to a heroic lover. The red room's mirror provides Eyre with her first vision of her own spirit as a type of the glittering moon goddess, a spirit that determinedly seeks to free itself and to realize its own powers. When Jane Eyre successfully rebels against the attempted mastery of St. John Rivers, she declares, in words evocative of the image of a rising moon, "It was *my* time to assume ascendancy. *My* powers were in play, and in force" (p. 370).[4]

When we last meet Eyre, at the end of her wanderings, she is happily married at Ferndean and basking in the June midsummer moonshine.[5] The lovers have achieved their long-awaited dream of "the paradise of union" (p. 224). For all its rawness, Ferndean is a wonderfully Dianesque paradise, for it has "brilliantly green" and "cheerful" fields, a "sparkingly blue" sky, and a "wet and wild wood." Here Eyre leads her refound Rochester by hand (p. 387).

Eyre's quest ends when she has joined the ranks of Keats, Dante, and Apuleius as a lunatic, lover, and artist in a paradise. During this quest, she realizes her fullest potential, as they do, to be a new *hero*.

The Modern Hero: She Who Can "Make"

The poetic power of the Diana-hero lies in her being derived from the goddess of the moon, the planet which rhythmically enacts a cycle of waxing and waning, of natural deconstruction and reconstruction—*of the making of new life.*

This natural cycle gives to the Diana-type her potential to be reborn and to be fatal, each complementary to the other. Jane Eyre, true to her nature as a type of Diana, always engages in the act of making, of constructing and destructing, of shaping and re-shaping ideas, feelings, visions, and homes. She sits before the clear embers of a dying fire, and in its flames there is "...the fiery mosaic I had been piecing together and scattering too..." (p. 104). Critically, Eyre herself "constructs" the novel, for she is the "author" of the tale, her autobiography. She is also—like Charlotte Bronte herself—a graphic artist who sketches the scenes, the life, and the characters around her. In short, Eyre constantly commits acts of "making," an act that from time immemorial has been a main symbolic power of the moon goddess.

This idea of a Diana-hero as "maker" has natural poetic applications, for the power of creation lies in words within many myths. The Christian God is *logos*, his word, and he "makes" by speaking: "Let there be light." This power of words led Tasso to claim that none merited the title of "creator" but God and poets. And, from godly inspiration does prophecy—the charmed words of priestesses and priests—spring.

Jane Eyre has this charmed relation to words. She can "read" Rochester like a "witch" (p. 247). She partakes, in short, of the poetical nature of the priestess, the sibyls and the prophets, and their magical abilities with words. When she appears to Rochester as if she were "a dream or a shade" in the "twilight," and she informs that she has come from the realm of the dead, he accurately observes, "A true Janian reply!" (p. 215).[6]

Eyre not only harbors a poetic power to "make," she asserts this power as her own to the men in the text. She creates all types of visions, of images, through words or on paper. Eyre proudly informs Rochester, a teaser who questions her artistic capabilities, that her artistic subjects she has seen with her own "spiritual eye," and each sketch is a "pale portrait of the thing I had conceived." The sketches are brilliant colors and tints of ships sinking, of a rising woman's shape reflected in the moonlight, and of a pale crescent of white flame—all reflections of her own moon-inspired spirit and moon-guided journey. Through her art does Rochester first come to perceive her true nature and love her.

Importantly, the chaste nature of a Diana-type aids her powers of poesis, for the chaste condition gives her the ability to complete her arduous and creative journey. "Chastity," or "virginity," is the Christian name for the moon goddess's energy, not sterility. Northrop Frye explains in *A Natural Perspective* that the notion of "chastity" is *contained* natural energy. To be chaste is to discipline natural powers, in the manner of Perdita's "chastity" in *A Winter's Tale*. Hers represents not the purity of nature but nature as a pulsating power contained within proper and natural rhythms, a power which finds condoned and blessed expression in the miracle of springtime renewal (pp. 151–53). Chastity, in short, not only harnesses chaotic energy but effects its metamorphosis into ordered creation.[7]

A few Diana-types may possess the strict "chastity" of eternal maidenhood, as does Virgil's Camilla, a maiden warrior reared and cherished by the goddess Diana, but Camilla's physical chastity serves mainly as symbol of her heroic and harnessed energy that makes her such a fierce warrior.[8] Many other Diana-types pass naturally into a properly "chaste marriage," a common enough literary epithet. Shakespeare's heroines like Perdita and Miranda do, as does Jane Eyre, and from their blessed unions and natures will new and pure life be born.

Moreover, the opposite of "chastity," in philosophy and in *Jane Eyre*, is the grossly "unchaste" state of those such as Bertha Mason (p. 270). This state also has an emblem in the illegitimate offspring, Adele Varens, of a notably unchaste union. In this context, the "chaste marriage" of Eyre offers to Rochester redemption from past "unchaste" liaisons and the salvation of true love and proper heirs.

Myriad implications of this ideology resonate throughout Bronte's text. There are repeated statements in *Jane Eyre* indicating that Bronte favored the idea of the pagan Diana's chastity over the Christian Mary's. In the Greek scheme, Diana's chastity more strongly derives from the natural world. Pagan authors celebrated that world while Christian philosophers often sought to distance themselves from it. Charlotte Bronte praises the life force of "Diana" Rivers, whose first name indicates her origins, over the lesser vitality of "Mary" Rivers. She even praises Diana's spirit, at times, over that of Jane Eyre, who is cousin to and a hybrid of the natures of both Diana and Mary Rivers:

> If in our [Rivers] trio there was a superior and a leader, it was Diana. Physically, she far excelled me: she was handsome; she was vigourous. In her

animal spirits there was an affluence of life and certainty of flow, such as excited my wonder, while it baffled my comprehension (p. 308).

Or,

> Diana had a voice toned, to my ear, like the cooing of a dove. She possessed eyes whose gaze I delighted to encounter. Her whole face seemed to me full of charm. Mary's countenance was equally intelligent—her features equally pretty: but her expression was more reserved; and her manners, though gentle, more distant (p. 302).

A variation on this idea is embodied in the Ingram sisters, who are modelled on the same Diana-Mary dichotomy as the Rivers sisters. "Blanche" indicates one sister's roots in the white moon goddess, as does the first name of her sister "Mary" point to her roots in the Virgin:

> Mary had a milder and more open countenance than Blanche; softer features too, and a skin some shades fairer (Miss Ingram was dark as a Spaniard)—but Mary was deficient in life; her face lacked expression, her eye lustre; she had nothing to say, and having once taken her seat, remained fixed like a statue in its niche (pp. 151–52).[9]

Blanche Ingram, however, is headstrong, and Diana Rivers shares a touch of this trait. Jane Eyre, the hybrid, contains the natural spirit and passions of these Diana-types, but one mitigated somewhat by the Christian idea of the humility of Mary. It is this ability of the hybrid Eyre to tame her passions and powers that allows in the end for her heroic success.[10]

The Solitary Wanderer

The Diana-type's chaste and poetic power to "make" her world combines with yet another factor in the myth of the moon goddess, one that increases her desirability as a hero for the modern world. Diana is the goddess of those who wander, for her planet is thought to wander through the heavens. Diana is thus the natural protector of travellers. She bears the title Trivia, or Goddess of the Crossways, because in Rome *Trivium* indicated the place where roads met, a public square, and *trivia* was "that which comes from the street," strangers and wayfarers.

This role of Diana appeals to the many moderns who share the dark vision of Celine, one author who conceived of our life as a night through which one must journey, alone. In the modern world which has more rushing cars than living faith, humans are isolated, rootless, and rushing.[11] Diana-types, who derive from the goddess that protected travellers yet who are themselves wanderers, are well-suited to endure in the struggle for order and direction in the confused modern world. The various "cross-ways" that exist in *Jane Eyre* and other texts are literal and metaphorical, as the authors chart the crises and turning points of a character and her realm.

The wayfaring of Jane Eyre fits specially the idea of a challenging, Dianesque journey. Terms and images repeatedly point to a pattern of this idea in the text. In her crisis, Eyre finds herself at a cross-ways, one the same color as the moon, especially that gloriously white moon which will later guide her out of Thornfield:

> Whitcross is no town, nor even a hamlet; it is but a stone pillar set up where four roads meet: (pp. 283–84).

When she arrives in the regions of the Rivers' Moor House, she thinks, "I had, by cross-ways and by-paths, once more drawn near the tract of moorland " (p. 290). She announces to the Rivers, "I will tell you as much of the history of the wanderer you have harboured..." (p. 305).

Where shall the questing Diana-hero find a home for herself in the modern world? In many texts, the free-spirited Diana-hero searches for her own "space," reflected in her journey through many houses. Jane Eyre begins at Gateshead and proceeds through the unsatisfactory homes of Lowood, Thornfield, and Marsh End. Each is a prison to Eyre.

The name of Gateshead itself indicates the extent to which Eyre feels trapped in this unsympathetic home. Lowood is not only a prison in a sunken location, but it is a place of death for many young women. At Thorfield, Rochester tries to snare Eyre into a false marriage with him. He already has one bride imprisoned in his attic, and strong hints of Eyre's possible entrapment permeate the scenes at Thornfield. In the charade, images of a bride are linked to Bridewell, a literal prison (p. 162).

Only after a lot of hardship does Jane Eyre find herself married and happy in the raw Ferndean, a fit place to make a beginning, a place of open fields and freedom from a stagnant society. Thus, finding a satisfactory "structure" in which she can live happily and express herself is one of the greatest challenges for the modern Diana-hero.

Intriguing is one final image of the text, that of Eyre holding her new-born son in her arms. Eyre's quest so centered on finding a space for herself as a female. She fled the harsh oppression of the Reverend Brocklehurst at Lowood, the crushing pressure of Rochester to be his mistress at Thornfield, and the oppressive will of St. John Rivers at Marsh End. When Eyre has finally achieved her own space and life, her son can be read as signifying her acceptance of the male principle. In "On the Moon and Matriarchal Consciousness," Erich Neumann has delineated that the Great Moon Mother's son-lover, and her consort who is frequently a dark moon god, has long represented the male element within, for all humans share elements of a matriarchal and a patriarchal consciousness (p. 224). At the end of Eyre's quest, she has arrived at an androgynous psychic wholeness.

Other signs in *Jane Eyre* expand the motif of Eyre as a wayfarer, as a hero on a long and difficult journey. The text is replete with nautical imagery. This is also particular to the archetype of Diana, for from ancient times, Diana was depicted as steering her boat through the starry waters of the night sky in her monthly pilgrimages through heaven and hell (Briffault, III, pp. 65–66).

Jane Eyre opens with interwoven moon and ship imagery, and this motif continues throughout the novel. The text begins with Eyre entranced by pictures in a book of a ship wrecked and sinking in the frozen, white Arctic, beneath a cold and ghastly moon (p. 6), and that picture is a perfect emblem of her frozen state in Gateshead, a cold hell. Later, when Sarah Reed is about to leave this earth for lower regions, Jane Eyre sketches in her mind's eye a full moon, with a ship crossing its disc (p. 204). Or, Eyre introduces her struggling and questing spirit to Rochester with three sketches, one of a pale woman in the moonlight, one of a pale crescent of white flame, and one of a sinking ship in a world in eclipse (pp. 110–111).[12]

Taken together, the images of ships adrift and lost wanderers in eerie moonlight heighten the idea of Eyre as a Dianesque wayfarer afloat in a difficult world. Her quest is especially arduous, the journey to the "crossways" of Whitcross being a three-day trial of near death from starvation, cold, and rain. In the tradition of wandering heroes, from Ulysses to Dante, Eyre has truly struggled. There is little rest for her, but, for the passionate and chaste Diana-hero, there is also no feebleness of heart. Hers shall be heroism, not disgrace.

The "Woman" Jane Eyre

The Queen Moon was above all "heterogeneous," and yet another element in her mytheme added to the suitability of the Diana-type to be a new hero. In the modern world, the revolution in gender ideology fuelled new interpretations of all goddesses, and of the revived pagans, Diana was the most independent and free-spirited female. There was a singleness of being to her. She was the maverick, the huntress free in the chase, and this green-spirited Diana-type could rebel against and regenerate a stagnant society.

Charlotte Bronte was seeking this type of hero. In her preface to the second edition of *Jane Eyre*, she honors Thackeray as the "first social regenerator of the day" (p. 2), and she cries against those who attacked her novels: "Conventionality is not morality" (p. 1). Within the text, Bronte has Rochester praise Jane Eyre for being one "cast in a different mould to the majority" (p. 118). St. John Rivers repeats this praise: "You *are* original!" (p. 330).[13]

Moreover, Diana traditionally had the role of protector of women in general. She is the goddess most beneficial to other females (Plutarch, *Moralia*, XII, pp. 167–69). She is a model for women wishing to be free and strong, and thus a hero in her vein serves well for authors examining the question of the New Woman in the 19th and 20th centuries. Eyre fits this revolutionary mold. She rebels against her imposed "master" John Reed (p. 9), she protests when Rochester pricks her pride as he asks if she learned her art under a "master," and she refuses to allow St. John Rivers to achieve mastery over her.

This motif applies to other women in *Jane Eyre* as well, especially to another Diana-figure. When Jane Eyre labels St. John an "exacting master" who wants to deprive her of "liberty of mind" (p. 350), she admires "Diana" Rivers for her strong will:

> ...*she* was not painfully controlled by his will; for hers, in another way, was as strong (p. 350).

The theme of female rebels against "masters" points to another important reason that Bronte preferred her "Diana" Rivers over "Mary" Rivers. St. John Rivers states that the Christian god is *the* "Master" of our society (p. 398). To counter this, one must need a "Mistress," and Diana, the moon goddess, possesses a famous tradition in literature of being the free huntress and the shining equal of her brother and sun god, Apollo.

Accordingly, Dante used the symbols of the moon and sun as being naturally and spiritually egalitarian entities. He opens canto XXIX with an elaborate simile in which "Latona's children," Diana and Apollo, achieve "perfect equilibrium" in the sky, like the pans of a balance (*Paradiso*, ll. 1–6; Oldcorn, p. 416). The image fulfills his idea of spiritual equality for men and women.

In a manner that also accords perfectly with this tradition, Charlotte Bronte has Jane Eyre flare up in the full moonlight and declare herself the equal of the Rochester at that exact moment when "sunset is thus as meeting with moonrise" (p. 219).

Her insistent will to live on these equal terms proves the redemptive force of the novel. Through all her trials, she holds onto her best self, and returns with this self to Rochester, who himself had to survive purgatorial fires. Eyre's insistence on nothing but a righteous life has ended in the realization of this new life and joyful marriage, for herself and for her groom. Just as Isis restored vision to the "blinded" Apuleius, and just as the moony Beatrice illuminates Dante, so Jane Eyre finds the wounded Rochester at Ferndean, and her radiant presence restores light to his afflicted eyes.[14]

His first new sight is of Jane Eyre in her pale blue dress and bearing a golden timepiece (p. 397)—the traditional signs of a virgin goddess of the skies and her role in the millennium.

Revelations

In the hands of Charlotte Bronte, the heterogeneously-natured Jane Eyre attains such a heroic synthesis of her powers that she becomes an apocalyptic force.

Bronte emphasizes the extraordinary difficulty of realizing apocalyptic powers through a multitude of other females in the novel who, for various reasons, have fragmented powers, ones which do not possess the synthesis needed to achieve the apocalyptic task. Upon close examination, each of these females has certain elements of the archetypal moon goddess, and a comparison of these variations to Jane Eyre, a figure who fits so perfectly into the idea of a Diana-hero, both clarifies and stresses her unique victory.

The first, deciding factor of a Diana-type's ultimate victory or failure in her quest for renewal, lies in the same source as the idea of apocalypse: religion. Jane Eyre, with her heterogeneous nature, is a hybrid who synthesizes myriad forces, especially ones traditionally allied in literature with the two main configurations of the moon goddess, the pagan Diana and the Christian Mary. The other Diana-types in the text have a nature which encompasses only one, segregated force of each of these goddesses they embody an idea typically linked either with the pagan Diana or the Christian Mary, but rarely with both.

The strongest literary precedent for the hybrid motif lies in the Italian Renaissance, the era when Christian artists interfused Diana's light with that of the Blessed Virgin. It was common enough at that time to add the glory of ancient Greece and Rome to the glory of Christianity, using the former to foreshadow, and therefore demonstrate, the inevitable coming and superiority of the latter. In this framework, Diana was typed to prefigure the Virgin. In Boccaccio's *Nymphs of Fiesole*, the "Blessed Lady" Diana prefigures the awe-inspiring virginity of Mary. In Dante's *Purgatorio*, Mary reigns supreme in the skies as Holy Chastity while Diana reflects Mary's virtue on earth, reigning as Natural Chastity.

This literary heritage is critical to understanding *Jane Eyre*. The Rivers sisters of the novel are, for instance, created on the same idea. The soft-spoken "Mary" Rivers marries a clergyman, a man devoted to the heavenly sphere, while the active "Diana" Rivers marries a gallant officer, a man seeking earthly conquests (p. 398). Mary Rivers is a quiet and gentle heroine whose pale brown locks are braided smoothly while Diana Rivers is a vivacious and robust heroine whose darker tresses cover her neck in thick, natural curls. Their pattern conforms to the literary, especially Renaissance, tradition of the relation between the Christian Mary and the pagan Diana, between holy versus natural chastity.

Jane Eyre, the synthesis, possesses the best elements of both Diana and Mary Rivers, of both goddesses whose archetype each of the sisters fit. From this, one can reasonably deduce that Eyre specially represents a union, not a segregation, of holy and natural chastity. "Eyre" may link her with airy sphere of the moon and paradisiacal realms, but references to the natural realm indicate that Eyre is a hero of life-on-earth, too. Her figure encompasses chastity of both the celestial and the natural realms. This kind of dual imagery constantly surrounds Eyre in the text. When she comes to Rochester at the end of the novel, she proclaims to him that she comes "in Mary's stead" (p. 385). But, she has come to him on earth, and when Rochester physically entwines her, she proclaims, "You touch me, sir—you hold me, and fast enough I am not cold like a corpse, nor vacant like air, am I?" (p. 382).

There is another aspect of Eyre's hybrid nature, one that encompasses both pagan and Christian elements, which should be noted for the sake of correctness—and because it opens up a fascinating vista on *Jane Eyre* and the exact shape of its modern Diana-hero. "Jane" is the feminine of "John," and that is her "brother" and "namesake," St. John Rivers (pp. 338–39). I take it that "Jane" and "John" not only allude to and ally the two characters with the great St. John, author of the Western world's central apocalyptic text, but their shared name points to their close and critically important personal relationship, too. Indeed, one reason for St. John's temporal failure in his quest lies in his unsuccessful courtship with Jane Eyre, while one reason for her temporal success in her quest lies in her successful rejection of his marriage proposal.

As a true Christian soldier, the most militant chastity in the novel belongs to St. John Rivers. He sets out to regenerate the human race with the Christian creed. Bronte rewards his noble ideal by having his apocalyptic cry end the novel:

"My Master," he says, "has forewarned me. Daily he announces more
distinctly,—"Surely I come quickly!" and hourly I more eagerly respond, "Amen;
even so come, Lord Jesus!"

These last words are a direct quote of the last words of St. John's The
Book of Revelation.[15] That work's goal, the realization of paradise on
earth, is the work for which St. John Rivers exclusively lives, and for this
enormous task he remains celestially chaste. Is St. John, then, the text's
more apocalyptic *hero* than Eyre?

When Jane Eyre seeks earthly happiness in a marriage to Rochester,
St. John Rivers urges that she forsake this mere mortal bliss to become
a fellow missionary with him in the grueling scene of India, for this labor
will earn her heavenly recompense. "Diana" Rivers, queen of the natural
realm, protests that St. John prefers Eyre to be "grilled alive in Calcutta"
(p. 366). Eyre chooses to realize comedy on this earth, and there are
subtle textual indications that hers is the better choice. Bronte rewards St.
John Rivers with the final cry in the novel, but it is the cry of a dying
man. His call to the apocalypse is admirable, but it is a call to an
apocalypse never realized. More textual details indicate that St. John's
inability to realize his desired apocalypse derives from his own flaws,
from his lack of the kind of true heroism that Jane Eyre possesses. Her
heroism is more viable in that it is the one better suited for the realities
of our modern and secular world.

St. John Rivers's flaw lies in his own nature, which is hybrid like Jane
Eyre's. Though Christian elements in the main constitute St. John's
portrait, pagan elements are also present. He is Eyre's "adopted brother,"
and if she is a Diana-hero, this makes St. John a type of Apollo. The text
directly identifies him as such: "Apollo ... tall, fair, blue-eyed and with
a Grecian profile" (p. 389). The text repeatedly hints at this connection.
Eyre is struck that St. John has such "a Greek face, very pure in outline:
quite a straight, classic nose quite an Athenian mouth and chin. It is
seldom, indeed, an English face comes so near the antique models as did
his" (p. 303). At one point, Jane Eyre even indicts him as a "mere pagan
philosopher" (p. 330).

Rivers replies that she "missed the epithet" and he alleges that he is a
Christian philosopher. Here is the key to St. John's flaw. He would be
like other grand Christian philosophers, such as Dante, except that unlike

Dante, St. John never admits his Pride and humbly offers himself to the love and the light of the guiding female soul, like Beatrice. Instead, St. John Rivers lets Reason solely—*not Feeling*—be his guide (p. 330).

When he gives this priority to Reason, he favors the pagan Virgil, the philosophical guide, over the Christian Beatrice, the guide of redeeming love, of the wellspring of feelings. In this he is the "mere pagan philosopher" Eyre perceives him to be. But he does not acknowledge that Eyre is right in her chastisement; indeed, he does not even acknowledge her greater, and more important, gifts as a potential Bride.

Both brides of Dante and Bronte, Beatrice and Jane Eyre, have the same luminous green eyes of hope and fertility; those eyes are glistening symbols of the rebirth that their "bridegrooms," be they literal or figurative, will find in them. In "On the Moon and Matriarchal Consciousness," Erich Neumann notes that green has long been the color of the moon, for green is the symbol of the moon's reign over vegetation, and thus over birth and development (p. 220). The moon controls water, all the oceans, streams, and lakes that give life to our green earth.

Every soul needs a bride, and in this case green-eyed brides who inspire with the light of the moon goddess: Apuleius swoons for Isis, Dante swoons for a radiant Beatrice, the Red Crosse Knight weds the glistening Una, and Rochester despairs for Jane Eyre. But what of St. John's deeply inspired and inspiring beloved? He rejects the idea of such a love with Jane Eyre.[16]

St. John's cold vision of earthly life and love, in his utilitarian relationship with Jane Eyre, is echoed in his relationship with Rosamond Oliver. Oliver almost becomes the bride of St. John Rivers, too. Upon his rejection, she marries a soldier, just as the natural Diana Rivers marries a soldier, a man of this earth. This latter detail that Oliver shares with Diana Rivers hints that there are elements of Diana in Oliver's portrait, too.

In fact, St. John partly rejects "Rosamond" because she is a Diana-hybrid, one who combines elements of Venus, not Mary, with elements of Diana.[17] He knows that "She is well named the Rose of the World, indeed!" (p. 331), the worldly rose being, typically, Venus.

Even so, the elements she possesses of an inspiring Diana-figure would also be unacceptable to the high and celestially chilled ideals of St.

John. Rosamond delightfully canters about this natural earth on her pony. She sports an "Amazon's" cap from which the "wild grace of natural curls" of her chestnut hair cascades, as flow the curls of Diana Rivers (pp. 323–25). She is like a delightfully mild, mildly mocking, and all-too-human version of Virgil's Diana-heroes, his suprahuman maiden warriors, Penthesilea, the Amazon queen with her crescent shield and Camilla, reared by the goddess. She is a very mortal and flitting version of past female heroes.

There are also certain imagistic similarities between the two potential Diana-brides of St. John, Rosamond Oliver and Jane Eyre. Jane Eyre feels much sympathy for Rosamond, and she takes an "artist-delight" in sketching this "radiant" model with "natural" curls in a "dark-blue silk dress" (p. 325). These details associate Oliver with celestial goddesses, conforming to the text's pattern of having a disguised deity, like Jane Eyre, appear in a blue dress when she comes to Rochester "in Mary's stead" (p. 385). Nearly every description of Rosamond reinforces a kinship with Jane Eyre and her derivation from moony spheres. Oliver's voice is a "silver bell," she appears at moments dressed all in white, and like Eyre she is "fairy-like" (pp. 319; 321).

But, Eyre perceives quickly that Oliver is only a radiant sketch-model, not a profoundly interesting mortal. Rosamond is that which her name implies—a quick bloom of this earth, a more ephemeral vision of a goddess, perhaps, whether she fits the archetype of Diana, at one moment, or of Venus, at another.

Thus, St. John Rivers is right when he recognizes that to embrace the "Rose of the World" would be to lose heaven. He aptly titles his passion for her a "fever of the flesh," and he confesses to Eyre: "So much has religion done for me; turning the original materials to the best account; pruning and training nature. But she could not eradicate nature: nor will it be eradicated 'till this mortal shall put on immortality'" (pp. 330–31). St. John's love embodies, in this sense, the paradigm of troubled earthly love. Unlike Eyre, he never works toward and thus discovers a successful resolution.

In the light of the May moon, St. John's cherubic voice read to Jane Eyre The Book of Revelation in the unselfish hope that she, too, would answer God's summons (pp. 366–67). But Eyre had another mysterious summons issued to her that same night, the seraphic voice of ardent love, the voice of Rochester crying, "Jane! Jane! Jane!" (pp. 369).

A Symphony of Revelation

The choreography of brides and grooms in *Jane Eyre* is even more intricate, especially as *every* female in the novel to some extent possesses elements derived from the archetype of the moon goddess: Mrs. Sarah Reed, her daughters Georgiana and Eliza, the Reed's maid Bessie, Eyre's teacher Miss Temple, her schoolmate Helen Burns, Rochester's wife Bertha Mason, Mason's guardian Grace Poole, Eyre's rival Blanche Ingram....

In short, *Jane Eyre* possesses a "symphonic structure" of characters and themes, a structure like that of Dante's *Divine Comedy* and Virgil's *Aeneid*. An analysis of the Diana-types within these structures, of the *Divine Comedy* and the *Aeneid*, clarifies the brilliance and complexity of this in Bronte's text.

At the opening and ending of the *Aeneid* are the tragic falls of Diana-queens. Before Dido falls prey to venereal passions, she is a noble, chaste, and powerful queen. Aeneas first sees Dido after he has studied a mural of the war-like queen Penthesilea and her chaste Amazons with their "moon-like" shields, for they bear the emblem of the goddess whom they worship above all others. This Dianesque imagery carries over into Aeneas's vision of Dido:

> ...And just as, on the banks of the Eurotas
> Or though the heights of Cynthus, when Diana
> Incites her dancers, and her followers,
> A thousand mountain-nymphs, press in behind her,
> She wears a quiver slung across her shoulder;
> and as she makes her way, she towers over
> All other goddesses; gladness excites
> Latona's silent breast: even so, Dido;
> so, in her joy, she moved among the throng,
> as she urged on the work of her coming kingdom. [*sic*] (I, ll. 702–11)

The final, grand, and tragic female hero of Virgil's epic is Camilla, and she is both a high priestess of Diana and a figure surrounded by imagery of Diana, the Amazon Penthesilea, and the moon:

> But at the center of the struggle, like
> An Amazon, one breast laid bare for battle,
> Camilla with her quiver charges, wild;
> and now she showers stout spearheads, and now
> untiring, she takes up a two-edged ax;
> the golden bow and arrows of Diana
> clang, loud upon her shoulders. Even when
> she has been driven back, she turns to cast
> her flying shafts; she is ringed by chosen comrades—
> virgin Larina, Tulla, and Tarpeia,
> who brandishes a brazen ax, all three,
> Italian girls, whom the divine Camilla
> herself had picked to serve as guard of honor
> and true attendants in both peace and war:
> a band just like the Thracian Amazons
> when they ride hard upon Thermodon's shores
> and fight in gilded armor, whether around
> Hippolyte, or when Penthesilea,
> Mars' daughter, in her chariot, returns,
> a victor, and with shrill and shrieking clamour
> her women troops run wild with half-moon shields. (XI, ll. 854–74)

Moreover, in the *Aeneid* another Diana-hero exists who bears relevance to the Diana-figures of Dante and Bronte. This is Deiphobe, who rules in "Diana's grove," for she is a priestess of "Apollo and Diana" (VI, ll. 14–18; 50–51). This Diana is clearly the Triple One, indicated by the various references in the scene, such as to "Hecate" ruling the sacred grove (ll. 162–65). The importance of Virgil's Sibyl and her prophecy of a coming messiah to Christians has been long established, rendering her one of the first Diana-hybrids, a figure of pagan and Christian meaning. The Sibyl especially gained importance in English literature from her brief but pointed role in Dante's *Inferno*.

Beyond the figure of the hybrid Sibyl, in Dante's the *Divine Comedy* Virgil's other Diana-types also receive high praise. In the *Inferno*, Dante first encounters Virgil, who cites various Italian heroes. Of these, Camilla, the purest Diana-type, is the only female, and she is singled out for her great gallantry. Along his journey Dante sees Camilla and the "Queen Amazon" Penthesilea among the pagan heroes in limbo (IV, ll. 124–5).

Importantly, these two women may be taken as antecedent to Dante's grand Christian and heroic females, such as Mary and Beatrice, based on the well-established fact that Dante purposefully absorbed pagan heroes, heroines, and themes into his Catholicism (Ciardi, *Inferno*, p. 39). Thus, the female heroes of Dante, from Camilla to Beatrice, have as one germinal seed the idea of the moon goddess, and taken together they, with the others, would form a resonating symphony.

Considered in the light of this literary tradition, the moon goddess as one germinal seed of women in *Jane Eyre* acquires greater significance, for it connects Bronte's text with a grand literary pattern, with the mighty scheme of truth which all poets seek to discover and to reify.[18] Bronte's text is filled with allusions to the "unity of source" of humans and the "germs" and "seeds" from which spring all natures. Eyre observes many times the "strange recurrence of one image" (p. 194) which shapes and re-shapes itself in myriad forms in the "ever-shifting kaleidoscope of imagination" (p. 204). Sketches of even the most minor female characters are imbued with thematically unifying allusions to the moon. Bronte describes the women of Rochester's party at Thornfield:

> There were but eight, yet somehow as they flocked in, they gave the impression of a much larger number. Some of them were very tall, many were dressed in white, and all had a sweeping amplitude of array that seemed to magnify their persons as a mist magnifies the moon (p. 150).

Or, the name of "Bessie," coupled with her ballads and tales of elves and fairy lands, hints that she belongs to the fairy realm of Elizabethan Diana-types, exemplified in Shakespeare's *A Midsummer Night's Dream*. Shakespeare's Diana-Queen was "Titania," an epithet of "Diana" made known with George Sandys's then-popular translation of Ovid's *Metamorphosis* (III, pp. 169–211). Sandys claimed that "Titania" was the epithet indicating the goddess Diana's descent from her grandmother, a Titan. The point here is that, once more, Bronte's Diana-heroes can be connected with the grand scheme of English literature.[19]

One more critical analogue exists between Dante's symphonic structure and Bronte's. Throughout *The Divine Comedy*, Dante used an extensive and complicated scheme of the moon and the sun derived from medieval astronomy. Dante launches his journey when the sun is at the vernal equinox, the moon is full, and it is dawn of the Easter season, and these "three compound into a massive symbol of rebirth. All things are at their regenerative peak" (Ciardi, p. 340). Dante repeats this image of the sun and moon, in perfect equilibrium, and in specific reference to Diana and Apollo, when he reaches Paradise (XXIX, ll. 1–6). He also applies this sun and moon imagery to the heroes and heroines of his *Comedy*, as when he identifies the fiery Beatrice with the moon goddess Diana (X, l. 67) and God with sun god Helios (XIV, l. 96).

Bronte employs similar imagery of the moon and sun in perfect equilibrium. Not only are her female characters all touched with images of the moon goddess, and the males with imagery of sun gods, but the union of the two, of the sun and the moon, is a symbol of regenerative love and marriage. The nighttime scene where Jane Eyre and Rochester first declare their passion for one another is a symbolic moment in a symbolic landscape. Rochester entices her to remain in the garden with him, for "no one can wish to go to bed while sunset is thus at meeting with moonrise" (p. 219).[20]

In conclusion, it has been said that Dante's *Divine Comedy* is a work in which all figures are variations on the same theme, with each one standing in meaningful relation to one another and acquiring kaleidoscopic dimensions that each would not have as isolated figures, and it has been further said that the development of such structural correspondences is an enlarging source of power in the *Divine Comedy* (Ciardi, *Purgatorio*, pp. 349–50). Given the correspondences between the symphonic structures of the *Divine Comedy* and *Jane Eyre*, then the same can be said of the latter, and especially it can be said that Bronte's text resonates with variations of moon goddesses and sun gods, whose interrelation is an enlarging source of power in the novel.

A knowledge of this symphonic structure gives the greatest understanding to the significance of each character's role and its meaning in the text. For example, the chilly aspects of a purely classical Diana-type, with no Christian elements mixed in, are embodied in the coolly false and calculating brides like Blanche Ingram or Georgiana Reed.[21] They are singularly like the pagan Diana who was the lethal huntress of the green chase.

Blanche Ingram is a haughty huntress of Rochester's heart, the vain coquette Georgiana Reed is a silly huntress of any heart, and both view their men like "prey," ones whose nobility only adds to the glory of their female slayer. The two create a stark contrast to the warmly true bride Jane Eyre, whose arrows of love and redemption, not power and conquest, more silently but surely pierce Rochester's heart.

Every image associated with Eyre is, in the end, somehow reflected and deflected in other females. Charlotte Bronte has Georgiana Reed spend much time before mirrors, wherein she vainly admires her own reflection; Jane Eyre spends important moments looking into mirrors, as in the red room, but her more powerful spirit experiences awesome visions. Further, all the mirrors in the tiny nursery at Gateshead belong to the childish Georgiana, whereas the gleaming mirrors which belong to Eyre are located in the red room and in her bedchamber at Thornfield. And, as Jane Eyre wanders lonely but honestly through the raw countryside in a struggle to hold onto her real self, to refuse to surrender her integrity under any trying circumstances, the degenerated Georgiana Reed roves continually, in search of change, excitement, and a series of foppish loves, in the worn-out world of fashion (p. 207).

This kaleidoscopic pattern of imagery begins to hint at the idea that Diana-types fall into a pattern of manifesting one of the Triformis's three realms. Georgiana Reed represents the Diana-type who is closest to the idea of the pagan goddess of the green chase. Thus, of the Triformis who rules earth, and heaven, and hell, Reed fits neatly into the configuration of the first. This idea takes on further meaning when one considers that Jane Eyre's last name affiliates her with the airy sphere of the Triple Goddess, and her first name affiliates her with The Book of Revelation.

A parallel contrast between Blanche Ingram and Jane Eyre gives more substance to this observation. When Eyre first meets Ingram, for example, she declares, "...Blanche was moulded like a Dian. I regarded her, of course, with special interest" (p. 151). This "Diana" Ingram is clearly molded after the Greek Diana, too, for she has a specifically "Grecian neck and bust," and, like the Greeks' huntress, she spends her time futilely shooting "Arrows" which glance off Rochester's breast, vainly fancying that each of her shafts hits the mark (pp. 141; 164). Eyre, however, knows that arrows shot by a surer hand would have quivered keenly in Rochester's heart. This "silent conquest" Eyre herself shall win. The lower world of vanity and fashion belongs to Blanche Ingram, as opposed to the higher and silent realm of pure love where Jane Eyre reigns.

Even stronger parallels and contrasts exist between the three Diana-types Blanche Ingram, Jane Eyre, and Rosamond Oliver. Jane Eyre not only sketches Rosamond Oliver, the rival bride for St. John Rivers, but she also sketches Blanche Ingram, the "golden rose" and rival bride for Rochester (p. 141).[22]

Then, Eyre chalks her own portrait for comparison (p. 141). This makes Eyre the artist of potential Diana-brides—herself, Blanche Ingram, or Rosamond Oliver. And Eyre makes the portraits of the rival, and false, brides Ingram and Oliver when she herself is on the brink of making a false step in marrying, first the unredeemed Rochester, then the cold philosopher St. John Rivers. Thus, the identities of these types—Jane Eyre, Blanche Ingram, Rosamond Oliver—are intimately connected, however heterogeneous they may appear to be on the surface. To be heterogeneous is to partake of the nature of the Myriad-Named. The characters are variations on one opalescent idea, each figure adding to the resonance of Bronte's text.

Even moreso, all three of the vain Diana-types, Blanche Ingram, Rosamond Oliver, and Georgiana Reed, occur at the three places which Eyre must leave behind in her quest: Gateshead, Thornfield, and Marsh End. At each of these places, Eyre also meets and rebels against a male character allied not only to herself but to one of the three shallow Diana-types as well. At Gateshead, the child Jane Eyre rebels against the tyrannical John Reed, who is Eyre's cousin and the brother of Georgiana Reed. At Thornfield, Eyre flees from Rochester, a potentially bigamous bridegroom to Ingram and herself. At Marsh End, Eyre refuses to give her hand to St. John Rivers's, who almost joins his hand with Rosamond Oliver's.

Considered in this light, Georgiana Reed, Blanche Ingram, and Rosamond Oliver do more than merely represent the earthly configurations of the Triformis. They themselves form a triangle within the text, indicating the novel has an increasingly intriguing symphonic structure—one whose complicated pattern possesses striking affinities to the archetype of the Triple Dian.

The Conflagration

The last sphere of Triple Dian, that of the underworld, is the realm of potent black magic. A Diana-type embodying the dark mysteries of this realm completes the triple-layering of types in *Jane Eyre*. Bertha Mason is such a Diana-type, a female who harbors the darkly pulsing powers of the underworld. In the archetype of the moon goddess, the title for this configuration is frequently "Hekate," meaning "inspired madness." Indeed, the etymological root of "moon" (*men*) and "madness" (*mania*)—and even of "prophecy" (*manteia*) which springs from inspired madness—is the same (Neumann, p. 211–212).

Mad is a fit word to apply to Bertha Mason. The etymological connections go even deeper, however. "Bertha" means "bright," "white," or "to shine," and this allies Mason to the mytheme of the moon goddess in a text full of Diana-types who bear such names as "Blanche" Ingram or Jane "Eyre."

Throughout, Bertha Mason's identity parallels the image of Hekate. Hekate is the dark and hidden side of the moon, and Bertha Mason is, literally, the dark and hidden lunatic of the novel. When Jane Eyre first meets Bertha Mason, she labels her "the lunatic" (p. 260), as does Rochester title her the "lunatic" wife, descended from a "lunatic" mother (pp. 256; 269).

There is another critical link between Bertha Mason and Jane Eyre, too, one that corresponds to the myth of Diana, for it is the fires both females possess. Mason sets the fires that engulf Rochester's bed, and eventually Thornfield, and fire imagery is typically associated with the moon and Jane Eyre, the "fire-spirit" of the novel (p. 230). The key difference, which renders Jane Eyre heroic, is that she learns to discipline her mad outbursts of rebellion with her coolly chaste will, while Bertha Mason's fires continue to rage out of control until they engulf her in lunacy. Thus Bertha Mason, like Blanche Ingram, Georgiana Reed, or Rosamond Oliver, forms another parallel figure and variation on the text's central hero, Jane Eyre.

Jane Eyre and Bertha Mason also share the text's symbolic mirrors. Eyre first sees her own rebellious spirit in the mirror of the red room, and she first sees Mason, Rochester's first bride, in a mirror. The fiery Mason is one more reflection in mirrors of Eyre's own heterogeneous nature, and in Mason's case she brings the revelation to Eyre of a dark and hidden part of her own nature, of the passions that constantly threaten to overwhelm Eyre, as they did in the red room and as they now tempt her into an adulterous love with Rochester if she remains at Thornfield.

Especially, glistening ebony curls and eyes signify the cloaked, dark passions and powers of the Bride which give her the black magic of love and fertility. Thus comes the black beauty of the Bride of the Canticles.[23] Her dark powers, however, must be disciplined by chastity. This makes entirely appropriate the revelation and warning to the future Bride Jane Eyre of her passions, when she sees the "mad" Bride Mason in a dark mirror. In the shadowy lustre of this reflector, Mason dons the bridal veil which Eyre herself will wear in the false wedding ceremony with Rochester:

> ... she threw [the veil] over her own head, and turned to the mirror. At that moment I saw the reflection of the visage and features quite distinctly in the dark oblong glass (p. 249).

Apuleius's description of the Triformis in *The Golden Ass* reveals another point on which Bertha Mason and Jane Eyre conform to the archetype of the moon goddess. Apuleius beseeches Isis under her myriad titles:

> ...or whether Thou be called terrible Proserpine, by reason of the deadly howlings which Thou yieldest, that hast power with triple face to stop and put away the invasion of hags and ghosts which appear unto men, and to keep them down in the closures of the Earth, which dost wander in sundry groves and art worshipped in divers manners; (p. 541).

Eyre first knows Mason by such "deadly howlings" which rend Eyre's night in twain (p. 181), just as Mason will later rend Eyre's bridal veil—and life—in twain. The moon goddess, whose cycle emblems birth and death, has always had these two powers, and two titles, one for her power to join together and one for her power to divide asunder. Eyre, who uses her poetic powers to bring images and lives together, fits the idea of Diana "Ilithyia," She Who Joins, while Mason, who uses her hellish powers to howl and rend, to rip apart the tissues of life, fits the idea of Diana "Artemis," She Who Sunders (Plutarch, *Mor.*, XII, p. 221).

Jane Eyre, as the most powerful hero, as the one who most fully realizes the idea of Diana as the goddess of earth, and heaven, and hell, possesses enough power to reign over her own fires and, as a corollary, over all subsidiary females, including the howling dark queen of the text, Bertha Mason. Only Jane Eyre is capable, as Rochester says, of facing the deadly Mason, of standing "so grave and quiet at the mouth of hell, looking collectedly at the gambols of a demon" (p. 258). This symbolic reign that Eyre possesses, to traverse and to conquer fiery hells, surfaces elsewhere in the novel. Rochester says upon Eyre's return from the deathbed of Sarah Reed, "She comes from the other world—from the abode of people who are dead!" (p. 215). This idea leads to another profound point of kinship between Eyre and Mason.

In *De Iside and Osiride*, Plutarch analyzed the symbolic relationship between the bright configuration of the Egyptian moon goddess, Isis, and her chthonic, dark counterpart, Nephthys:

> Nephthys is what is below the earth and invisible, while Isis is what is above the earth and manifest (*DIO*, p. 189). When the light shines of Isis and her husband Osiris, whom she saves, the entire earth is cloaked in their radiance; however, Isis and Osiris are rhythmically wounded and eclipsed by the dark side of the moon's powers—Nephthys and her husband Typhon. Then, the world is benighted, and Isis's task is to quench Typhon's mad frenzy (p. 159).

That is a task not unsimilar to Eyre's. Her quest, her revivification of a profoundly wounded Rochester, her quenching mad passions and fires, the redemption she and Rochester find from his past union with the dark and hidden Bertha Mason, these factors coalesce to re-enact in Bronte's text a parallel to the ancient story of the eclipse and regeneration of moon goddesses such as Isis and their spouses.

There are other engrossing parallels. The rhythmical wound and eclipse of Isis's moon was a critical transitionary point, from death to rebirth, and on this level it was identical with her planet's monthly rhythm of death and rebirth. The rituals of these transitionary times are emblematic of this fact, for they are held at the "crossroads" of the moon goddess to honor her monthly "cross" from death to re-birth.

Similarly, Jane Eyre passes through "Whitcross" on her journeys to and from Thornfield, the haunt of the deadly Mason. Moreover, Hekate in particular was partial to these crossroads, where she could manifest her spirit to ravish and sunder in wild dogs who circled wolfishly (Kerenyi, p. 33). That is precisely the act of Bertha Mason; on all fours, she snatches and growls like a wild animal; her hair is dark and grizzled as a "wild mane"; she is a "hyena" who rears herself on her "hind feet" (pp. 257–58).[24]

Moreover, "Bertha" Mason, who shines darkly and embodies all that can rip apart the world about her, conjures through her name images of that most famous Bertha, the mother of the Roman Emperor Charlemagne. He was a figure so critical in the creation of the Holy Roman Empire and in the preservation of classical literature, among other achievements, and his image in Western literature for quite a long time was an important one, especially given the imaginative portrait of him in *Chanson de Roland.* Especially, the image of Charlemagne underwent a revival in the literature of Victor Hugo and certain Romantics, the immediate precursors of Charlotte Bronte. The name "Bertha" can be wonderfully evocative of all this within the context of our literature.

Once this idea arises, one begins to note the varied allusions to the Roman Empire throughout Bronte's text. When these allusions are culled from the text, they point to an important scheme of pagan versus Christian systems in *Jane Eyre.*[25] For example, Christian Rome may have been the glory of the Church, but pagan Rome under the Emperors was the Church's murderous persecutor, and Bronte raises this issue in the opening pages of *Jane Eyre.* When Eyre rebels against the tyrannical John Reed, she dubs him a "murderer...a slave-driver...like the Roman emperors" (p. 8).

Over the course of her quest, Eyre leaves behind the Romanesque figures of John Reed and Bertha Mason. On this level, she is journeying from pagan passions to Christian values. Eyre's redemption, then, her forging of the best destiny for her true self, comes with her acting out a quest typical in Western literature: the progression from old pagan Rome to the new Christian Rome.[26] Eyre's nature as a Diana-hybrid would particularly suit her for this journey. The goddess of Old Rome was the moon goddess Diana, to whom Horace sang "Rome is your handiwork" in his "Centennial Hymn," and the goddess of New Rome is Mary, the Moon of the Church. Once more, Eyre's identity and journey can be placed neatly within the mytheme of the moon goddess.

Reference to Virgil's *Aeneid* reveals more on this typical progression. Dido, the majestic Diana-queen, falls prey to a mad passion and ends consumed in her own fires: "...she is eaten by a secret flame" (IV, l. 3). Before Dido perishes, she curses the hero Aeneas that bold foes plague him and that his friends die useless deaths. Dido prays to "Hecate, the triple-shaped Diana, the three-faced virgin" to grant these curses (IV, ll. 707–08), and her curses become prophecy, for Aeneas suffers them before he succeeds in his quest to wed his new Bride Lavinia and found the New Rome.

In notable ways, Mason's life parallels Dido's. When Rochester meets Bertha, she is physically royal, molded like the other aristocratic Diana-types of the novel. Rochester describes Mason as "...in the style of Blanche Ingram; tall, dark, and majestic" (p. 268). Similar to the onset of the royal Dido's madness, Mason's passions grow and grow until her chastity melts in a furnace, too; she becomes "unchaste" (p. 270). In the end, Mason's fires are unleashed, as Dido's were, along with a string of curses on the hero Rochester. Her curses also come true, for she creates, temporarily but literally, a flaming "hell" at Thornfield, one similar to the fiery tropics whence she derives (p. 264).

Curses echo thematically around Mason's figure throughout the text. When Rochester reveals his old and cursing bride to his new and blessed one, Jane Eyre, the vision conjures up an inner voice that warns of the Biblical curse: "You shall, yourself, pluck out your right eye: yourself cut off your right hand: your heart shall be the victim...." (p. 261). That Biblical curse comes true to the letter on Rochester, precedent to his redemption with marriage to his new bride, Jane Eyre, at their new home.

Crucially, however, Rochester is not actively engaged in this quest. It is Eyre, in the main, who carries out the Aenean journey from Old Rome to the New Rome. It is the new Bride Jane Eyre who realizes her best self, then redeems her bridegroom from the curses and fires of his old life and bride Mason. Rochester's spirit may parallel hers in its movement from his "infernal union" with the "unchaste" Bertha Mason to his new marriage with the chaste and redemptive Eyre (pp. 268–70), but the actual physical and arduous questing of the novel belongs to Eyre. The movement that belonged to Aeneas in Virgil's epic now belongs to Jane Eyre in Bronte's novel. She is the modern hero. Bronte, through Jane

Eyre, revises centuries of this type of male heroism by assigning it in the main to the woman.

One more important, and intimate, tie exists between Bertha Mason and Jane Eyre. Every one of Mason's appearances is heralded with lunar imagery. One of the first nights Eyre has gone to Thornfield, the moon's powerful beams call Eyre out from peaceful sleep to hear Mason's demonic howling:

> ...when the moon, which was full and bright (for the night was fine), came in her course to that space in the sky opposite my casement, and looked in at me through the unveiled panes, her glorious gaze roused me. Awaking in the dead night, I opened my eyes on her disc—silver-white and crystal clear. It was beautiful, but too solemn: I half rose, and stretched my arm to draw the curtain.
> Good God! What a cry!
> The night—its silence—its rest, was rent in twain, by a savage, a sharp, a shrilly sound that ran from end to end of Thornfield Hall (p. 181).

Even Mason's fiery red eyes are likened with the fierce nights of the West Indies and its sulphurous moon "broad and red, like a hot cannon-ball" (p. 271).

Moreover, on that strange night when Eyre, half sleeping and half awake, sees Mason for the first time, imagery of the lunar goddess is subtle but horrific—and "horrific" is the key word here, one that explains a point previously considered baffling in the text by many critics. To begin, the triune moon goddess, in her benevolent "Diana" configuration, was the protector of new life and childbirth; she was the mother of the nine muses, and the sender of dreams of bridegrooms to young maids. However, in her malevolent "Hekate" aspect, she was destroyer of new life and children, the mother of the nine-fold terrors, the wolfish one who rips apart (Neumann, pp. 227–28). This side of the Triple Dian arises in horrid manifestations, like the "Night-Mare" who is Shakespeare's Hekate:

> Swithol footed thrice the wold
> He met the Night-Mare and her nine-fold,
> Bid her alight and her troth plight,
> And aroynt thee, witch, aroynt thee!   (qtd. in Graves, pp. 25–26)[27]

This Night-Mare's hostility toward new life had to be appeased. The ancient Romans propitiated this Hekate with torches of hawthorn, her sacred plant, at weddings so that she would not pay demonic visits to newlyweds, bringing death and curses (pp. 69–71). Considered in the context of this myth, the doomed bridegroom Rochester's description of "the nightmare" Mason is appropriate (p. 182). Jane Eyre, who will at one point find herself a doomed Bride, similarly speaks of Mason's midnight and nightmarish visitations: "Yes, that was ever the hour of fatality at Thornfield" (p. 375).

This knowledge is critical to explaining the meaning of Eyre's "Nightmare" of Thornfield as an Underworld full of bats and owls. In her bad dream, it is a "moonlight night." Eyre clutches a wailing changeling and frantically searches for Rochester, "a speck on a white track, lessening every moment." This pale "nightmare" serves as a mere "preface" to the real-life nightmare of Bertha Mason, a "foul...spectre" who rents the wedding veil of Eyre and the nights at Thornfield (pp. 248–50). The dream echoes Jane Eyre's current inability, as a Bride, to marry her Bridegroom and give birth to new life, who will be her son with sparkling black eyes.[28]

At the time of the dream, Eyre's quest for union with her bridegroom is frustrating, and thus Rochester rides farther and farther away from her. This also parodies the Biblical idea of the Wedding, especially of the Canticles, where the bride serenades and pursues her groom until they be united (Gustafson, p. 100).

The central dream of *Jane Eyre*, which has so long puzzled critics, can thus be said to belong to a well-known literary tradition: the demonic parody. It is a nightmare of the Greek Endimion fleeing his savior Diana, of the Egyptian Apuleius fleeing Isis, of the Christian Bridegroom of the Canticles fleeing The Bride, or of Bronte's Rochester riding from his moon-bride Jane Eyre. Paradise can never be reborn in these nightmares of separation, not union, of the bride and groom.

Rochester's first marriage also points toward this dream as a demonic parody, which has been his fate in unions so far. He and Bertha possess the jet-black hair and eyes typical of the Bride and Bridegroom of the Canticles, only the two are joined in an "infernal union." Rochester almost makes a second fatal union with the false Bride Blanche Ingram, also possessor of gleaming black hair and black eyes, and the name "Ingram," "Angel-Raven," indicates that Blanche also partakes of the demonic realm, the "night-raven" being the black guardian of Hekate, her hell, and her bewitching magic.

The nightmare of Jane Eyre's futile pursuit of Rochester, the Bridegroom, who flees her on horseback along a moony-white track, is also a parody of their first meeting. In the moonlight "waxing...bright," Rochester rides his horse, takes a fall, and Eyre comes to him to offer help (pp. 99–100). Eyre's nightmare, then, mocks an event that took place in waking life, and that renders it neoplatonic, too.

Plato offered the idea in *Theaetetus* that the features of the two states of sleeping and waking "correspond exactly, like counterparts" (p. 26). Significantly, he also explained that the realm of sleep belongs to Diana, a deity much admired then, and he proceeds to develop his idea of "Socratic midwifery" by analogy to Artemis and her charges (p. 12). An ancient midwife's chief duty was to make offerings to the moon goddess of childbirth to ensure the bringing forth of fruits (Harding, pp. 23–24). Thus, the symbolic link between Artemis and Socrates is that both are concerned with this bringing forth the fruits (Plato, p. 13). Plato even repeatedly boasts in *Theaetetus* of the fame of Socrates and his mother, one as a philosophical, and one as a literal, midwife, whence he learned his skill (pp. 15; 109).

Overall, both *Jane Eyre* and *Theaetetus* deal with questions of dreams and madness and wisdom; of knowledge and judgement; of true and false births. On this level, Jane Eyre, as the new hero, is questing to find a "space" free of the fetters of false appearances and values so that she may give birth to a heroic life for herself. She seeks to leave the prison of a nightmarish reality to discover a home that will allow the fullest expression of her best self. The text's constant images of changelings and lost infants reflects the frustration and difficulty of the female hero's struggle to midwife her own destiny. Especially, this motif identifies Jane Eyre's nature as inherently radical, for a midwife, as a bringer forth of new lives, is an agent of change, not a transmitter of fixed states (Hairston, p. 192).

Importantly, neoplatonism was influential on Bronte's precursors, the Romantics, whose texts were replete with neoplatonic and prophetic dreams and nightmares. It is no coincidence, therefore, that Bronte's text is also full of neoplatonic dreams and nightmares that have Keatsian imagery and bear reference to his Dian.

Eyre asks herself the famous Keatsian question, "Did I wake or sleep?" in the surrealistic Sibyl episode with Rochester (pp. 172–77).[29] Moreover, the Keatsian allusion is repeated in the surrealistic episode with Bertha Mason, when Rochester attempts to explain away Eyre's midnight vision by falsely blaming Grace Poole:

> It was half dream, half reality: ... In a state between sleeping and waking you noticed her entrance and her actions; but feverish, almost delirious as you were, you ascribed to her a goblin appearance different from her own: the long dishevelled hair, the swelled black face, the exaggerated stature, were figments of imagination; results of nightmare: the spiteful tearing of the veil was real: and it is like her (p. 251).

In this scene, Rochester is being false, not true, which is apt for his life up to this point, a life cursed by Bertha Mason, a wife taken for monetary gain. His life has been a nightmarish parody of true life and love. He will be exposed as the unredeemed Bridegroom he currently is by the very forces he lies about: his demonic Bride and her family.

Charlotte Bronte, with her creation of Bertha Mason, transformed the stereotypical "madwoman in the attic" of her Victorian society into the moon goddess in all her raving lunacy, her unquenchable thirst for human blood, her dark and hidden passions, her ghoulish nightmares and demonic parodies, which haunt the novel—and lead to its darker truths.

The Rose

Lastly, the heterogeneous nature of Jane Eyre includes the mysterious powers that Diana, goddess of celestial and redeeming love, shares with the goddess of earthly love, Venus. Diana is often titled the Celestial Rose. Later, Mary retained this title, as the Rosa Mystica. Venus is similarly titled after her sphere, for she is the earthly rose, the Rose of the World, the "Rosamond." All three goddesses bear a rose as their emblem, a hint to the symbolic import of their sisterhood, in myth and in *Jane Eyre*. Many of the text's females are linked with rose imagery.[30] Moreover, the variations of the manner in which a female character fits the pattern of the archetype of Diana and Venus, whether each woman conflates or segregates the natures of each goddess, determines their comedic—or tragic—end.

Traditionally, in literature, tragedy can spring from a pathological insistence on an exclusive devotion to either Diana or Venus. Euripides's *Hippolytus* illustrates this tragic fault. Its hero, despite the advice of wise elders, refuses to pay any homage to the altar of Venus. He will only honor Diana. His flawed judgement is echoed in reverse by his stepdame Phaedra, who also fails to achieve a balance. She becomes the slave of Venus and forgets all chastity. As Trachey has observed, Hippolytus's fanatical devotion to Diana is contrary to the procreative function demanded by society, and Phaedra's enslavement to Venus is contrary to the stable existence of family demanded by society (p. 105).

One achieves comedy when one strikes a balance between the forces represented by Diana and Venus. Where Hippolytus and Phaedra meet tragic ends, Eyre meets a comedic one because she balances the powerful forces of passion and chastity within her nature. She uses her cool will to discipline the fires within her—especially her passion for Rochester.

This theme has many precedents and variations in literature, which in total create a grand tradition in Western literature. Tragic Dido perishes in the fires of her mad passions, but *The Aeneid*'s comic hero, Aeneas, successfully wrestles with the forces of both Diana and Venus. Susan Finkel Smith has delineated the manner in which, on his quest, Aeneas comes to terms with his heroic identity and descent through this device: he meets his mother, the goddess Venus, disguised in the garb of a mortal Diana-type.[31] This idea is played on in reverse when he meets the tragic Dido. She is a mortal Diana-type, one who appears chaste, but she is ultimately consumed by the goddess Venus within. Moreover, Dido falls while in Diana's garb and on a hunt, a poignant reminder, I would add, of the ideally chaste vows she is about to break.

For Aeneas, two females, the goddess Venus appearing in Diana's train and the Diana-queen Dido harboring a Venus within, constitute his first feminine encounters. Together, they suggest that the hero is resolving the relationship between Diana and Venus within himself. Especially, these encounters and their resolution anticipate his third feminine encounter, with Sibyl, the priestess of Diana's wood, who guides him in his heroic journey to the Underworld (pp. 46–47).

The comedic progress of Aeneas is not unlike Dante's. Dante follows Beatrice, who turns out to be a Diana beneath her appealing Venus-exterior. Dante's transformation comes with his movement from worship of the pagan Lord of love, represented by his troubadour's devotion to the mortal Beatrice, whom he perceives as a kind of Venus, to worship of his later ideal of Beatrice, whose beauty he now sees as an earthly glimpse of a greater Love, the love that leads to him to the highest worship, of God, who is Love. He gradually devotes his heart to this celestial Beatrice, now perceived as a kind of Diana (p. 63).

There is a second relation between Diana and Venus in literature, however, that can determine a character's fate—and will determine, partially, Eyre's. A devout Dante obtained spiritual salvation and experienced celestial bliss by progressing from a Beatrice perceived as a type of Venus to a Beatrice perceived as a type of Diana, but Trachey shows that *earthly* happiness can be achieved by a reverse process of progression and synthesis. For many a mortal woman, a comedic life arrives when she completes a journey from the maiden chastity of Diana to the womanly love of Venus, when she arrives at the well-known literary paradigm of "chaste marriage."

In Chaucer's "The Knight's Tale," Emelye prays at the altar of Diana to remain free and single, but she is fated to pass into a full life and marriage with Palamon, who prays at the altar of Venus to win Emelye as his wife. The goddess Diana cares for maidens up to and after the central event of marriage. Upon marriage the maid must be passed, within limits, unto the domain of Venus; this allows for earthly passions and procreation within the frame of "chaste" marriage.[32] After marriage, the woman, once again, returns to Diana, patroness of childbirth (p. 124).

Sir Philip Sidney's *Arcadia* offers a paradigm of this idea of achieving a balance between the forces of Diana and Venus to realize earthly happiness. He shapes the heroine Pamela as a Diana-type, one in contrast to her sister Philoclea, a Venus-type.

Philoclea has a "loving" mind, and, unlike her majestic sister Pamela, Philoclea struggles against a "fall" from the Venus within (p. 241). In heartache, Philoclea appeals to the moon, to its chastity and immortal realm, to save her "virgin" life from a likely earthly "stain" (pp. 240–41). Philoclea prays to overcome those passions which are most forceful in her nature, for she desires to be more like her nobler sister Pamela, "a Diana apparelled in the garments of Venus." She wants to reach, like Pamela, the "highest point...the holiness of marriage" chaste and sanctioned (pp. 352; 692). When various lovers of *Arcadia* finally achieve this state of balance and harmony between the powers of Diana and Venus, they have discovered earthly comedy, and it is celebrated in a hymn to "chaste marriage":

> From holy marriage, sweet and surest mean
> Our foolish lust in honest rules to stay.   (pp. 709–10)

Achieving this harmony is a hard-won goal through literary tradition, and it is an heroic achievement for Eyre. Upon close examination, one can discern textual allusions to Venus subtly mixed in and around the Diana-hero Jane Eyre. For instance, Eyre refuses the proposal of St. John, a column of celestial chastity, a blue-eyed "Apollo" of the skies, for Rochester, the dusky "Vulcan...brown, broad-shouldered" (pp. 388–89). Vulcan is the husband of Venus, so by marrying the Vulcan-type Rochester, Eyre is clearly passing into Venus's realm. She does so on her "honeymoon" (pp. 396).

As Jane Eyre knows, humans are "sublunary things" (p. 76), and as Rochester intuits, the mortal Jane Eyre has two natures: "fairy-born and human-bred!" (p. 386). As living creatures, Eyre and Rochester want to achieve comedy while in *this* world's frame. Eyre tells Rochester: "To be your wife is, for me, to be as happy as I can be *on earth*" (p. 392) (italics mine).

In short, a heroic woman can aspire to the ideal of the Celestial Rose and the Rosa Mystica, but to aspire to them alone is not to arrive at earthly comedy but to arrive at the earthly tragedy of Helen Burns. She literally consumes herself and dies with ardor for the spiritual world. One must accept this life "*on earth*" to find balance, harmony, and happiness here. The hybrid Jane Eyre, within whom blooms the roses of Diana, Mary, and Venus, singly brings the powers of comedy and marriage to her mortal world.

The Conception and the Crown

Not only does the mytheme of the myriad-natured Diana offer an explanation of the structure of *Jane Eyre*, and of the identities of its female characters, but each of these is interrelated to the others through a pattern of kinship or marriage. For example, Diana Rivers, Jane Eyre, and Georgiana Reed are a triangle of cousins, and Bertha Mason, Jane Eyre, and Blanche Ingram are a triangle of brides at Thornfield. This not only reinforces the idea that all females derive from the same germinal seed, that of the moon goddess, but that they exist in a symphonic structure.

Once this pattern has been noted, one can discern other manifestations of it and, finally, decode with success the structural patterns of *Jane Eyre*. In a text full of symbolic names, "Grace" can be read as an echo of John, "the grace of God," which bestows upon Grace Poole associations with St. John. Through "Grace" and "John," Poole is also linked to "Jane" Eyre, for "Jane" is the feminine name for "John." The Christian implications of these names then echo throughout the novel. Especially, Dante notably expounds upon the meaning of "Grace" in *Paradiso* (XII, ll. 79–81), for that is the book where all is revealed to him—and Grace Poole certainly hides the revelation which haunts, and awaits, Eyre. Thus, the three figures of "Grace," "John," and "Jane" form a triangle on the theme of revelations, the revelation that each hides or reveals, seeks or experiences.

Moreover, Dante surrounds the radiant Beatrice with "pool" imagery because she is the center of the circle of glorious souls, just as the moon is the center of a glowing halo. The waves of this kind of "pool" can move from rim to center or center to rim (Mandelbaum, p. 360).

In exactly such a manner does the suprahuman laughter of Grace "Poole" radiate outward through Thornfield and disturb its inmates, inversely guiding their thoughts like reverse ripples back to the inward, secret chambers she guards. Grace Poole is dubbed a "mystery of mysteries" (p. 178), and at Thornfield Jane Eyre, her doppleganger Bertha Mason, and Mason's guardian Grace Poole form another triad, another mystery to be fathomed and revealed.[33]

Bessie is also a kind of earthy surrogate mother to Jane Eyre, or she is at least the closest that lonely orphan ever comes to such a figure at Gateshead. As such Bessie, an Elizabethan Diana-type, forms part of yet another triad of surrogate mothers in the novel. Sarah Reed is stepmother to Jane Eyre at Gateshead. Reed's cold grey eye "glimmered...devoid of ruth" (p. 30), and this identifies her, with other images, as a Hekate-type. She is mistress of a particular hell, Gateshead. Hell is also the place to which she is doomed to go because, like all the damned souls in Dante, Reed dies unconfessed. Jane Eyre's third surrogate mother, Maria Temple, is a type of the moon goddess, her first name and last indicating her affiliations with the Christian Moon of the Church. Beneficent moon imagery heralds her entrance:

> We had not sat long thus, when another person came in. Some heavy clouds, swept from the sky by a rising wind, had left the moon bare; and her light, streaming in through a window near, shone full both on us and the approaching figure, which we at once recognised as Miss Temple (p. 61).

In addition, female characters who are more exclusively types of Mary, the Moon of the Church, fit into this triad pattern. Mary Rivers is a positive configuration of Mary, one who marries a spiritual man. The vain Mary Ingram is a silly earthly devolution of Mary. The cold nun Eliza Reed is a vindictive, hellish distortion of Mary. All three are sisters to Diana-types, Diana Rivers, Blanche Ingram, and Georgiana Reed.

And, those female characters in the novel who have not literal sisters have symbolic sisters. Helen Burns is a kind of surrogate sister to Jane Eyre at Lowood, and Helen Burns fits perfectly into the pattern of types of the moon deity.[34] "Burns" indicates Helen's ability to consume herself with her own feverish visions, and in this she is a symbolic sister of the flaming lunatic, Bertha Mason, whose madness consumes her, and of Jane Eyre, who struggles to master her own mad passions. "Helen" reinforces this idea because the root of "Helen" is swel, to shine. The suffixed swel-ena, from which Selene and Helene spring, means "Torch." "Helen" is a torch of the night, like Bertha Mason, the moon, and Hekate, a bearer of hawthorn torches.

Over and over, a pattern of triplicates groups and re-groups itself like a kaleidoscope through *Jane Eyre*. At the hellish Gateshead, Eyre lives with a trinity of cousins. John Reed is a tyrant who uses his power to abuse the helpless, and so he is a mockery of the truly redemptive St. John. Georgiana Reed is a dilettante who uses her beauty to hunt a foppish husband in the world of fashion, so she is a mockery of Diana as goddess of the green chase. Eliza Reed is a cold nun who uses her power to judge others, so she is a mockery of the gentle *dame du ciel* Mary. These three form a hellish trinity, who eventually expulse Eyre from Gateshead into Lowood, a bed of death.

Much later, Eyre finds shelter at Marsh End, the home of three new cousins, a heavenly trinity who give her new life. The truly redemptive St. John Rivers raises Eyre from the threshold of death and welcomes her with his warm-hearted and open-armed sisters, Diana and Mary. Eyre has completed an hegira, therefore, from Gateshead and its demonic trinity to Marsh End and its heavenly trinity.[35]

Eventually, Eyre herself discerns and declares that there has always been a complicated but clear pattern to her tale:

> Circumstances knit themselves, fitted themselves, shot into order: the chain that had been lying hitherto a formless lump of links was drawn out straight,—every ring was perfect (p. 338).[36]

As the central Diana-hero, around whose life every ring falls into perfect order, Jane "Eyre" is the novel's "heir." That phonetic variant of her name reminds one that Eyre is the inheritor of a legacy, one which she divides equally with three persons who signify the three main elements of her identity: Diana, Mary, and St. John Rivers.

There is a literary tradition of female brides and heirs, too, ones whose spirits hail from "airy" spheres. The latter entitles them to be the former. Bronte's Jane Eyre is, in the end, like Spenser's Una, who was her father's "onely daughter, and his onely heyre." Una's birthright is no less than Eden, and so with the advent of the *hieros gamos* is the inheritance of Eyre and her groom the raw paradise of Ferndean, the home where they achieve "perfect concord" (p. 397). Upon this inheritance can a new world be built for the two.[37]

In the high tradition of literature from ancient Egypt to modern times, Eyre triumphs over all like the garland-crowned Una; both discover themselves to be like the crescent-crowned Triformis who reigns in harmony:

> There also the image of Diana, wrought in white marble, stood in the midst of all, holding all in balance, which was a marvelous sight to see...[38]

HESTER PRYNNE: THE AMERICAN TRANSFORMATION

"...thou hadst great elements"

At the same time Charlotte Bronte was shaping and revising the figure of Diana to mold a dynamic female hero for British literature, Nathaniel Hawthorne was envisioning and creating the first female hero of America. He also engaged in a fresh vision of this woman as a new type of the ancient moon goddess, as a new woman for, literally, a New World. By the end of his novel, the Diana-hero herself engages in visions of a radically different future and world for humans.

Diana-types are always complex, composites derived from the many elements found—and united—in the myth of the moon goddess. Hester Prynne is, like Jane Eyre, a hybrid of the moon goddess's configurations, especially in two cultures, the Christian and Classical. In *The Scarlet Letter*, Nathaniel Hawthorne associates Prynne with both "Divine Maternity," or Mary (p. 1698),[1] and with the figure of witch in the moonlit forest, or Diana. Also like Bronte, Hawthorne laces his Diana-hybrid with imagery of Venus.[2] The sum of creative powers Prynne inherits from these deities make her, as they make Eyre, a prime actor, shaper, and illuminator in her world.

Lastly, the child whom the visionary Prynne gives birth to is not a male saviour, the traditional Christ-type of her Puritan community, but Pearl. She is, like Bronte's Jane Eyre and Spenser's Una, the heiress and future bride of her world, and her name derives from the perfectly round, white, and opaline stone symbolic of the moon, the one stone that Jane Eyre wore throughout her arduous quest.

Symbols and Labyrinths: Romance, The Scarlet Letter, and Jane Eyre

The Scarlet Letter is America's first symbolic novel, with critics far and near applauding its allegory as one of the richest and most enigmatic levels of the novel (Perkins, pp. 1564–65). Words like "type" and "symbol" recur frequently: Hester is a "type of sin," weeds that grow in a grave "typify some hideous secret," the rosebush at the prison door "may symbolize some sweet moral blossom," and Pearl is "herself a symbol" (Perkins, p. 1668 n.).

Other examples from the text make manifest Hawthorne's intent not only to write allegorically but to instruct the reader to look toward this level for interpretation. In "The Custom-House," he pronounces the faded scarlet letter to be a "mystic symbol" harboring a "deep meaning in it, most worthy of interpretation." In its secret meaning, "treasure would here be brought to light" (pp. 1684–85). The letter is a "scarlet symbol" of the "singular woman" of his novel (p. 1686).

The tale is not only placed on the level of a "parable" (p. 1802), but an important element of that parable is the Romantic. Hawthorne titled his masterpiece, *The Scarlet Letter: A Romance*, presumably for the transfigurations it records. Like the struggling Endymion of Keats or the wayfaring Jane Eyre of Charlotte Bronte, the figures in Hawthorne's landscape are on a difficult romantic quest.

Their goal is the famous one of Romantic questors: to discover "the inmost Me behind its veil" (p. 1670). The scarlet letter first provides Hawthorne with a quasimystical experience of the Romantic kind: "there was some deep meaning ... streamed forth from the mystic symbol, subtly communicating itself to my sensibilities" (p. 1685). Hawthorne penetrates this "deep meaning" and its attendant mysteries in his text. He also announces that at least one context in which the figures of his tale be perceived is that of romance, moonlight, and the dream worlds:

> Moonlight, in a familiar room, falling so white upon the carpet, and showing all its figures so distinctly,—making every object so minutely visible, yet so unlike a morning or noontide visibility,—is a medium the most suitable for a romance-writer to get acquainted with his illusive guests (p. 1687).

And,

> Glancing at the looking-glass, we beheld,—deep within its haunted verge—the smouldering glow of the half-extinguished anthracite, the white moonbeams on the floor, and a repetition of all the gleam and shadow of the picture, with one remove farther from the actual, and nearer to the imaginative. Then, at such an hour, and with this scene before him, if a man, sitting all alone, cannot dream

strange things, and make them look like truth, he need never try to write romances (p. 1688).

Importantly, Hawthorne's images of haunted glasses, moon spirits heralding a dream world, and mortal warmth bring to mind images of Jane Eyre in the red room. On this level, the tales of Jane Eyre and Hester Prynne are similarly structured. The two are mortal and passionate women, erring and wandering, and guided by cold spirituality, glass reflections, and inner fires. The goal of each heroic woman's struggle is that of all inward romantic quests: to realize the potential of the soul, the heart, the spirit.

That goal of questors, be they medieval or Renaissance, Romantic or Victorian, be they Endymion or Eyre, Prynne or Dimmesdale, is no less than paradise regained. It is the lost green Eden, the paradise, happier far, that can be regained from a revolution within. From the preface of *The Scarlet Letter* on, there are constant allusions, both serious and despairing, to this ideal and the possibility of realizing it in the modern world: "...as if the natal spot were an earthly paradise," "...Neither the front nor the back entrance of the Custom-House opens the road to Paradise" (p. 1674–75), or The Puritan fathers of olde Boston intend to found a "Utopia" (p. 1693).

Hawthorne uses the image of the human heart for the paradisiacal grail of his questors, and this points to another Romantic element in his text. In the "Custom-House," Hawthorne states that the "singular woman" Hester Prynne was sought after in olde Boston for advice in matters "of the heart" (p. 1686). The minister praises Hester in the opening scene: "Wondrous strength and generosity of a woman's heart!" (p. 1704). Prynne's heart, however, in the grey landscape of olde Boston, grows "sick and morbid" (p. 1709). The novel centers on the possible healing and regeneration of her sadly "tomb-like" heart (p. 1762) and Dimmesdale's. Like Keats's Diana, and like Keats himself when he faces Moneta, the warm nature of Hester has become numb, reflected in her face "frozen" in "marble quietude" like "a dead woman's features" (p. 1785). Her heart seeks a re-awakening. This is promised, as in *Jane Eyre*, and as in Romantic and alchemic literature, by the sacred union of the Bride and Groom—only that union is sadly unviable in the world envisioned by Hawthorne.

Even the diabolical figure of the text, Roger Chillingworth, also seeks no other treasure than the heart: "He now dug into the poor clergyman's heart, like a miner searching for gold; or, rather, like a sexton delving into a grave, possibly in quest of a jewel that had been buried on the dead man's bosom..." (p. 1735). The secrets of the heart are the "revelation," the illumination, the gold of the physician's "quest." He is on the same quest as the other characters, only his has taken on a perverted twist.

But one key to the text's Romantic and alchemic motifs lies here, for Chillingworth is an alchemist (Gross, pp. 51; 52 n.; 54). Through him the theme of alchemy imbues *The Scarlet Letter*, and Hawthorne's interest in alchemy has roots in Romantic symbolism. Various works, such as Charles Swann's "Alchemy and Hawthorne's *Elixir of Life Manuscripts*," Luther H. Martin's "Hawthorne's *The Scarlet Letter*: A is for Alchemy?" and Itala Vivan's "An Eye into the Occult of Hawthorne's Text: The Scar in the Letter" document Hawthorne's fascination with alchemy and the symbolic use of that science in his texts. Swann points out that Hawthorne's hero Septimus, as an alchemist seeking to interpret ancient manuscripts to obtain the golden secret of immortality, is a meditation by Hawthorne of the Romantic quest, as defined by Abrams in *Natural Supernaturalism* (p. 372).

Abrams explains the significance for a Romantic questor of the links between mystical theology and alchemy: "the inherent tendency to return to the one origin is expedited by the Philosopher's Stone, the principle of transformation and unification which it is the task of the alchemist to disengage and purify. In the ultimate transformation, man will be transfigured and will circle back to his point of departure" (p. 159). Both the alchemist and the Romantic hero strive to achieve original unity, the lost harmony of Eden.

In addition, Jung has shown that alchemy has a history of frequent use in discourses because it affords "us a veritable treasure-house of symbols" (p. xviii). Medieval questors preferred and perfected the ideas of alchemy because they were in "a highly peculiar state of mind in which Christianity and alchemy" interpenetrated (p. xv). The themes of both alchemy and Christianity—the redemption of the original and black sin, the divine revelation of a golden truth, and so on—ran parallel, and this made alchemy become "a very great deal to people like Albertus Magnus and Roger Bacon, and also to St. Thomas Aquinas" (p. xvi). The

Romantics, among others, inherited and appreciated this history, passing it onto their own legatees.

Hawthorne employs the motif of alchemy in this spiritual sense in *The Scarlet Letter: A Romance*. The quests of Chillingworth, Prynne, and Dimmesdale are simultaneously alchemic, Romantic, symbolic. All are studies of inner workings and hoped-for transformations. Most important, Swann has explored the manner in which Hawthorne constructs an alchemic-Romantic-Puritan triangle in his works as an emblem of the artist's quest.[3] That triangle in *The Scarlet Letter* will emerge, in the end, as an emblem of Hawthorne's own quest as an artist, a state transferred to his "artist" types such as Hester Prynne.

Lastly, the text's language is linked inextricably with the Quest. The Pentecostal tongues of flame are those which can—like Hawthorne's tale, Dimmesdale's election sermon, or Prynne's final consolations to women in the novel—address the whole of humanity and bespeak its sympathies (p. 1742). Toward the height of this language do heroes aspire because it is the language of truth, of human hope and of God's knowledge (p. 1768). To grasp the mystery of the tongues, therefore, of words, is to grasp the mystery of the heart, and that is to realize the Romantic, the medieval, and the alchemic quest—now transferred to modern literature, and one of its grandest woman, Hester Prynne.

The Roots of Transformation: Alchemy and the Colorful Bride and Groom

On one level, the colors of black, red, and white embody the transformative quest of Prynne, Dimmesdale, and Chillingworth. Not only are these the colors of the Triple Goddess, of her planet's rhythmic birth, death, and re-birth, but both Jung's *Mysterium Coniunctionis* and Fred Gustafson's *Black Madonna* offer detailed explorations of the manner in which the ritual passage of the moon, from its waning black crescent to its new white crescent, with the lustrous reddish-gold full moon in between, evolved into a highly important archetype to alchemists, who sought to transmute black dross into gold through a process of white purity.[4]

Firstly, black as an emblem of the ritual of mortification which precedes rebirth, is an emblem which points toward birth as well as sin, evil, and death. In the opening pages of *The Scarlet Letter*, this kind of symbolism is at work. The prison is labelled the "black flower of civilized society"—an image of darkness and of blossoming (p. 1693). The image is reinforced again and again: "Let the black flower blossom as it may!" (p. 1759). The physically striking Prynne has "deep black eyes"—an image of darkness and of beauty, and one that is directly reminiscent of the dark but fertile powers of the Bride of the Canticles (p. 1696).

Especially, the Puritan clergy reproach Hester Pyrnne for the "blackness" of her sin of adultery (p. 1702), but that sin leads to the birth of the beautiful Pearl and to Prynne's and Dimmesdale's growing knowledge of themselves and humanity. Moreover, the sin of Prynne and Dimmesdale sprang from being "possessed" by Satan, whose living type in the novel is Chillingworth, the "Black Man" of the forest, and that is the novel's repository and grand symbol of a dark but teeming nature (pp. 1705; 1729; 1765).

That Chillingworth is the "Black Man" of the forest points to his intimate role with both the sin and subsequent transformation of Prynne and Dimmesdale. As Jung notes, in alchemic symbolism there is typically an innocent young lover and evil old man, a motif derived from the myth of the moon goddess. When Jung's description of this innocent young lover and evil old man is applied to Dimmesdale and Chillingworth, it can offer insight into the relationship between them:

> "Ostensibly it is the wicked thief that hinders the youth in his love for the chaste Diana, but in reality the evil is already lurking in the ideal youth and...his chief fear is that he might discover himself in the role of common sulphur. This role is so shocking that the noble-minded youth cannot see himself in it" (p. 168).

Appropriately, Chillingworth, the evil old man of Hawthorne's text, can claim that "portion" of the young lover Dimmesdale which is already sulphur, the subtle alchemic "poison" within him, as Dimmesdale's sin, his mortal passion for Hester Prynne, lies within his own body, and that is a fact mortifying to him (p. 1769).

Importantly, for this work, the alchemical relation between Chillingworth and Dimmesdale, as the evil old man and idealistic youth, points toward Hester Prynne as a type of the moon goddess, the bride of this tradition.[5] Hester Prynne has a bewitching nature, in accord with a type of the dark moon goddess; she has the rich black eyes and hair typical of such figures. As her symbolic Spouse, Dimmesdale is a glorious soul who gives off sun-like spiritual rays to his community. On one level the alchemic bridegroom, a sun god, Dimmesdale must pass through a transformative phase from *Sol niger*, the "black sun," to a more glorious manifestation (Jung, *MC*, p. 95). During this dark passage, his life, along with his beloved Prynne's, must, typically, be haunted by Black Man.

The forest, another embodiment of black, and its powerful magic, especially that worked on Prynne and Dimmesdale, is "so black and dense" that it becomes a "mystery...primeval," one emblematic of a "moral wilderness." Through this the two lovers wander, literally and figuratively (p. 1763). In its depths were the two first led to commit their passionate sin.

But they do not only wander there. A natural version of the alchemical *coniunctionis* takes places in the forest's blackness. Sunshine pierces, floods, and gladdens the shadowy woods. It touches with joy "each green leaf, transmuting the yellow fallen ones to gold." This beautiful transfiguration prefigures Hester Prynne's transfiguration, moments later. Amid the "wood's heart of mystery, which had become a mystery of joy," the natural love of Prynne and Dimmesdale arises from the "deathlike slumber" of their entombed hearts. The "radiance" of their hearts is reborn and shines anew amidst the "great black forest" which embodies the "sympathy of Nature" (p. 1774). The dark forest, then, is a dual image of black error and blossoming, one that is both conducive to and emblematic of the struggles and future transformations of Prynne and Dimmesdale.

Especially, the work of minister and scholar Gustafson notes that Jung demonstrated alchemy is a highly developed psychological metaphor, and Gustafson's studies are well applied to *The Scarlet Letter* on many points of its alchemy, especially the alchemic role and identity of Hester Prynne. Gustafson makes enlightening commentary on the dark figure of the Black Madonna as a religious and psychological metaphor. Her figure is usually located in a dark forest, a place of natural, mysterious, and cathedral-like majesty (Gustafson, pp. 5; 28; 82-83; 86-99). Now Prynne is, exactly, a darkly shadowed figure of Divine Maternity from the opening pages of the text (p. 1698). She is, archetypally, a wonderful living idea of a Black Madonna, one with special affinities to the wild, dark forest (p. 1709), and in this sense she fits perfectly the idea of a Christian Moon of the Church who has reclaimed to herself the entire spectrum of powers—black as well as white—alloted to the original triune moon goddess.

A second color important to Hawthorne's text, and alchemy, is red. Scarlet "fire" kindles and sears the souls of all three main characters. Like black, the red of such fires not only points to destruction but to renewal. In alchemy, these fires refine the elements that they engulf for entry into a higher state (Gustafson, p. 38). They have this effect on Hawthorne's creations. Chillingworth, the novel's alchemist, labels his wife's letter the "bale-fire...of our path" (p. 1707), for it signals indeed that they have started on a path. As an alchemic journey, it is necessarily scorching.

Prynne finds that the "fatal symbol," the burning letter, has given her a "new sense." With her searing mortification comes a "sympathetic knowledge of the hidden sin in other hearts. She was terror-stricken by the revelations that were thus made" (p. 1713). She is receiving "intimations," for her feverishly heightened perceptions embody "truth," that Romantic gold (p. 1713). As Vivan states, "Fire, which alone makes for transformation, is within the letter" (p. 79), and it is Prynne who is bearer of this letter, publicly as well as privately, throughout the text, pointing to the central heroism of her role, especially as an agent of change.

Further, in the text's interwoven imagery of scarlet and black, touched with sun-gold, lie more indications of Prynne as a fulfillment of the idea of a Diana-bride, and a truly dynamic one. Jung and Gustafson observe that blackness plays a special role with the Bride of the Canticles in the alchemical tradition. Commenting on the Song of Songs, Gustafson writes, "Many alchemical writings pick up on this love dialogue, as described in Jung's *Mysterium Coniunctionis*, where the Shulamite corresponds to the "nigredo," the black initial stage of the alchemical process.... She is that which must be transformed. In the end, there is to be a union of bride and groom, sun and moon, where the Shulamite will take on the attributes of the sun—that is her head will be of gold. The

hair of the [Black Madonna] of Einsiedeln is also tinted with gold."
Typically, her clothing is also embroidered with tinges of gold (p.101).

In Hawthorne's novel, Prynne, as the alchemic woman, is this bride,
and a hint is that her scarlet letter, derived from her black sin, is touched
by flourishes of gold thread. Critically, these significant colors are created
and united in her own art. She works the transformations. And the
outcome of her creative fancies, her golden embroidery, proceeds to
enrich the "sable simplicity" of her community (p. 1710). She is, indeed,
emerging as figure who could be a transformative "poet" of her world.

Ultimately, one of the grand tragedies of the novel is the impossibility
of *coniunctio* in this lower world, of Prynne, the black-eyed Bride, to
achieve earthly union with her lover, Arthur Dimmesdale. From the union
of their equally poetic natures spiritual wealth could have sprung. Hester's
greatest dream was that someday she and Dimmesdale would achieve a
"union," a "marriage-altar" of any kind, even if it be, for their earthly sin,
a "joint futurity of endless retribution" (p. 1710). Their entrance into the
Jerusalem of the next world is assured by the end of the text, but while
on earth the Bride and her Beloved will forever lie beneath the same
tombstone, but separate. Paradise will not be regained in olde Boston.

One last image of alchemy places Prynne and Dimmesdale within the
context of the tradition of the Bride and Bridegroom in Western literature,
especially as they are imaged in the Canticles. Repeatedly, Prynne is
labelled the scarlet woman, and Dimmesdale the sainted white minister.
The texts of alchemy contain numerous allusions not only to the Song of
Songs, but to its particular details, especially its cry, "My beloved is white
and ruddy" (p. 17). Much of alchemy, therefore, came to allude to a
unification of the red woman and white man, or the white woman and red
man, as the states of the archetypal moon-bride and sun-groom begin to
rhythmically change (pp. 50; 69; 129; 230; 377)—and here we have the
scarlet woman and the sainted white minister.

Moreover, the alchemic process begins with the ritual wounding of the
bridegroom derived from Song of Songs: "Thou hast wounded my heart,
my sister, my spouse...." (pp. 31; 50). That is an apt description of
beginning of the novel, which opens with the freshly wounded hearts of
two lovers, especially the lover Dimmesdale who keeps continually his
hand over his sore heart. Their wounds indicate the beginning of the
process of healing and transformation.

Moon Magic

Black Magic, Scarlet Magic, and White Magic. In *The Scarlet Letter*, the triune colors play a crucial role in the nature of Hester Prynne as a poet. First, Hawthorne not only singles out black as a symbol both diabolical and powerful, but one reason for this is that the underworld aspect of Diana, or Hekate, is the most potent configuration of the Triformis.[6] For example, the Black Man Chillingworth is a type of warlock, for his powers are those of the shadowed underworld sphere and its witches. Hester early on perceives that Chillingworth is The Black Man associated with the witch sabbaths in the forests surrounding olde Boston (Gross, p. 55 n.), and Hester must know for her scarlet letter is the token of her own attendance in the dark forest (Gross, p. 163). In this sense, Chillingworth is properly the husband of Hester Prynne as a Diana-hero, one whose beauty so bewitches and leads herself and Dimmesdale into the dark forest.

The theme is a carefully crafted one for Hawthorne. Associations between the Black Man and witches are strong elsewhere in Hawthorne's writings. "Young Goodman Brown" would be one good example. Other allusions within *The Scarlet Letter* itself suffice to demonstrate the strength of this idea in the text. The Puritans believe in the superstitions of witchcraft and think Pearl is a "demon offspring," a child of Satan or his emissary, who is The Black Man. Their real belief is echoed and quite strengthened by the allusions to real life figures in the early American drama of witch persecution. Ann Hibbins, a figure who appears and reappears throughout the novel to remind others of witch sabbaths, and particularly to remind Hester and Pearl of their close tie to The Black Man, was actually "put to death as a witch in 1656," for instance, and Increase Mather, who earned "dubious fame as a persecutor of witches," is considered a model of success for Puritan priests in olde Boston (Gross, pp. 37 n.; 55 n.; 69 n.; 81; 161 n.; 164).

Moreover, Chillingworth is not only Prynne's husband, but he is so in an occult manner, for it is a secret between them. When Chillingworth comes to Hester, he immediately informs her of new secrets learned in his old trade. He talks to her of both his old identity as an alchemist, and his new one: "My old studies in alchemy...and my sojourn, for above a year past, among a people well versed in the kindly properties of simples, have made a better physician of me than many that claim the medical degree.... I have learned many new secrets in the wilderness, and here is one of them—a recipe that an Indian taught me, in requital of some lesson of my own, that were as old as Paracelsus"—the latter a Swiss alchemist (pp. 1705–06; 1706 n.).

Hawthorne also associates Chillingworth with Sir Kenelm Digby, a fellow "correspondent" and "associate" in the "supernatural" and "occult sciences," and with Dr. Simon Forman, a notorious necromancer and concocter of love philters and poisons (Perkins, p. 1731; 1731 n; Gross, pp. 88 n.). When Prynne encounters her husband at the shore, he is gathering belladona and henbane, plants believed to possess magical power and used, with dogwood, in the potions of witches (Gross, p. 120 n.).

This constant attention to secrecy and the occult points to Chilling-worth as the proper husband of Prynne on an even deeper level, for it is her occult and spell-binding sexuality that secretly has joined in sin with Dimmesdale's. In fact, both "husbands" of Prynne commit the same error, and it is one centered on Prynne, Pearl, and their bewitching natures. Chillingworth and Dimmesdale harbor the Black Man within and hide this fact, especially in their refusal to acknowledge either the bewitching Prynne or her issue Pearl as their own.

When the novel's action is resolved, both acknowledge Pearl as their own, for to her comes the inheritance of the minister's blessed kiss and the physician's hordes of gold. She becomes the "richest heiress of her day" (p. 1803). The black magic of sinful love began an alchemic struggle for Prynne, Chillingworth, and Dimmesdale, one that led to the height of human poesis, to the white magic of a new bride and heiress.

Other transformations occur in a manner that has affinities to the mytheme of the waning moon goddess and her powers of poesis. Prynne experiences a near-magical "transfiguration" (p. 1753) in the forest. She metamorphoses into the "very heart of womanhood"; her hair is darkly rich and luxuriant; her majestic form glows with youth and sex (pp. 1773–74). This scene of Hester's transfiguration in Hawthorne's lawless forest, one whose dark beauty is as spell-binding as hers, and beneath whose shadows Prynne and Dimmesdale first fell into their catalytic sin, brings to mind the realm of waning moon goddess.

Hawthorne's forest itself has this weirdly wonderful but transforming, feminine nature of the waning moon goddess, of a witch. It takes Pearl, Hester, and Arthur into its wild "bosom" so that they may be "newly born" (p. 1774). It is Hawthorne's "mother-forest, and these wild things which it nourished" fill with vibrant and luxuriant beauty many forest scenes (p. 1775). Clearly, Prynne embodies over and again the forest's dark, perhaps, but fertile powers. In his crisis, Dimmesdale throws himself onto the forest bed to rise "up all made anew" in the strong arms of the forest's "better angel"—Prynne (p. 1773), this scene blending the maternal powers of the forest and of Prynne.

Hawthorne's feminine and heathenish forest, then, can be read as an archetype of the black, potent, and transformative witch-mother, whether in her form of Hekate, Circe, or the Black Madonna. Prynne, one of its periodical inhabitants, and one whose nature is in sympathy with its forces, fits at these times this type of the moon goddess, a figure in whom the triple colors of black, red, and white are contained and take turns manifesting themselves. Many critics have noted this "symbolic ambivalence" of Prynne, a woman simultaneously allied with the white and "sainted Anne Hutchinson," the scarlet fires of the letter, and the dark figure of the "old Hag" Mrs. Hibbins (Vivan, p. 73). But this ambivalence is really the continual heterogeneousness of any type of Diana Triformis. In Prynne, the "ambivalence" in her figure can be understood as a sign of her symbolic wholeness as a Diana-hero, one modelled on the Myriad-Named goddess emblematic of change.

Gustafson notes that our culture experiences "turmoil" when confronted with this "ambivalence" (p. x). This truth—of the poetic power of the dark side of the feminine and the turmoil it causes in our society—manifests itself in *The Scarlet Letter*. In doing so, it points to another reason why Hawthorne may have favored alchemy as the science of his text. Alchemists emphasized the underworld nature of the moon, of Luna, so ever-present a force in Hawthorne's text.[7]

This nature was an opening beyond "the patristic allegories" in which the Western world's overriding "masculine judgement" engaged in a lopsided over-evaluation of the white side of the "beauteous bride" at the expense of her three-sided nature as Triformis. The scarlet- and black-natured Prynne, as a type of this alchemic Luna, is this kind of puzzling antithesis to the Puritan fathers and their lopsided judgements (p. 175).

Exemplary on this point are Hawthorne's allusions to the real life figure of John Wilson, the "chief clerical opponent" of Anne Hutchinson, to whom Hester Prynne is allied in her imprisonment and exile (Gross, p. 47 n.). Prynne is one opening into dark, perhaps, but deep mysteries, ones that make a human sadder but wiser, ones that the Puritan fathers fiercely—and erroneously—banish from their presence and theology.

Importantly, these Black Madonnas, these Hekates and Circes in Hawthorne's texts, and his bewitching Hester Prynne, can offer in their wholeness and their powers a "healing force" to societies that are overly "rational and masculine" (Gustafson, p. xi). The grey Puritan community of olde Boston is in need of such healing, and it is a sad comment that the fathers exile Prynne to a thatched cottage on the outskirts of their society.

Once again we see the dilemma of the Diana-hero: where shall she find a home for herself in our world? When the tale begins, Hester Prynne is literally in a prison. She could leave olde Boston, but she voluntarily makes a small "space" for herself in a cottage that is an emblem of her banishment. Later, she urges Dimmesdale to flee with her, only to discover that there is no escaping the past. Her old husband Chillingworth will accompany them. After Dimmesdale's death, Hester seeks freedom in the rest of the world. She ultimately returns, however, for the emotional reality of her life lies in Boston.

Her return may indicate her acceptance of her life, but it is an unsatisfactory end for she lives in her cottage once more, such a small and isolated structure for a woman who possesses great gifts. The Diana-hero has embraced her role in our world, an act full of courage for she knows that her role is a constricted one. Hester's gifts are still imprisoned by her society, which allows her speech to flow freely only within the limits of a small structure, a cottage that exists outside the limits of that society. Her quest ends with her located on the fringes of our civilized world, and nearby the natural world of the ocean and the forest.

Thus, Hawthorne locates Prynne geographically in a manner that echoes her spiritual role in the novel, that of a mysterious angel exiled and earth-bound. The parameters given for her expression are small indeed. Her "magic circle" shall remain small (p. 1789).

There is also evidence that Hawthorne's scheme in *The Scarlet Letter*, which places the dark forces of the witch in contrast to the cold powers of the male lawgivers, derives at least partially from Greek archetypes. A study of the images of Hecate, Circe, Pandora, and Prosperina in Hawthorne's *A Wonder-Book* and *Tanglewood Tales* lead McPherson to conclude that Hawthorne shaped these women as a "Dark Lady," a figure that surfaces and re-surfaces in Hawthorne's major works; these are dark and fecund types of whom Hester Prynne is one (pp. 14–15; 20; 99; see esp. "Hawthorne's Character Types," pp. 213–220).

McPherson reaches the conclusion:

> ...she is a very strong personality. If her creative energies were given full scope in society, she might serve as a benign creative force. But men keep denying her, and when her daylight creativity is denied she may enter the dusky realm into which Hester was forced by her Puritan judges; and here she can appear to be a witch, a destructive force which haunts men's dream. In mythology she is Gorgon Medusa, Medea, or Circe.... (p. 223).

In addition, scarlet, the second color of alchemy and of the triune Queen Moon, also points to Prynne's transformative nature. The prison that Prynne enters for her black sin is called civilization's "black flower," and this image, both mysterious and blossoming, is repeated in another outside the prison door, the "wild rose-bush" whose roses "offer their fragrance and fragile beauty...of Nature" (p. 1693). The image of "wild" red roses blooming beside the "black flower" gains deeper ambivalence when the reader learns that it sprung from the footsteps of "sainted" Anne Hutchinson. Eventually, Prynne's soul, like the heroic soul of Hutchinson and like her "wild" roses, will be refined until it comes to "symbolize some sweet moral blossom" in Hawthorne's dark tale (p. 1694).

Moreover, the richest heiress of the novel, the grown-up Pearl, is called the "Red Rose" of the novel. She tells the Puritan fathers that she was "plucked" by her mother off the wild rose-bush at the prison door (1725–26). She, too, will undergo a process of refinement. Her creative nature reaches its own apotheosis. She becomes her society's richest heiress and bride. The rose imagery links Pearl, Prynne, and Anne Hutchinson in a manner that renders it a symbol of the promise of feminine salvation, however misperceived initially by the community.

A study of Hawthorne's alchemy indicates another important aspect of flowers, gardens, and colors in his text. In *Elixir of Life*, the key to the alchemist-hero's quest lies in decoding the enigmatic inscription, "Plant the seed in a grave...." (Swann, p. 377). Such images of seeds and graves, from the wild rose-bushes by the tomb-like prison to the domesticated rose-bushes in the Governor's dying garden, or to the black weeds which spring from a Puritan grave, are critical in *The Scarlet Letter* as well as *Elixir of Life*.

In *The Scarlet Letter*, the image points to the mortification of the feminine powers. The Puritan fathers falsely decode it as a pure equivalent of frailty and sin. They exile the scarlet flowers of their community, banishing the scarlet Prynne and her child, the "Red Rose" (p. 1725). They have forgotten that Christ took the scarlet woman into his fold, an act which enabled her transformation into a glorious saint. The Puritans focus solely on the story in the Bible of the Scarlet Whore of Babylon. In essence, they do not accept the scarlet side of feminine nature, as did Christ within limits, but they single out its scarletry to condemn it.

Hawthorne, on the other hand, constantly conflates and makes inseparable the three colors that are symbolic of Prynne's heterogeneousness. When we first see Prynne upon the scaffold, Hawthorne likens her to "the image of Divine Maternity" (p. 1698). He writes that Prynne calls to mind "that sacred image of sinless motherhood, whose infant was to redeem the world." Yet, this allusion to a pure white nature Hawthorne simultaneously blends in her character with strong elements of red and black. Hawthorne writes that Prynne has the "taint of deepest sin," and the world is "darker for this woman's beauty" (p. 1698). And, she bears the scarlet letter. Thus, Prynne from the first is a mixed image of (1) the Virgin Mother, the white Moon of the Church, (2) the Scarlet Whore of Babylon, and (3) Hekate, the dark witch of the forest. All three aspects constitute Prynne's feminine nature, in all its ambivalent powers.

Such images of ambivalence re-occur throughout the text. The scarlet in Pearl's nature beautifies her with its natural "fiery lustre." The traditional Christian "pearl" of stainless Mary had a calm, white, and unimpassioned lustre (pp. 1714-15)—much like the blanched Mary Ingram of Charlotte Bronte's *Jane Eyre*. But it is the streak of the moon goddess's mid-month fires restored to "Pearl" that makes her shine.

In fact, the scarlet fires which Pearl inherits "out of Hester's [erring] heart" are the flames of life itself. Hawthorne writes of the scarlet "fire" in Pearl: "The spell of life went forth from her ever creative spirit, and communicated itself to a thousand objects, as a torch kindles a flame wherever it may be applied" (pp. 1717; 1720). Pearl is "the very brightest little jet of flame that ever danced upon the earth." Pearl's fires are like the scarlet columbines that will grow out of rock (p. 1766)—everlasting, regenerative, inspiring.

The last color of the triad, white, is the least obvious in the text. Nonetheless, it plays a significant role. Hester is touched by white, from her past maidenhood to her recalling the image of Divine Maternity, but white is significant in the main by its noted absence in Hester's portrait. It is regulated to an irrecoverable past, that time before her initiation in the dark but creative moonlit realm of human error and frailty, but also of creativity and imagination. This absence forms a marked contrast to its visible role of white in the being of "Pearl."

Further, Prynne's fantastic embroidery, with its golden and artistic flourishes, becomes the fashion of the Puritans. The people employ her needle for all occasions but one: "But is it not recorded that, in a single instance, her skill was called in aid to embroider the white veil which was to cover the pure blushes of the bride" (p. 1711). White, then, is once again noticeable for its loss. White, the ideal color, one of purity, innocence, and youth, is neither a central nor viable color to image Hawthorne's maturing and complex human characters.

This idea is critical to understanding Hawthorne's commentary on America and its treatment of its Bride, its feminine hero. Gustafson notes that the cults of the Black Madonnas were spurred by Christianity's Virgin Mother having a nature with a "too one-sided 'white' and pure aspect" (p. 83). He concluded that if one does not acknowledge the nature embodied by the Black Madonna, then "Not to know that rhythm—the process of birth, life, and death—would doom anyone to naivete and sentimentality, to a world of undernourished piety and one-sided 'wisdom'" (p. 117). The Puritans' insistence that the Bride, Hester Prynne, be exclusively white and unstained, or be imprisoned, branded, and exiled, is an instance of such "one-sided wisdom."

Truly, the Puritan moral code fails to accord with the full extent of the human condition, and nature, as an invention of Divine Wisdom (p. 1714 n.), and the realm of nature is quite feminine in Hawthorne's text. The Puritan error of divorcing themselves from that which is or partakes of the natural world leads them to ban from their community passionate "Hester"—named for Esther, I assume, the woman who saved her people. The people in this case are the first Americans; they cast out their Esther. This is one manner in which they cast their "blackest shade of Puritanism, and so darkened the national visage with it" for years (p. 1788).

Pearl is the other female for whom the color white has a significant meaning. Hawthorne specifies that the white of "Pearl" is not pale but opalescent with the glint of other colors (p. 1714). This lustrous color of "Pearl" reveals more on Hawthorne's critique of America, for "Pearl" and her lustrous spirit are emblems of American Romanticism. That spirit is well evidenced in Emerson's "Self-Reliance":

> "What have I to do with the sacredness of traditions, if I live wholly from within?" my friend suggested, —"But these impulses may be from below, not from above." I replied, "They do not seem to me to be such; but if I am the Devil's child, I will live then from the Devil" (p. 1136).

In this Emersonian spirit of Romanticism in America, "Pearl" has the nature of a fiery and elfish child of the American forests, but her fellow Americans, the Puritans, condemn her opalescent nature. They narrowly perceive her as an offspring of the Black Man and will allow no positive consideration of the vibrancy and freedom in her nature (p. 1719). In reality, Pearl, infused anew with the scarlet fires of her mother and the ebony sin of her mother and father, harbors within her most fully the triple-nature of red, black, and pearl. She is truly an American Diana-child. She is a type of the maiden, opalescently powered, and creative Diana-bride, a creature who harbors red and black while retaining white. Hawthorne so clearly specifies these colors of Pearl's spirit:

> "...during that momentous period while Pearl was imbibing her soul from the spiritual world, and her bodily frame from its material of earth. The mother's impassioned state had been the medium through which were transmitted to the unborn infant the rays of its moral life; and, however white and clear originally, they had taken the deep stains of crimson and gold, the fiery lustre, the black shadow, and the untempered light, of the intervening substance" (p. 1715).

The heiress of the novel, "Pearl" has certainly received in full her tri-colored inheritance: white, crimson, black.

Moon Mirrors. Hawthorne gives specially to the Diana-maiden Pearl her traditional moon-mirror. Hawthorne clearly knew of or intuited of the idea in myth and literature associating the moon with the finest, clearest, and most magical of mirrors, for in his Greek tales, the image of the "moon-mirror" figures pointedly, embodied in such moon gods as Quicksilver (McPherson, pp. 16; 252). Reflected in Hawthorne's Greek moon-mirrors is the traditional glimpse of an "ideal...heavenly world" embodied by the moon in its harmonious and airy upper spheres (pp. 62; 109; 112; 215).

Hawthorne's American moon-mirrors still reveal mysteries, but ones beclouded by earthly shadows. Initially, in *The Scarlet Letter*, the youthful Hester beholds her own "girlish beauty...illuminating all the interior of the dusky mirror" (p. 1699). The "dusky" quality of mirrors intensifies as the novel progresses, in effect making its images more occult for humans. Hester perceives a reflection of her letter in a similarly distorted and earth-bound mirror, and it is Pearl who guides her to it:

> ...she saw that, owing to the peculiar effort of this convex mirror, the scarlet letter was represented in exaggerated and gigantic proportions, so as to be greatly the most prominent feature of her appearance. In truth, she seemed absolutely hidden behind it. Pearl pointed upward, also, at a similar picture in the head-piece; smiling at her mother, with the elfish intelligence that was so familiar an expression on her small physiognomy. That look of naughty merriment was likewise reflected in the mirror, with so much breadth and intensity of effect, that it made Hester Prynne feel as if it could not be the image of her own child....
> (p. 1723).

The more occult such visions are, the more they point to the text's alchemy and its promise of transformation, for its dusky images are often tinged with heavenly promise, the final transmutation into gold. Pearl points again to a mirrored vision of the letter, after her mother has tried to fling it aside: "The child turned her eyes to the point indicated; and there lay the scarlet letter, so close upon the margin of the stream, that the gold embroidery was reflected in it" (p. 1778).

Further, Pearl is the moon-mirror endowed with life, just as she is the scarlet letter come to life. Hester is haunted by "the small black mirror of Pearl's eye." Her imagination keeps trying to plumb into "the unsearchable abyss of [Pearl's] black eyes" (p. 1718). Indeed, Pearl's being, as that of a "visionary little maid," is one that admires reflections of its mirrored self in the pools of the forest:

> "Here and there, she came to a full stop, and peeped curiously into a pool, left by the retiring tide as a mirror for Pearl to see her face in. Forth peeped at her, out of the pool, with dark, glistening curls around her head, and an elf-smile in her eyes, the image of a little-maid...." (p. 1755).

Moreover, Hawthorne connects his moon-mirrors to The Book of Revelation. Both the mirrors of Hawthorne and the text of St. John provide us with the glimpse of another world. Over and over, the language of Hawthorne's text hints at this. The small brook, in which Pearl perceives herself, is a "mystery," and its surrounding forest serves to "mirror its revelations" (p. 1765–66).

The brook not only mirrors Pearl, but its power is identified with her: "Pearl resembled the brook, inasmuch as the current of her life gushed from a well-spring as mysteries, and had flowed through scenes shadowed as heavily with gloom. But, unlike the little stream, she danced and sparkled, and prattled airily along her course" (p. 1765). Pearl is all mysteries, be they the scarlet letter or the moon-mirror, come alive, revealed.

Continually, Pearl, the Diana-child, the one who partakes of the white, crimson, and black, has a heterogeneous nature that constantly shifts, reshapes, and reveals itself anew in a host of magical mirrors:

> And beneath, in the mirror of the brook, there was the flower-girdled and sunny image of little Pearl, pointing her small forefinger too.
>
> ...In the brook, again, was the fantastic beauty of the image, with its reflected frown, its pointed finger, and imperious gesture, giving emphasis to the aspect of little Pearl.
>
> ...alone as she was in her childish and unreasonable wrath, it seemed as if a hidden multitude were lending her their sympathy and encouragement. Seen in the brook, once more, was the shadowy wrath of Pearl's image. (p. 1777).

In the end, it is the "gold" promise of transfiguration emblemed in flourishes around the scarlet letter to which Pearl, the text's princess of mirrors, points, reveals, and foretells for others in *The Scarlet Letter*.

The Promise of Transformation: Marriage and Re-Birth

The legend of King Arthur is a legend of promise. The greatest Western king lies asleep in a mysterious cave somewhere, whence he will emerge when someone discovers and blows the trumpet he lost in his last battle. On King Arthur's head is the golden crown of a sun king. His wife is "Guinevere," the White Crescent, the Moon-Bride.

So the legend of "Arthur" Dimmesdale is one of promise, a promise as mythical and other-worldly as King Arthur's, but also as full of frustration while on earth as were the lives of King Arthur and his bride Guinevere.[8] "Dimmesdale" is a constant reminder of this fate, a poignant one for shining heroes, whose only happiness must lie in some future, distant resurrection of himself and his bride. The ill-fated union of Dimmesdale and his Bride, Hester Prynne, whose heroic nature is equally dimmed and cloaked, points to further levels of Christian and alchemic allegory in the novel.

Hester's fate, as the black-eyed Bride, is one of loneliness and yearning after her groom that is as heartfelt as that of the wandering Bride of the Canticles. In this context, Hester, like the Bride of the Canticles, can be perceived as a symbol of the earthly state of the Church, who must yearn after her groom, Christ. Traditionally, the Church is a type of "widow" for she "lacketh a husband, lacketh a man." Her bridegroom has not yet come (Jung, *MC*, p. 22). Indeed, exploration of this theme in the text reveals the exact manner in which Prynne holds the promise of poetic transformation, specially as a type of the moon goddess.

The Church remains in her "widowed" state, in both alchemy and Christianity, until the Second Coming, when the Messiah arrives and restores all to its lost original unity (p. 23). Before this, all will stay fragmented and divided. Significantly, even the dust of the graves of Prynne and Dimmesdale can not mingle, on this earth, and that is a sign of Hawthorne's vision of earthly life, so divided and fragmented, and so in accord with alchemy's and Christianity's idea of the widowed Church, her separated Groom, and our earthly state.

A host of sacrosanct imagery of the "Bride" of the Canticles, who is the "Church" in much Christian tradition, hints that Hester fulfills this role. Like the Bride of the Canticles, she has "dark" and "glossy" hair, "a burning blush," "deep black eyes," and a "beauty" that shines so holily it can even make "a halo of the misfortune and ignominy in which she was enveloped" (p. 1696). Just as the Bride of the Canticles is linked with fertile images of wheat fields and future regeneration, so is Hester identified with the natural "forest-land" and "new birth" from the start of the novel (p. 1709). There is a "sacredness" about her that converts the scarlet letter into a "cross on a nun's bosom" (p. 1753). She declares her union and Dimmesdale's had a "consecration" of its own (p. 1770). Always, she yearns toward the "marriage-altar" that she and her Spouse may arrive to in the next world (p. 1710).

Separated, the powers of the two are stifled and hidden, hers beneath the stiff and grey dress and cap, his beneath a dark cloak. Importantly, the forces of the Bride, of her dark but fertile and sacred nature, initiate the healing of Dimmesdale, who has become a "poor, forlorn creature" (p. 1741).[9] In the bosom of the black woods and in the arms of his bride, Dimmesdale throws his "sorrow-blackened" self down on the earth, then rises up anew (p. 1773). This dark chapter is entitled, appropriately, "A Flood of Sunshine." The Groom and Sun-King has confronted his natural Spouse and child, his own mortal love and destiny. This purgative truth smites him to the point it excites his soul to achieve Pentecostal tongues of fire (p. 1742). His "anguish" shall be the one "truth" of his life that saves his soul (p. 1744).

At this crux, his identity as a type of the sun king further manifests itself in the text's symbolism. As Dimmesdale writes the prophetic Election Sermon, the golden sunrise beams into his study (Male, p. 114). Or:

> The sun, but little past its meridian, shone down upon the clergyman, and gave a distinctness to his figure, as he stood out from all the earth to put in his plea of guilty at the bar of Eternal Justice (p. 1799).

He then bares his scarlet letter in the "mid-day sunshine" for all to see. His life rises to the truth of its parable (p. 1802), making possible his entry into the "golden pavements of the New Jerusalem" (p. 1731). Sunny golden is the color bathing Arthur Dimmesdale when he acheives his limited victory on earth.

Hester, the bride, is concurrently suffering from her sin with, and her subsequent divorce from, Dimmesdale. This is often imaged through a lack of sunshine on her being: "Mother," said little Pearl, "the sunshine does not love you. It runs away and hides itself, because it is afraid of something on your bosom" (p. 1764). Pearl again voices the shadowed state of her mother's life:

> "What a strange, sad man is he! ...In the dark night-time, he calls us to him, and holds thy hand and mine.... And in the deep forest, where only old trees can hear, and the strip of sky to see it, he talks with thee.... But here in the sunny day, and among all the people, he knows us not; nor must we know him!" (p. 1787).

Eventually, the public proclamation of the union of Prynne and Dimmesdale will be a kind of "triumphant ignominy" (p. 1801), Hawthorne's earthly fate for the Bride and Bridegroom, and this fate conforms to the pattern of medieval Christian and alchemical archetypes of the Moon-Bride and her Sun-Groom. In this tradition, the Bride, as the wafer new moon in darkness (Luna), is the symbol of the Church in the nuptial embrace. Luna so symbolizes the Church in the nuptial embrace because the moon is the gateway to heaven from earth. In this context was the Church essentially lunar and feminine (Jung, *MC*, p. 176). The long-awaited union of this Luna, who is the Bride and the Church, with her groom, who is Sol and Christ, begins with a ritual wounding of the groom because Christ upon the cross was wounded for his love of the Church (Jung, pp. 32–33). His crucifixion was also an earthly event of ignominy but, ultimately, heavenly triumph.

On this archetypal level, Dimmesdale's symbolic wounding and mortification is allegorically parallel to Rochester's in *Jane Eyre*. The structure of both stories parallels the primeval myth of the solar king and son who is rhythmically wounded, dies, and is reborn in the arms of the moon bride and moon mother, who are frequently the same (Jung, *MC*, p. 100). Alchemy, especially, pivoted around this "metaphorical designation of Christ as Sol" (*ibid*), and this was the Christ who is not only an archetype of resurrection, but the Christ who derives from the primordial dying and renewing spouse of the moon mother.

Like this kind of dying and reviving son of Luna, Dimmesdale walks his final steps to Prynne with "the wavering effort of an infant, with its mother's arms in view" (p. 1798). Dimmesdale gains strength to confess independently, and, having done so, dies in maternal arms: "Then, down he sank upon the scaffold! Hester partly raised him, and supported his head against her bosom" (p. 1800). In the opening pages of *The Scarlet Letter*, Prynne stood as "Divine Maternity" (p. 1698), and she closes Dimmesdale's life with this image, too. She is a type of Black Madonna, a shadowed Moon on the Church on earth, from the first to the last pages.

The community's relation to Hester Prynne, when we perceive her as a type of the Bride of the Canticles, a shadowed Moon of the Church, is further revealing of Hawthorne's criticism of America's founders. The Puritans place the letter "A" on Hester's breast, and, significantly, not only Hester, but the "A" itself, takes on new meanings for the community during the course of the novel. Their "A" initially labels her an "Adulteress" but eventually her true identity manifests itself even to the stubborn townspeople, who begin to perceive that the letter stands for "Angel."

Prynne spends her time entering freely into any household darkened by poverty or sickness, and all those within find comfort from the glimmers of the "unearthly ray" of the "A" (p. 1752). Perceiving Prynne as a "Sister of Mercy" whose nature is "warm and rich," the Bostonians also begin to understand that the "A" is more a "symbol of her calling," one that signifies "Able" for "a woman's strength" (p. 1752).

The Puritan people initially cast out this shadowed Bride, however, because they fully believe women to be, mainly, a symbol of "frailty and sinful passion" (p. 1709). This belief leads them into the highest irony of the text: their self-righteous banishment of her from Boston. They exile the earthly embodiment of Luna—the Church—from their New World community. It is no wonder olde Boston does not become the Utopia the Puritans pridefully envisioned.

In a novel with an alchemic framework, Prynne's banishment is even more damning. In that science, the sacred wedding of the Bride and Groom gives birth to harmony:

It is the moral task of alchemy to bring the feminine, maternal background of
the masculine psyche, seething with passions, into harmony with the principle of
the spirit—truly a labor of Hercules! (Jung, *MC*, p. 41).

Moreover, both alchemy's and Christianity's sacred wedding is parallel
to "the marriage in the Apocalypse" (pp. xiii; 371; 457). The alchemists,
like other Christians, viewed their "art on the level of divine revelation,"
so the manner in which one figures in the drama of the divorce and union
of elements, symbolically of the Bride and the Groom, is an extremely
telling factor on one's success in "the work of redemption" (pp. v; 254).
The Puritans figure only in the divorce, not the union. Hawthorne further
emphasizes the grievous nature of their error when he declares, "The
angel and apostle of the coming revelation must be a woman" (p. 1804).

In short, the Puritans have separated themselves from the feminine.
Death, sadism, and sterility—these are consequent plagues of their hopeful
but erring community. On the midnight that the members of the separated
family—Prynne, Dimmesdale, Chillingworth, and Pearl—linger at the
scaffold, two windows open upon the scene of their distress. The first
reveals the lamp of the Governor, and the second Mistress Hibbins, "also
with a lamp" (pp. 1746–47). Both the witch and the Governor illuminate
the scaffold scene, and they illuminate the theme of sterility, of two
bachelor figures, male and female, who rule olde Boston. Perhaps, on this
level, all the humans in the text are seen as the children of God, divided
and straying from each other and their Parent during their earthly stay.

Hawthorne's world may be "only the darker for this woman's beauty"
(p. 1698), but it is also enriched by this hybrid, who gives birth to Pearl,
olde Boston's heiress and the novel's "Red Rose" and emblem of Eden
(pp. 1711; 1714; 1725). Prynne intuits that her love, however unsanctioned by Puritan law, "completes a sacrament of Nature" (p. 1774 n.). In
sum, the Puritans can frown upon Prynne as a "scarlet woman, and a
worthy type of her of Babylon!" (p. 1725), but in truth only her heart
creates the "magic circle" of love and new life that is part of our *natural*
life (p. 1774).

When the Puritans brand Prynne as the Scarlet Whore, blinding
themselves to that element of her which is evocative of "Divine
Maternity," they end by completely divorcing themselves from this natural
life. They exile the Bride because her soul is in an erring, earthly vessel.

On this kind of error, of opting for divorce over union, Gustafson notes: "Psychic wholeness becomes a possibility through the symbolism of the Black Madonna, thus preventing psychic splits that can lead to neuroses or psychoses. In the same way, through her, a person does not let his or her libido (energy) go off in projection on other people—a projection that would take on dark characteristics, such as racial prejudice, witch hunting, and class oppression. Whenever people or individuals do not accept their own dark side, it is projected onto the nearest, most convenient object of personality" (p. 115).

Hawthorne depicted well the roots of Puritan evil that plagued his imagination: his ancestors' role as fierce judges in the Salem witch trials. In his study of the bewitching and banished Prynne, Hawthorne dissected the psychology of New England's founders, and pictured the fate this entailed for the heterogeneous-natured Diana-hybrid in America. Prynne is a woman whose scarlet A casts a spell that encloses her in her own "magic circle" (pp. 1789; 1796). This isolation of Prynne from her bleak community is emblematic of the extent to which the Puritan law was an "incomplete morality" (p. 1789).

Prynne, alone, discovers at the end a more complete morality, and she returns to olde Boston to share this. Her growth began with the spiritual mortification heralded by her "deadly symbol" (p. 1778). Her forbidden love for Dimmesdale always struggles "out of her heart, like a serpent from its hole" (p. 1710), but what is a serpent? The emblem of the dark moon and its ritual powers of rebirth. The serpentine sin of Prynne, a Luna-type, rhythmically leads, in seven years, to her being a "wiser and better" woman, one who can rear well and afresh her child (p. 1725). It leads her and her lover to a "truth" (p. 1758), however purgative, and it does so in a novel whose final wisdom is "Be true! Be true! Be true!"

Her mortification and rebirth, like that of most Diana-heroes, is a personal apocalypse. The "fatal symbol" brings with it a "new sense" of human nature. It endows Prynne with the power of "revelations" and "intimations," comprising her initiation into a "mystic sisterhood" (p. 1713). In these new discoveries, Prynne begins to know a wisdom and perception that transcends Puritan law. The "fatal token" and its strokes of "sudden death" are bringing her golden knowledge, hinted at by the gleam of the fringes of her letter (p. 1718). In turn, the gold fringes and golden knowledge hint that they are her path to the golden pavements of the New Jerusalem. Hawthorne asserts this is Prynne's destination (p. 1714).

The realm of apocalypse belongs to Prynne's child, too. The "clear, wild laughter" of the sin-born but Edenic Pearl rises from the Puritans' "burial-ground" (p. 1737), and she decorates her infant bosom with a scarlet letter of "eel-grass"—making that letter "freshly green" and revealing to all the world its true "hidden import" (p. 1761).[10] The hidden import which she reveals, green, is birth and hope. Pearl is green potential in the grey community. Green has long been "supposed to be the color of the moon; it is because of the moon's inherent kinship with vegetation" (Neumann, p. 220). The moon has always controlled water, the tides, the rivers, and the dew which give life to our green earth.

Thus is green an appropriate color for the Diana-maiden Pearl. Within her is new life, both literal and symbolical. In her nature is the "richest" heritage for the "New World" (p. 1803). In the clear waters of her soul resides a "perfect image" of fresh beauty in a "ray of golden light" (p. 1776). She is another soul destined for the New Jerusalem, for that true apocalypse of new life.

Importantly, the novel's apocalypse take a specifically modern form. Nathaniel Hawthorne, like Charlotte Bronte, brought down to earth his Luna-figure and her Bridegroom. Theirs is not the unqualified joyful bliss of the Romantic Endymion and Diana, who ascend into ethereal realms. Paradise is promised to Prynne, Pearl, Dimmesdale, and even Chilling-worth, but it is one far distant in the skies.

During the novel, Prynne's and Dimmesdale's ideas and beliefs in the apocalypse are truly heroic, but the novel closes with the death of their individual dreams. As Puritans, each was tutored to strive to realize in the New World "the relation between the Deity and the communities of mankind, with a special reference to the New England which they were here planting in the wilderness" (p. 1796). That is true heroism, but doomed heroism in Hawthorne's vision. In short, the only path left for his characters to reach the New Jerusalem is that of tragic heroism.

The figure of Pearl also fits neatly into this paradigm, but in a manner that offers a touch of promise and progression. She possesses physical perfection worthy of "Eden"—after the world's first parents had been driven out (p. 1714). Hawthorne thus identifies her nature as beautiful, but postlapsarian. She inherits Hester's, and in an analogue Adam and Eve's, original sin (p. 1715). While walking in the Governor's garden, Pearl calls out for the "red rose," echoing humanity's eternal passion for the forbidden fruit (p. 1723 n.).

However, considering Pearl as a Diana-child opens up another perspective on this paradigm. She continually flits between "two worlds" (p. 1776), that of the dark forest and the sunlit community, that of heathen lawlessness and Puritan law, that of demonic darkness and heavenly light. Like her name, symbolic of the moon, the planet that is intermediary between earth and heaven, "Pearl" crosses the "boundary" (p. 1776) sphere between two worlds. In alchemy, too, the maid of the moon "stands on the border-line between the eternal, aethereal things and the ephemeral phenomena of the earthly, sublunar realm" (Jung, *MC*, pp. 25; 145; 322).

This nature, as a moon-child who crosses and re-crosses boundaries, explains why Pearl receives a double inheritance: material wealth from her stepfather and spiritual wealth from her natural father. She inherits to herself the blessings of two worlds. These inheritances make manifest Pearl's full identity, for they establish her, like Charlotte Bronte's Jane Eyre or Spenser's Una, as the new heiress. Like them, she is the new moon of the text, the crescent promising a new life.

In alchemy, and in the manner that science evidences itself in the text, Pearl is even moreso a figure of promise. As the mediating child of the "circle of the moon," the realm between this earth and that of the immortals (Jung, pp. 25; 172), she would signify, and indeed she is, the "virgin soil" born anew, i.e. the field which can be the site of a Utopia (p. 1693). True to this concept, Pearl does succeed in realizing a happy marriage, unlike Hester, her old moon mother. In this, one could argue that Pearl is an emblem of human progression. She is happier in her earthly life, and the promise of transformation does not seem so remote.

Brides of the Apocalypse: Pearl and Hester Prynne

Pearl: The Child-Bride of the Apocalypse. Like the traditional Bride of the Canticles, Pearl has eyes that are "wild, bright, deeply black" (p. 1716) and hair that is "deep, glossy...akin to black" (p. 1720). Her radiance and her name indicate that she can be read as the Christian "treasure...of great price," and that, like the medieval Pearl, she is a "radiant 'bride of Christ the lamb'" (pp. 1716; 1716 n.; 1726). Her dress, like her "imagination," is "abundantly embroidered with fantasies and flourishes of gold thread" (p. 1720)—gold signifying the light and the pavement of New Jerusalem in Hawthorne's text. Pearl possesses the Bride's powers of apocalypse, of "transformation," for she is an "ever creative" spirit who can shape out of air a "visionary throng" (p. 1717). Pearl is the text's "gem" of apocalyptic brilliance: "...resembling nothing so much as the shimmer of a diamond, that sparkles and flashes" (p. 1786).

Pearl's creating a "visionary throng" also points to her as a poetic type of Diana. Hawthorne states in "The Custom-House" that "Moonlight" is the "medium most suitable for a romance-writer to get acquainted with his illusive guests" (p. 1687), and Pearl, with her "visionary throng," is analogous to Hawthorne conjuring his "illusive guests" in the moonbeams. Both are Diana-heroes in that both are romantic poets, with Hawthorne inspired by the light of the moon.

In "The Custom-House" Hawthorne also states that the "magic moonshine" of romantics possesses a "cold spirituality" which needs to be mingled with the "warmer light" of earth (p. 1688). He then proceeds to mingle the "white moonbeams" (p. 1688) of Pearl's nature, which are of a "hard, metallic lustre" (p. 1764), with the "deep stains of crimson and gold, the fiery lustre, the black shadow" of her mother's earthly sin (p. 1715). He touches her with an mortal grief to "humanize" her (p. 1764). In sum, Hawthorne shapes a humanitarian Diana-bride.

Like many Diana-brides, from Titania to Jane Eyre, Pearl is an "airy sprite" who works "witchcraft" (p. 1716). The traditional images of the moon and its sphere—harmonious airs, witchery, fairies—surround Pearl. She has an "airy gayety" and "music" in her soul (pp. 1716; 1786).[11] She has an "elf-smile" and the light ability to fly "away like a bird" (p. 1755). She sparkles with an "effervescence" that makes her "flit with a bird-like movement" (p. 1786). Pearl has a magically "light, airy, childish laugh" which thrills the hearts of mortals (p. 1747).

The redemptive power of Pearl's nature is capable of shining through the sombre Puritan crowd. Pearl's "glistening ray" alone gives cheer to the

Puritan crowd; to them she is like "a bird of bright plumage" that "illuminates a whole tree of dusky foliage by darting to and fro" (p. 1794). The source of Pearl's redemptive and joyful nature is hinted at by its seeking to return, naturally, to its airy, upper spheres: Pearl is "like a wild, tropical bird, of rich plumage, ready to take flight into the upper air" (p. 1725).

Moreover, this bird imagery places Pearl within the idea of the moon-bride of alchemy, for in that science, the union of the moon-bride and sun-groom brings forth the final treasure of the process, and that is often the "scarlet" bird. This alchemic bird proceeds through the same triple colors of the text and of Pearl, for it begins as black, ritually molts to white, and then to red, which signifies the end and successful transformation (Jung, *MC*, p. 194).

In addition, the alchemists' *lapis philosophorum* is exactly what Pearl is—"one pearl of great price" (Jung, *MC*, pp. 372; 436; 473). It is a "treasure," like Pearl, a lustrous stone that harbors the precious secret of the mystery of the individual. As a gem containing all of human mystery, the white stone is androgynous, a union of male and female spirits, just as Pearl is a mingling of the elements of Prynne and Dimmesdale. She is the symbol of their "material union" and its "spiritual idea" in whose being the Bride and Groom will dwell "immortally together" (p. 1776).[12] In Hawthorne's work, Pearl is the mystery endowed with life. She is, truly, an apocalyptic bride.

Textual images reveal Pearl has roots in the moony brides of the Renaissance poets, too, particularly Spenser. Hawthorne puts the novel in this historical framework by allusions to the Elizabethan era. Early on he notes that its women stand "within less than half a century" of and bear a strong resemblance to the dames of that era (p. 1695). Of the Puritan fathers, Hawthorne reminds us that they were "native Englishmen, whose fathers had lived in the sunny richness of the Elizabethan epoch" (p. 1787). The "merriment" of Elizabethan times was full of "witch craft" (p. 1788), which the stern Governor identifies with the delightful little Pearl (p. 1725).

In Pearl lies all that is "phantasmagoric," the purest image of all the magical "dance," "fancy," "transformation," "wild energy," and "fantastic...conjuration" in the novel (pp. 1716–17). Her home, Boston, borders on the "antique wood" to which Pearl is a "nymph-child...in closest sympathy" (p. 1775), and in this sympathy, the "imp" Pearl, "whose next freak might be to fly up the chimney" holds a "secret spell" (p. 1719) in the midst of grey olde Boston.

The Dianesque nature of Pearl's magic, especially of its Renaissance quality, is clearly depicted in the forest scene. There, like Una in the forest, or Lady Comus in the wilds, or a type of the bewitching *potnia theron*, Pearl's natural spirit needs have no fear in the woods:

> A fox, startled from his sleep by her light footstep on the leaves, looked inquisitively at Pearl, as doubting whether it were better to steal off, or renew his nap on the same spot. A wolf, it is said,—but here the tale has surely lapsed into the improbable,—came up, and smelt of Pearl's robe, and offered his savage head to be patted by her hand. The truth seems to be, however, that the mother-forest, and these wild things which it nourished, all recognized a kindred wildness in the human child (p. 1775).

This scene also reinforces the parallels between Pearl's role and that of the moon-bride in alchemy, for one of that science's main directives is to have the youth wed Luna because she possesses magical powers over nature; she is its *potnia theron*:

> Here may Diana be propitious to thee, who knoweth how to tame wild beasts (Jung, p. 168).

Moreover, the airy-spirited Pearl, who flits between the two worlds, of the forest and of Boston, brings intelligence from the former world to the latter. In "front of the meteor/sign, on the scaffold of extreme revelation, Pearl speaks 'in a tongue unknown to the erudite clergyman'" (Vivan, p. 82). She whispers mysteries, which the Reverend can not yet grasp, apocalyptic mysteries not to be revealed to those of the narrow Boston sphere only.

In the end, the union of opposites is the essence of the sacred wedding, whether that be the wedding of the Bride and Bridegroom of the Canticles or of Sol and Luna in medieval alchemy:

> The sun and moon come together in a...dramatic embrace. The coming together of these two principles [black eclipse and brilliant gold] and the drama of their struggle gives birth to a third and new thing (Gustafson, p. 59).

The third and new thing, who unites and reveals all the mysteries of alchemy, who embodies all the drama of the love, sin, and salvation of Hester Prynne and Arthur Dimmesdale, is Pearl. She is the "lovely and immortal flower" whose "innocent life" redeems the earthly sin of her parent and points her the way to be a "blessed soul" in heaven (p. 1714). Pearl is so special that for her kiss, the kiss of "My little Pearl," the Reverend Dimmesdale asks in his death throes (p. 1800). His great soul intuits that she is the "true" treasure of great price, the pearl that bespoke the immortal truth "in a tongue unknown" to him, Boston's most "erudite clergyman," that midnight on the scaffold (pp. 1750; 1802).

Like her ancestress of revelation, the medieval Pearl, Hawthorne's Pearl guides her grieving father over the waters to the New Jerusalem.[13] At that moment, she fulfills her dual role as a human child and as a "messenger of anguish" from the other, the ideal world (p. 1800). Happy will be any mortal who is "illuminated by the morning radiance" (p. 1715) of this bride, who lives in the "absolute circle of radiance" about her (pp. 1714–15).

Hester: The Woman-Bride of the Apocalypse. Hester Prynne leaves behind the "stainless maidenhood" of virgin brides (p. 1709), but such purity is also identified negatively with the "cold snow" of the frigid bosoms of the Puritan matrons (p. 1713) and with the heavenly but "cold" moonbeams devoid of any "human tenderness" (p. 1688). Hawthorne does allow the Puritans' cold and hard law to triumph over the pagan force of nature, but he condemns the Puritans for failing to come to terms with this force, and he paints Nature in such brilliant colors that it, like Hester, can signify profound beauty as well as profound wildness in earthly life.

Prynne is, even moreso than her daughter Pearl, touched by earthly grief, and so she is a poignantly humanized Diana-hero. Her beauty and her vulnerability are key to her heroism. Critics have noted that *The Scarlet Letter* is "so deep, so dual, and so complete" like no other book, particularly in the figure of Prynne, whose "dual role as sinner and saint" makes possible the peak of her heroic and artistic development, of her becoming "[e]very inch a woman" (Male, pp. 90; 97).

From the start, Hawthorne focuses on Prynne's heroic and creative nature, and on the consequences she suffers for this in the New World.

In the first scenes, Prynne is labelled "haughty" (p. 1697), but she is also in her pride likened to the "sainted" Anne Hutchinson. That reference condemns the Puritans more than Prynne, for Anne Hutchinson was a gifted woman banished by the narrow-minded Puritan governors. The opening remarks of the Puritan matrons, who wish to see Hester wince in pain, to bear the "brand of a hot iron" and even "die," further condemn the vein of sadism and misogyny toward a proud "woman" like Prynne or Hutchinson (p. 1695).

Hawthorne constantly alludes to this idea that Prynne is condemned in part because of her proud and gifted nature is less acceptable to her society when found in a woman. The link between Anne Hutchinson and Hester Prynne is repeated. He writes that Prynne could, with her active intellect, very well have been a similar "prophetess" or "foundress of a religious sect" (p. 1754). Prynne's life in general is similar to Hutchinson's: "a spiritual counsellor to Puritan women, interpreting to them the best of the male theological mind; now a prophet in her own right, giving voice to a new spirit of freedom and embodying within herself a new awareness of female intelligence and social power" (Colacurcio, p. 22). One of the main movements for Prynne is from undisciplined private speculation to unsanctioned public prophecy. The reader leaves her when she has found a way to make public, quietly, her ideas about sexual justice (p. 22).

Thus, in Nathaniel Hawthorne's *The Scarlet Letter*, any true "impulse to challenge the Puritan theocracy's dominant (and socially conservative) assumptions about 'visible sanctity' evidently comes from a fairly deep and powerful source. It seems to be coming from—'the woman'.... Evidently, in Hawthorne's view, fully awakened women accept the inevitability of a given legal order far less easily than their male counterparts. And clearly this is the central issue" (Colacurcio, pp. 22–25).

Moreover, Prynne's potential as an agent of change, as a seer—like Jane Eyre—of a newer, better order, is made in *The Scarlet Letter* to be equally powerful to a man's. In addition to Prynne's links to Anne Hutchinson, Hawthorne links her to male prophets. In her transcendental ideas contrary to the Puritan ethic, she is said to be like the censored Luther (p. 1719). Prynne herself ponders that her fate has come to her as a female, for her genius presents a "dark question...with reference to the whole race of womanhood" (*ibid*). Chillingworth notes that Hester's "spirit" has a "strength" that bears the burden of sin and the scarlet letter better than Dimmesdale's (p. 1757). He sees that even in her despair she has a "quality almost majestic," and he cries, "Thou hadst great elements!... I pity thee, for the good that has been wasted in thy nature" (p. 1758). In short, Prynne has all the makings of a hero, and indeed she is heroic, but that role is neither allowed her nor acknowledged by her society.

Hester Prynne's heroic nature is strengthened by another factor. Allusions connect Prynne to the grand female hero and royal virgin of the Western world, Queen Elizabeth. Hawthorne's first reference places Prynne in the Boston community of women who are like the "man-like Elizabeth" (p. 1695), and Prynne, for all her beauty, is strong and tall and no exception to this.[14]

In her "man-like" nature, Hester seems as invincible as Queen Elizabeth.[15] Strangers, who see Prynne stand alone with her glittering letter as if in a magic circle, think her some magically unconquerable "great lady" (p. 1722). The Indians believe that Prynne "...must needs be a personage of high dignity among her people" (p. 1796). Reports circulate that when an erring Indian drew his arrow against her "badge" the missile struck the letter but fell harmless to the ground. This latter report is similar to myriad famous images of chaste Elizabethan heroines, an example being Shakespeare's portrait of the Queen Elizabeth as a virgin vessel against whom Cupid's arrows fall helpless (*MND*, II, i, 155–65). These allusions to Elizabethan heroism flow smoothly with Prynne's identity as an alchemical hero, too, for in *Felton*, Hawthorne states that "secret writing" is an element "for which...the age of Elizabeth was so famous and so dextrous" (Swann, p. 379).

Prynne's figure is interwoven with allusions to yet another Western female icon, Mary, the Moon of the Church. She is "the image of Divine Maternity" (p. 1698), however shadowed. Critically, the "rose-bush" outside the prison door is sprung from the footsteps of the sainted Hutchinson (p. 1694). The rose and rose-gardens in Christianity and in alchemy symbolize Mary, the most sainted female, as the locked *prima materia*, and by analogue the rose can be seen as the symbol and link of Christian female saints to the grand idea of Mary. This rose, however, is a dualistic phenomenon, for while it embraces human beauty and virtue, its very beauty creates lust and must be guarded.

Such dualistic imagery of the archetypal Black Madonna and of Hawthorne's dark image of Divine Maternity is parallel in their costumes, too. The clothes of each are emblems of the transformative powers and process of these dark queens. Prynne wears a fiery scarlet letter embellished with glittering gold flourishes, and the Black Madonna of the Finsterwald wears a rust color dress with gold hems and a gold belt (Gustafson, p. 46). In alchemy, in medieval literature and elsewhere, the transfiguring Luna bears this fiery dress, with its gold flourishes pointing toward the golden pavement of Jerusalem, for her sovereignty is of the heart, red and alive, and filled with feelings, especially ones inconsistent or beyond the scope of the narrow letter of the law (p. 57).

One discovers this archetype of scarlet dress to signify the transformative female hero in the red dress of Dante's Beatrice of *Vita Nuova* and her transforming dress of "live flame" in the *Divine Comedy*, too (Wright, p. 117). The same kind of miraculous creativity lies beneath the black robe and multicolored flames of Isis in the Apuleius's *The Golden Ass* (p. 86). As Hawthorne pronounces for his scarlet woman, creative in her very deviance, "The world's law was no law for her mind" (p. 1754).

Hawthorne clearly places Prynne within this tradition elsewhere in the text. To her belongs "Passion," whence her power of "transfiguration" (p. 1753) and her ability to "read" the minister's "heart more accurately" (p. 1769), like Eyre's gifted power to "read" Rochester. Prynne's banishment results in a freedom for these powers, and thus for her genius, a freedom unique in the text:

> ...Hester Prynne, with a mind of native courage and activity, and for so long a period not merely estranged, but outlawed, from society, had habituated herself to such latitude of speculation as was altogether foreign to the clergyman. She had wandered, without rule or guidance, in a moral wilderness; as vast, as intricate, and shadowy, as the untamed forest.... The tendency of her fate and fortunes had been to set her free....
>
> The minister, on the other hand, had never gone through an experience calculated to lead him beyond the scope of generally received laws;... As a priest, the framework of his order inevitably hemmed him in (p. 1772).

Prynne might go amiss in her free visions, but they nonetheless render her an original thinker. Her mind and powers are not "hemmed...in."

Prynne's strength and visions not only make her a "poet," in the Romantic sense of a doer, seer, and artist, but one of the longest-standing points of intrigue in Hawthorne's novel is that all three adult characters, Dimmesdale, Chillingworth, and Prynne, are artists of some sort. This makes *The Scarlet Letter* charged with the theme of poesis, and these powers endure most in the figure of Hester Prynne.

Prynne's artistry appears touched by the Romantic. Hawthorne indicates his text is a romance in both its title and its preface, and immediately Prynne's artistry is marked with Shelleyan "fancy" when she appears on the scaffold with her letter A. Her art has "fantastic flourishes of gold thread," and is "so artistically done, and with so much fertility and gorgeous luxuriance of fancy" that it achieves "splendor" (p. 1696). So high is Prynne's art that it literally "illuminated" her (p. 1697). Further, as a woman, Hawthorne hints that Prynne is, inherently, a romantic artist for he identifies her genius as "womanly fancy" (p. 1699).

Other critics have noted Prynne's important role as an artist. Vivan concludes that Prynne's "magic thread...illuminates" the whole novel, its death and funerals, its forbidden passions and its erring Puritan law (p. 85). The fantastically embroidered letter even inflames the indignation of the Puritan matrons, for Prynne's needle is functioning as a "medium by which she converts the scene of shame into 'a kind of lurid triumph,'" one which is, in essence, an occult transformation (p. 86).

Prynne's needle, the tool of her art, links her to another configuration of the moon goddess, Minerva, and her genius: "Hester, in her New England life, has become like Minerva—a goddess of needle and loom, an intellectual who voyages boldly in the dusky region of mind" (McPherson, pp. 177–78).[16] A survey of Hawthorne's Greek tales shows that Minerva falls snugly in an overall pattern with other moon deities in Hawthorne's major works (pp. 124–25), the beings who offer creative glimpses of a silvery world.

Vivan goes on to discuss Prynne as a heroic woman-artist:

> Hester is a woman and her magic tool is the needle in Hawthorne's eye, a symbol of the feminine condition—; her pattern of experience might therefore be read as the path of suffering and transformation of women, historically bound to

reach a new status, a new nobility which will redeem the destiny of humanity as a whole.... Hester's role also includes a reference to the mission of the artist. She creates art in the only possible way for a Puritan, by redeeming experience and making it a type of biblical heroism. Her very name, *Hester*, shows her as the type of feminine saviour in the New Canaan, like Hester was in the Old Testament (p. 86).

The text directly supports these conclusions on Prynne as a woman-artist: "She possessed an art that sufficed.... It was the art—then, as now, almost the only one within a woman's grasp—of needle-work" (p. 1710). Prynne's gifted fingers not only "could have embroidered a monarch's robe" but combined with her "nature ...warm and rich," they turn out a highly-wrought embroidery that achieves an "unearthly ray" (p. 1752). Over and again, Hester Prynne is imaged as a radical artist.

Tragically, not only is Prynne's "delicate and imaginative skill" in needlework the sole outlet for her powers, but the artistic exercise of her needle makes Prynne feel guilty because it bestows upon her life a "passion" that like "all other joys" her Puritan upbringing has caused her to regard—and reject—"as sin" (p. 1711). She persists, however, from necessity as well as inclination, and her romantic art ends by bestowing a "richer and more spiritual adornment of human ingenuity" to the costumes of olde Boston as well as her life (p. 1710).

Importantly, Male demonstrates that through her art and its letter, Prynne comes to know the truth of her life and her sin. After the pillory scene, with the letter fresh on her bosom, Prynne puts off her old life and finds a new self in art, for she novelly earns her living by her needle, expresses her passion through it, and even employs it as penance by doing clothing for the poor (p. 1711). In the privacy of her cottage, she perceives Pearl's magic, then uses her art to make Pearl a symbol, in her flame-colored dresses, of her meaning. In total, Prynne's needlework is an imaginative product, an act of penance, and a vehicle to become involved with birth, with death, and with the social hierarchy and all phases of her community's life (except marriage) (p. 105).

Prynne's art—especially in the form of Pearl's flourishing scarlet dress—eventually raises her above everyone else, to become their moral instructor:

> The superiority of Hester's artistic insight over the hollow rigidity of the orthodox is made clear when she and Pearl educate the highest members of the local hierarchy in the Governor's hall.... The stunned Governor asserts that [Pearl] is 'in the dark,' thereby provoking Hester into a heated illumination of his own blindness. '*See ye not*, she is the scarlet letter, only capable of being loved, and so endowed with a millionfold the power of retribution for my sin?'.... 'There is truth in what she says,' answers the minister, who has always been more responsive to the word than to the vision. Upon the Governor's request that he 'make that plain,' Dimmesdale teaches him what is expressed by Hester's art—namely that Pearl is both burden and blessing (Male, pp. 106-07).

In this sense, Hester's art has transformed her into a type of dark but illuminating Luna-Ecclesia of her society. The moon has always had many feminine configurations of wisdom, another well known one being Sophia (Neumann, pp. 211-212; 225). Hester Prynne is this type of configuration.

One more intriguing idea in the text points to Prynne as one of its heroes. Hawthorne writes in "The Custom House" that hers is a "now forgotten art" whose "mysteries" are "not to be re-covered" by any means (p. 1685). Her art, then, is itself a mystery, and its product, the letter, seems a "clue" that "has been lost, so that no one can now undo the spell which lies hidden in the letter, beyond all magic formulae" (Vivan, p. 75). This idea fits with the main idea in *Elixir of Life* of a single plant—the one that Septimus needs to achieve his goal—being extinct in the modern world. Hester's lost art, like Septimus's extinct plant, is key to Hawthorne's study of alchemic transfiguration of the modern world. Both Prynne and Septimus function as tragic heroes in this context—with the difference that Prynne encounters more success in and through her mysterious art by the end of *The Scarlet Letter*.

Further, Prynne gives birth not to the traditional male savior of Christianity, but to the highly dynamic Pearl. The future heiress of olde Boston is as female and poetic as her mother. In Christianity, the pearl is linked not only to the moon but to Christ, for in its white beauty it is emblem of the pure soul (Male, pp. 94-95). In sum, Pearl, who wears the living artistry of Hester, who is her artistic "A" endowed with life, and who is the future bride, becomes another signifier of Prynne's identity as a creative hero.

Especially, Pearl is a signifier of Hester as hero because it is in complement with Pearl that Hester comes to embrace an apocalyptic role. Vivan notes that through her relation with Pearl, Hester comes to function as an archetypal "*virgo* in whom is concentrated the redemptive mission of the quest and also of the individual woman. In short, the *opus* begins with the woman who is herself the *prima materia* and proceeds through her, as it were, towards another woman in whom she projects herself." This constitutes a cycle of feminine rebirth and transformation, one important—and indeed heroic—because it points towards a historical awareness of woman's role in the millennium (p. 79).

This highly symbolic relation between mother and daughter is enhanced by art, a woman's art, the needle. Pearl's inheritance from Prynne, her "rich and luxuriant beauty," her deep and glossy eyes, and her bright fires, are enriched by the "fantasies and flourishes" that Prynne's "imagination" creates in Pearl's crimson apparel (p. 1720). With Pearl's costume and Prynne's letter, derived from the same creative hand, Prynne makes Pearl emblem of their mutual nature and role, of her past sin and their future redemption. Prynne is "the very heart of womanhood," and she, through the dynamic Pearl, reveals this heart to be "the heart of mystery...become a mystery of joy" (p. 1774).

For Prynne to accomplish this revelation, an internal process must take place, transforming and refining her heroic nature. Not only does it occur, but it mirrors the one that her daughter experiences. Just as Pearl, an elfish child, eventually takes a place in the community, Prynne also moves from exile to participation in her community. Initially, Prynne's natural passion brings upon her the community's banishment and scarlet letter, which turns Prynne's life to "thought" (p. 1753). The result, a refined blend of her natural passion and subsequent knowledge, raises Prynne to the heroism of resistance and vision. She ends returning this to the misguided Puritans in Boston, and they, particularly the women, seek her out for counsel. This process of Prynne, Pearl, and the Boston women constitutes one on-going and expanding process of feminine rebirth and transformation.

Hawthorne, then, clearly shapes Prynne as a hero, a redemptive and artistic hero. Equally important, he re-evaluates traditional male heroism and artistry in its relation to hers.

In "Hawthorne's Psychology of the Head and Heart," Donald Ringe analyzes Dimmesdale's artistic powers. He admires Dimmesdale's fiery spirit and Pentecostal tongues as evidence of his creative powers, and he calls Dimmesdale's final triumph, the Election Sermon, "the supreme consummation of the artist's gift" (p. 93). Chillingworth also possesses artistic potential, especially in his task of alchemical poesis, though his powers are thwarted. Hawthorne clarifies that Chillingworth pursues the "rare case" of Dimmesdale "for the art's sake" (p. 1740). Chillingworth's means are artistic, too, as when he arranges to have a piece of art, the tapestry of David and Bathsheba, exhibited to afflict Dimmesdale's conscience. That tapestry, an elaborate piece of needlework, hints at a link in the artistic natures of Prynne, Chillingworth, and Dimmesdale. Its form connects the three as much as its subject.

Another critic, Roy Male, notes that the most significant forms of "expression" in *The Scarlet Letter* are achieved through these three in their arts: Hester's needlework, Chillingworth's psychiatric alchemy, and Dimmesdale's Election Sermon. Chillingworth "inhumanely" unites his intelligence with "amoral lore, both Indian and civilized, to perfect his art" (p. 103), thus making his art perverse. But Prynne and Dimmesdale strive for better art. Male notes that for Hawthorne the test of a true artist is whether the person succeeds in patterning her or his life "as a work of art...a parable to be the word incarnate." In this Prynne and Dimmesdale succeed, making themselves and their lives emblematic (pp. 102-03).

Moreover, the greatest artistry arises in the union of Prynne and Dimmesdale, for their union, however stained, results in deeper wisdom and in new life, Pearl. Hawthorne believed that an artist must be wedded to the human community and not isolated in his own egoism and gifts, so Hawthorne's artist-heroes, if successful, are 'married' in some fashion. That is the symbol of their spousal to the human realm, of their commitment to work creatively in it. Often, Hawthorne makes sexual love a metaphor for artistic fertility and for the creative use of the individual's power (McPherson, pp. 12-13).

The sexual love of Prynne and Dimmesdale can thus be read as a metaphor for their artistic fertility. Their sinful but passionate union not only heightens the artistic fertility of Prynne and Dimmesdale but increases their awareness of their intimacy with the larger human community. Both end sadder but wiser heroes, but Dimmesdale dies while

Prynne endures. This raises the question that Dimmesdale's art is also like the extinct plant in the *Elixir of Life* manuscripts. His art does not survive into his modern world. This leaves Prynne's art, however archaic in more recent times, as the most viable. Only Prynne's art endures. In another time, Hawthorne discovers it, faded perhaps, but beautiful enough to inspire, and her emblematic tale unfolds for us. More than one critic has suspected this kind of victory for Hester to be Hawthorne's intention. Ringe concludes that Hester's victory echoes most strongly the Romantic idea that the artist is the "poet" who re-makes his—or her—world:

> ...though Dimmesdale achieves the highest moral triumph that man is capable of, his is not the ideal solution. That solution rests in Hester, who does not achieve true insight until she leaves the colony and loses herself in the mass of men. She learns in time, however, that only in the colony does her reality lie, that the world of men is a meaningless sham. With this insight, she returns, assumes again her stigma, and reminds the people constantly of the omnipresence of sin. It is only in the Hester Prynnes of the world that gradual and perhaps continuing moral progress for man can be hoped for or sought (p. 93).

Prynne's endurance is also her unique gift as a woman. The "{W}ondrous strength and generosity of a woman's heart" is that which marks Hester off from Dimmesdale from the beginning, a fact that he recognizes and to which he pays tribute (p. 1704). In fact, in "Prometheus Ashamed: *The Scarlet Letter* and the Masculinity of Art," Scott Derrick argues wonderfully on the compelling theme of the gender struggles and ultimate frustration of the American male artist in the novel against the successes of women. He assesses that the so-called male heroism of the novel, whether it be Dimmesdale's artistic triumph or by analogy Hawthorne's, actually resides in the feminine side of their natures:

> The generative power of imagination is feminine through *The Scarlet Letter*, and feminine in a social sense.... The gesture which inspires the novel-writing project, thinly disguised through projection into the past, is an act of female identification. Hawthorne presses an *A* worn by an adulteress to his breast and feels a heat like a 'red-hot iron,' the explicit transmutation of the feminine into the phallic. The light by which Hawthorne will write is also feminine, the moon.
> ...The *A* functions for Dimmesdale in a way homologous with its Custom House function for Hawthorne himself: it leads to a speech, writing, creation, and, at least the author hopes, to fame. The letter confers on Dimmesdale a pentecostal gift of passion, which allows him to address his fellow sinners in 'the heart's own

language,' a language which seems related to the feminine, if we remember the dryness and dessication of the earlier male world.... Written through a passion which has its source in Hester, a passion reawakened in the forest scene in which Hester displays her own latent eloquence, Dimmesdale's sermon achieves not only a religious and artistic triumph, but a political one. He may be said to actualize symbolically an enduring dream of the American artist... (pp. 124–27).

Even Dimmesdale's triumph, however, paradoxically produces a return of that femaleness it is meant to finally transcend. As Chillingworth says, if Dimmesdale's guilt were revealed, his punishment would be "the gallows." He has not assumed the full punishment for his deed and his silence by revealing the A he has hidden; instead, he has sealed the extent of his identification with women.

Derrick concludes:

.... Confined to her own sphere, [Hester] surrenders and wins the right to speak, to her equally suffering sisters, a sentimentalized message of acquiescence in a world emptied of men. Dimmesdale's fame is secure: why should he care if she is a better orator than he? (pp. 124–27)

Derrick is perceptive that Prynne's message can be seen as escapist and segregational, but that it is also, in the main, a better art than Dimmesdale's.

In fact, Chillingworth, Dimmesdale, and even Nathaniel Hawthorne borrow the feminine forms of art—weaving and embroidery—to aid, shape, or advance their own work. Chillingworth employs a gorgeously wrought tapestry to mortify Dimmesdale's soul. And as Derrick notes, Hawthorne experiences creative emotion when he presses Prynne's "A" to his breast, an act Dimmesdale parallels in the "A" he keeps hidden on his breast. This "A" indicates Dimmesdale's strong identification with the feminine (pp. 124–27). In "On the Moon and Matriarchal Consciousness," Erich Neumann delineated well this kind of crisis for creative men in a patriarchal culture, for they must borrow from the feminine consciousness, whose symbol is the moon in all of its spiritual mysteries which belong to the realm of night, not the realm of daylight and rational logic (pp. 211; 221). The symbol of Prynne's imaginative consciousness is her gorgeously wrought needlework, and to these Chillingworth, Dimmesdale, and even Hawthorne turn.

Thus, Prynne's role in the novel—as woman and as artist—is both a complement to, model for, and a critical reflector on the artistry of the males. In the "Romance" of *The Scarlet Letter*, Prynne is one high model of a romantic poet who helps to shape her world, aid its progress, and envision its transformation into a New World.

A particular role of Pearl reinforces the idea of her mother as a romantic poet re-making her world. She is a "spirit-messenger" to every human in the novel (p. 1762). From her earliest days, Pearl is a "half-fledged angel of judgement" come to rout and instruct the sin-ridden Puritan community, and she, like her mother, accomplishes this "victory" to a certain extent (p. 1721). She is a moon-maiden who inhabits the New World, with the same characteristics as the medieval Pearl, whose wrath, chastening, and stern adherence to the truth can guide mortals to those heights.[17]

So, twice the female is a central—and apocalyptic—wonder of *The Scarlet Letter*. Specifically, Vivan identifies the image of Prynne as female hero allied to The Book of Revelation at the close of *The Scarlet Letter*: "The virgin, positioned at the end of the palingenesis, obviously recalls The Book of Revelation, to which there are various allied references: the eagle, the seven years' span of the narrative, and, of course, the seal and the letter" (p. 79).

In fact, Hawthorne writes this theme directly into the text. He shapes Prynne a woman-apostle who envisions the apocalypse and confirms that its herald must be female:

> She assured them, too, of her firm belief, that, at some bright period, when the world should have grown ripe for it, in Heavens' own time, a new truth would be revealed, in order to establish the whole relation between man and woman on a surer ground of mutual happiness. Earlier in life, Hester had vainly imagined that she herself might be the destined prophetess, but had long since recognized the impossibility that any mission of divine and mysterious truth should be confided to a woman stained with sin, bowed down with shame, or ever burdened with a life-long sorrow. The angel and apostle of the coming revelation must be a woman, indeed, but lofty, pure, and beautiful; and wise, moreover, not through dusky grief, but the ethereal medium of joy; and showing how sacred love should make us happy, by the truest tests of a life successful to such an end! (p. 1804)

When Prynne looks to the time when the veil will be lifted and the "new truth would be revealed," she is the model of an artist of the

Romantics and of Hawthorne. He, too, in "The Custom-House," speaks of revealing his own "inmost Me behind its veil" (p. 1670), and his works move inexorably toward "the day when all hidden things shall be revealed" (p. 1736), toward that apocalyptic cry, "It was revealed!" (p. 1800).

The final image of the novel is one of apocalyptic art. This is the gravestone of Prynne and her fellow artist Dimmesdale. When closely scrutinized, their gravestone's "sable field" is revealed to be a reminder of the text's alchemy, of its hidden levels, and especially of its poetic process of revelation, of unveiling and veiling, of heroic attempts at transfiguring (Vivan, p. 72).

The black gravestone possesses two more colors, equally significant. One, white, is carefully hidden in a manner that is itself emblematic. "Sable" is an animal with double fur, black on top and white underneath, and its figure is a common heraldic transcription and allusion (Vivan, p. 78). The white beneath the sable of the gravestone embodies the novel's unending duality (p. 80). The stone's last color is the "red" of the letter A. So, the gravestone possesses the tri-colors of the text; it is an entity which unites. Like the "philosopher's stone" of alchemic search, it is emblematic of final transformation (p. 80).

This stone also serves to lead the reader's eye back to the beginning, to the emblematic A, to its bearer Prynne, and the hidden mystery. In those opening pages, Prynne reminisced of her home in England with its "half-obliterated shield of arms," the emblem of her heritage in "antique gentility" (p. 1699). In essence, then, from the first to last, from the letter "A" to her family's arms and beyond to her tomb in Massachusetts, Prynne has been marked by heraldic allusions and symbols (Vivan, pp. 80; 91).[18] She, in turn, has marked the novel; she has been the bearer of its emblems and their mysteries.

Finally, "The Custom House" indicates the manner in which that emblematic A, and its bearer, come to function as a metaphor and a theory of art. All bearers of the letter—Prynne, Dimmesdale, and Hawthorne—are artists, and on many levels Prynne discovers for herself the same fate as Hawthorne does for being an artist. For example, in "Hawthorne's *The Scarlet Letter*: A is for Alchemy?" Luther H. Martin demonstrates that Hawthorne established the alchemical framework for the novel in "The Custom House" because, as a fanciful and romantic story-writer, Hawthorne is struggling to remove and transform the "black" curse and frowns of his severe Puritan ancestors. That is the same task Prynne will endure.

Hawthorne, like Bronte, embodies in one heterogeneously-natured woman the heroic forces of the triune Luna. She shines as the white crescent, grows into the reddish-gold full moon, and wanes into the black moon, preparation for her next creative regeneration. In this context can Prynne be read as a mysterious, creative, and dark beauty, a beauty of glossy black hair and black eyes, a beauty that leads to a scarlet sin which stains her white soul. Her offspring Pearl is a like united substance of the triple colors, and she serves to further unite myriad elements and powers. She becomes "the connecting link" between Dimmesdale and Prynne upon the scaffold and beneath a fiery comet in the night (p. 1749)—and into the future.

THREE

MOLLY BLOOM: THE HERO OF COMEDY

"Glimpses of the moon...."

James Joyce sought to create a text glimmering with momentary visions of a comedic New World. His idea of Molly Bloom, a female resplendent with music and dreams, constitutes a unique re-shaping of the myth of Diana, for Bloom is clearly a Diana-hero, one direly needed in a troubled old Dublin.

Molly Bloom is a complex Diana-hybrid, and in this capacity she is especially the queen of a comedic apocalypse, one that heralds earthly joy, not sorrow, for the New World. This comedic type successfully fuses the multiple powers of the moon goddess's myriad configurations, making it possible for her to be a strong regenerative force. Molly Bloom is identified, through the images of the red, earthly rose and the white, heavenly one, as a synthesis of the pagan goddesses of natural chastity or love, Diana and Venus, and the Christian ideal of celestial chastity, Mary. Bloom is further linked imagistically throughout the epic with the moon's perpetual cycle of birth, death, and rebirth. Herein lies Molly Bloom's comedy, for she embodies successive generation, the eternal process of creativity, the very nature of birthing a new vision and new life.

The Nature of Molly Bloom

Molly Bloom as a Diana-type. All women in Joyce's epic are Diana-types in that they are all associated with the moon, and this in turn indicates that the goddess Diana is the archetype for the female form in *Ulysses.* When Leopold Bloom embarks on his journey in the morning sun, he appreciates all women as "Glimpses of the moon" (p. 68).[1] Molly Bloom also uses moon imagery when describing women, as when she notes of another female "her beautys on the wane" (p. 618). A woman's body is typically "round and white" in the text (p. 638).

Or, Gerty MacDowell cuts her hair "on account of the new moon" (p. 286). Gerty's haircuts, based on the rhythm of the moon's phases, correspond to her menstruation, too, which begins with the new moon (p. 296). This connection between the moon's cycle and Gerty's is then contemplated by Bloom in relation to all women:

> How many women in Dublin have it today? Martha, she. Something in the air. That's the moon. But then why don't all women menstruate at the same time with the same moon, I mean? Depends on the time they were born I suppose. Or all start scratch then get out of step. Sometimes Molly and Milly together (p. 301).

At the close of the text, menstruation becomes Bloom's main physical act during her soliloquy (p. 632), so the text closes with Molly Bloom's cycle of creativity, one linked to the moon's rhythms.

Moreover, in the Nighttown scene, Leopold Bloom exchanges masculine-feminine roles with the many women in the scene, and his feminine transfigurations come under the realm of the moon goddess, with her triple powers. It is the "witching hour of night" in which Bloom wears a hat "with an amber halfmoon" (p. 364), and Bloom marries "the princess Selene, the splendour of the night" who appears "in moonblue robes, a silver crescent on her head" (p. 394).[2]

Another textual image in *Ulysses* is the mare, and the myth of Diana has always been replete with images, symbols, and motifs relating to horses, the tale of the life and death of her worshipper "Hippolytus" ("stampede of horses") being one well-known instance (Graves, I, p. 157).[3] Or, Diana was always the queen of Amazons, female warriors who bore moon-like shields as they rode their fierce steeds into battle. In fact, Joyce links mares with the configurations of a huntress and the Amazons. The Lady Mountcashel rides out with her "staghounds" to a fox hunt: "Riding astride. Sit her horse like a man. Weightcarrying huntress.... Strong as a brood mare some of those horsey women" (p. 131). In the Circe episode, Mrs Mervyn Talboys, with her "hunting crop" is an "amazon" whose eyes "shone divinely" (pp. 381–82).[4]

These associations accumulate, creating a fine web of interconnections in Joyce's text. "The witching hour" of the Circe episode is described as

"A pure mare's nest" (p. 373), a fairly traditional image in myth and literature, the Shakespearean "Night-Mare" that haunts *Jane Eyre* and other texts. In Joyce's realm of the dark moon goddess, a nightmare literally appears as "A dark horse...his mane moonfoaming, his eyeballs stars" (p. 467). Also, a new-moon bride appears to Bloom: "She follows her mother with ungainly steps, a mare leading her fillyfoal" (p. 338). In this vein, the image of Molly as "a gamey mare" (p. 193) points toward her roots in the moon goddess.

From the opening pages, images of Molly Bloom relate to the moon: "Night sky, moon, violet, colour of Molly's new garters" (p. 47). Molly's mother is "Lunita Laredo" (p. 627), whose first name identifies her with the moon. Importantly, Molly was born in September, the Virgin's month, be it Diana's or Mary's (pp. 615; 618), and Molly's "female issue" Milly enters menstruation in September, too (p. 606).

When Joyce has Milly commence her womanly cycle in her mother's month, a cycle he has already tied to the moon, and when he refers to Milly as "Marionette" (p. 366), a little Marion, he shapes Milly and Marion as an incarnation of the moon's rhythmical waning and waxing: "...recurrence known as the new moon with the old moon in her arms: the posited influence of celestial on human bodies" (p. 575).

Molly Bloom, like Hester Prynne, has thus engaged in an act of womanly generation that points toward an awareness of woman's role in the millennium; it points to the successive generation—within history—that moves toward the apocalyptic moment when the old world dies and the new is finally born. Molly Bloom has done so, specifically, as a model of the moon goddess; it is her act as a Diana-hero.

This idea surfaces in "Artemis: The Pre-Homeric Source of Marion Tweedy Bloom," an excellent study by Sally Abbott that explores Bloom's roots in the moon goddess. Abbott notes that the figure of Penelope, Molly's model, originates in the "virgin" goddesses such as Artemis, the word "virgin" being used in the ancient sense that the goddess refuses to have a single husband, for she embodies nature in its untamed fecundity, wildness, and regenerative powers.[5]

In addition, "Penelope" derives from "penelops," a water or marsh bird associated with Artemis. This mythical bird is man-devouring precisely because it signifies Artemis, the moon goddess who rhythmically destructures in order to prepare for growth and change (pp. 497–500). Marion Bloom, likewise, not only engages in physical generation, but she continually constructs and destructs images and lovers in her mind, just as Jane Eyre constantly constructed and destructed images of life before her homefires. In short, Bloom constantly engages in all aspects of regeneration.

This specific kind of Dianesque imagery surrounds Molly Bloom to the close of the epic, where it becomes a main symbol of the Blooms' marriage. Leopold contemplates the "special affinities" between the moon and women:

> Her antiquity in preceding and surviving successive tellurian generations: ...her constancy under all her phases, rising and setting by her appointed times, waxing and waning: ...her potency over effluent and refluent waters:... (p. 576).

He soon climbs into Molly's bed and settles into the imprint of another man, which spurs him into deeper meditations on the links between the moon and women. Both create constant cycles of life and love, and he muses:

> "To reflect that each one who enters imagines himself to be the first to enter whereas he is always the last term of a preceding series even if the first term of a succeeding one, each imagining himself to be first, last, only and alone whereas he is neither first nor last nor only nor alone in a series originating in and repeated to infinity" (p. 601).

In sum, Molly Bloom embodies the infinite process, the perpetual nature, of the Queen Moon's cycle of creativity. Bloom's famous "Yes" is the final, and eternal feminine, affirmation to unending nascency. Her "yes" embodies the Diana-hero's power of poesis, even in the perplexing, disconsolate, and temporal world of Joyce's Dublin.

Molly Bloom as a Diana-hybrid. Molly Bloom is a synthesis of the many configurations of the Myriad-Named moon goddess. Images in the text identify her as a Mary-Nymph-Martha-Bride-Rose-Muse-Isis-Penelope-Aphrodite-Juno-Gea-Tellus-Eve-Circe-Cleo-Athena-Cressid-Carmen-Mermaid-Siren-Sibyl-Leda-Victoria-Scarlet Whore-Star-Magdalene hybrid. She is the epic's "female form" incarnate in its "splendid proportions" (p. 521). She is the "full bloom of womanhood" who is "more than vi-

sion" of the female's "opulent curves," ones as beautiful as those of the
Grecian art in Dublin's museums (p. 533). In this complexity lies her
comedic powers.[6]

Myriad images synthesize Molly, women, and art, from sculpture to
music, throughout *Ulysses*. During Leopold's morning walk "in the track
of the sun" comes a beautiful image blending a mother, Molly, and a girl
with moonlight and music:

> A mother watches me from her doorway. She calls her children home in their
> dark language. High wall: beyond strings twanged. Night sky, moon, violet, colour
> of Molly's new garters. Strings. Listen. A girl playing one of those instruments
> what do you call them: dulcimers. I pass (p. 47).

A host of such images coalesce during the course of the epic to build the
symbol of one "Femininum!" (p. 359), the inspirational and harmonious
ideal "womancity" (p. 389), of which Molly Bloom is the terrific living
manifestation in the text.

One of the configurations in the ultra-hybrid Molly Bloom that makes
her nature so much of this comedic "Femininum!" is the Moon-Bride. Her
progenitor, Penelope, is Ulysses's Bride. She is in *The Odyssey* one
emblem of the "eternal question of life connubial" (pp. 532; 122, 165,
166). That is the question of joining over sundering, of harmony over
discord.

Joyce shapes the Greek's Bride to fit his Irish and Christian culture,
making Molly Bloom, on one level, "Marion" for Mary, the Moon of the
Church, Christianity's Bride. Molly's spouse, Leopold Bloom, witnesses
this fact, for his nature proves to be a synthesis of Sun-Groom
configurations from pagan and Christian myths. "Leopold" links Bloom
with the lion, the heraldic animal of sun gods such as Apollo, the brother
and oft times husband of the moon goddess Diana. Other images link
Bloom with Christ, Christianity's glorious sun king, and the true Husband
of Christians, typified by nuns who marry him and bear his wedding ring.
Various images in *Ulysses* confirm this idea: "The Christ with the
bridesister, moisture of light, born of an ensouled virgin, repentant
sophia...." (p. 152).

Moreover, Molly Bloom has the traditional dark eyes and "raven" hair
of the Bride (pp. 69; 262; 312; 359; 520), and she has the Bride's
Canticlean beauty, linked with images of golden wheat and female

fertility: "Naked wheatbellied sin" (p. 163). Molly, as this kind of Universal Christian Bride, in all of her biblical manifestations from "Eve" (p. 163) to Mary, can also be read as the Bride of The Book of Revelation, for not only is she the bride of re-birth, but the union of her and her spouse will herald the terrestrial paradise, the ultimate goal of the epic.

Moreover, the women in the text belong to a sisterhood of midwifery, another fact indicative of their role in perpetual life-giving, a role rooted in Diana, patroness of childbirth and midwifery since the moon was thought to control menstruation and labor. This Greek role is strengthened when conflated with Bloom's shape as a type of Mary, Moon of the Church, who can open the pathways to spiritual as well as physical renewal:

> ...Know all men, he said, time's ruins build eternity's mansions. What means this? Desire's wind blasts the thorntree but after it becomes from a bramblebush to be a rose upon the rood of time. Mark me now. In woman's womb word is made flesh but in the spirit of the maker all flesh that passes becomes the word that shall not pass away. This is the postcreation. *Omnis caro ad te veniet.* No question but her name is puissant who aventried the dear corse of our Agenbuyer, Healer and herd, our mighty mother and mother most venerable and Bernardus saith aptly that She hath an *omnipotentiam deiparae supplicem*, that is to wit, an almightiness of petition because she is the second Eve and she won us, saith Augustine... (p. 320).

Further, Joyce's bramblebush re-blooms as a rose because Mary is the "mystical rose" (p. 292), an image that surfaces over and over. Inspiring is the "whiterose scent" of Mary that Gerty inhales (p. 298). Such imagery is critical, for the images of roses blooming and the allusions to midwifery identify Joyce's women to be, like those of Charlotte Bronte and Nathaniel Hawthorne, agents of change.

With her choice of the red rose, Molly Bloom decides to work toward a terrestrial comedy. The choice is necessitated by her hybrid identity, composed of the varying configurations of the moon goddess, from the Christian Mary to the Greek Artemis or the Egyptian Isis, and it is necessitated by the schism between the celestial origins of these goddesses and Molly's mortal state. The images of moon goddesses and Molly are constantly parallel, except for a twist now and then that gives a mortal taint to Molly's. "Holy Mary" is linked with "Flowers, incense, candles melting" (p. 68), and Molly is linked with "full lips, drinking, smiled. Rather stale smell that incense leaves next day. Like foul flowerwater" (p. 52).

Moreover, while the white rose belongs to the Greek Diana and to the Christian Mary, so the red rose belongs to Venus. This not only indicates that Bloom's choice of flowers is a symbol of her famous choice between earthly love or heavenly, in either the pagan or Christian framework, but it points to her identity as a Diana-hybrid and allies her with others in the *Gestalt*. Bloom's possession of both roses signifies that her heroic nature is, like Jane Eyre's, capable of evaluating and balancing the heterogeneous elements in her nature. She, like Eyre, chooses the greatest happiness *on earth*.

This heterogeneous nature is central to Molly Bloom's construction as a Diana-hybrid. Not only do images of Venus surround Molly, in addition to all the images of Mary and Artemis, but, to a certain extent, Venus rules over the earthly sexuality in the epic (p. 143). Molly Bloom is titled its "Venus Metempsychosis" (p. 400). Also, from the first mention of The Scarlet Whore, Joyce seeks to embrace this configuration of earthly sexuality. He reminds us that Christfox "Women he won to him, tender people, a whore of Babylon" (p. 159). In the Christ-like Bloom's encounter with "O, the whore of the lane!" Joyce is equally accepting, adding the qualifier that the strange whore "Knew Molly" somehow (p. 238).

Abbott perceptively speculates that there is a symbolic scandal surrounding Molly's mother ("he hadnt an idea about my mother till we were engaged otherwise hed never have got me so cheap as he did" [p. 614]). Lunita Laredo retains her own name, never being "Mrs. Tweedy," which hints of no marriage, of Mediterranean mystery, and possibly of prostitution, all for the sake of linking Molly imagistically to the early Mediterranean fertility goddesses, who were moon goddesses (pp. 497–500).

Moreover, just as menstruation is linked to Artemis, so the erotic zone of female anatomy is imaged in allusions to the moon, whence derives Venus, too. The two are constantly blended. The mound of Venus becomes Joyce's "Mount of the moon" (p. 458). Joyce then juxtaposes this idea of pagan sensuality against Christian bliss, as when he writes of the Aphrodite in the museum: "Greek mouth...has never been twisted in prayer" (p. 165). Immediately, however, the pagan and Christian elements are conflated when Leopold Bloom views and responds to Aphrodite's statute: "His pale Galilean eyes were upon her mesial groove. Venus Kallipyge. O, the thunder of those loins!" (p. 165). Bloom also conflates spiritual-sensual forces in his perception of Molly: "woman's breasts full in her blouse of nun's veiling" (p. 144).

Joyce, like Charlotte Bronte, rewards his heroes who engage in a comedic resolution of conflicting forces, and it is this struggle of hybrid characters that he poses against the loss of other characters, who embody the antipodes of "stonecold" virginity versus "exhausted whoredom." Those are the enemies of joyful life in the epic, and Joyce gives the laurels to the hybrid Bloom, the "Marion" who chooses a sensual red rose. Bloom herself declares and celebrates this conflation of the sensual and spiritual: "...theres nothing like a kiss long and hot down to your soul" (p. 610).

Sally Abbott's work sheds more illumination on this idea of Marion Bloom as a complex hybrid. Mary, "star of the sea" (p. 284), derives from Marina and Myrrhine, ancient sea goddesses, so "Marion" Bloom is referential to both the Irish Catholic and Mediterranean pagan cultures. And Daedaelus, over whom Bloom fantasizes, was last seen by Bloom when she was in mourning over her own son—an image linking her to the moon goddesses who grieve ritually over their lost lover-sons (such as Isis and Mary). In sum, the sensuality of "Marion" Bloom becomes the grand conflict of female sexuality in Christian Ireland (pp. 497–500).

Ultimately, the full-natured Molly Bloom, the Spanish "Rose of Castile," chooses the red rose over the white, chooses earthly joy over celestial ideals. Like Bronte's Jane Eyre, who avidly chooses happiness "on earth," Molly and her choice, in Joyce's Ireland, were as radical in their day as Jane Eyre's choice was in hers. Theirs is the human condition—and struggle. Joyce captures this struggle, and its tragic triumph, in poignant cries throughout the epic. In the scene of renewal, in the maternity hospital, the realm of female labor, comes the cry "How mingled and imperfect are all our sublunary joys" (p. 331).

Molly Bloom as a Type of the Triformis. Marion Bloom, as a type of Diana Triformis, encompasses the choice not only of a white rose or a red one, but of a black flower that blooms within her, too. Specially, Joyce, like Bronte and Hawthorne, renders these colors emblematic of certain powers within his female protagonist, and he opposes each color, and the power it signifies, against one another, to heighten the epic's central tension.

To start, Joyce ties white to the "virgin moon being then in her first quarter" (p. 265). Leopold Bloom is entranced by the "Bluerobed, white under" sculpted curves of "Bassi's blessed virgins," a whiteness that belongs to a "goddess," each in the museum with their "cream curves of stone" (pp. 150; 213). *Ulysses* is replete with such images of and speculations on virginity, from this new moon to her virgins. Daedaelus early in the epic contemplates one, giving a "Keen glance" to the "virgin at Hodges Figgis' window" (p. 40), and Molly concludes that all men are absurdly troubled by a culturally-instilled desire for a virgin (p. 633). To this absurd desire The Bawd of the whorehouses panders. Joyce's mocking of an earthly fetish for snowy virgins, then, comes under the realm of the waning moon and its black Circe (pp. 352; 360–61; 440).

Joyce also associates virgins with light colors in general, not only white but pastels such as yellow. The "sacrificial butter" is the color of the pure Christ and his bridesister, "moisture of light" (p. 152). Golden caramel and butter are what the youthful Molly Bloom, behind a virgin's veil, ingests at the Sisters' Feast of Our Lady of Mount Carmel (p. 127). The moon itself is described as edibly golden in such epithets as "pineapple rock" (p. 137).

Joyce proceeds to develop the idea, however, that the colors white, gold, and yellow are beautiful but inadequate to encompass the spectrum of human life. Frequently, he has the mortal virgins of these colors go a bit off-color: the "otherwise carroty Bess, the gross virgin" (p. 168). The frustrated nuns, who are clothed in "white" habits, become so snowily chill that they invent barbed wire (pp. 127; 294). References to immortal virgins remain positive, from Saint Ursula (p. 278) to "holy Mary, holy virgin of virgins....Virgin most powerful, Virgin most merciful" (pp. 290–91). But mortal virgins, who deny their own humanity and its rainbow of natural colors, "go mad in the end" (p. 301). Their denial of life's myriad colors leaves them with only the "chastity of the tomb" (p. 321).

Joyce's mortal virgins can blossom into life, not madness, if they embrace the realm of red. It signifies the "womanly bloom" of marriage and motherhood (p. 329), one crucial role for females in *Ulysses*, from its various human mothers to the textual emphasis on *Amor matris* (p. 23). Red encompasses a mother's labor and "ruddy birth," the "wombfruit" of human life she produces (pp. 314; 347). This ruddy birth earns Mina Purefoy the sacred "chalice" on her swollen belly (p. 489). The young maids whose "lily virtue" still belongs to Mary may be clothed in "white and saffron," but upon the night they are wedded, the night of their "deflowering," theirs becomes the red "stain" (pp. 321; 633). Crimson blood also serves as an allusion to female menses, the "bloodflows" of Molly and others (p. 316), red flows which make ruddy births possible.

The color white is not only juxtaposed against red but black, and in many episodes, such as Nighttown, the two come together, with the dark subsuming the light for the moment. In one instance, the milk of motherhood is first identified with whiteness, paradise, and fulfillment:

> Drink, man, an udderful! Mother's milk, Purefoy, the milk of human kin, milk too of those burgeoning stars overhead rutilant in thin rainvapour, punch milk, such as those rioters will quaff in their guzzling den, milk of madness, the honeymilk of Canaan's land. Thy cow's dug was tough, what? Ay, but her milk is hot and sweet and fattening. No dollop this but thick rich bonnyclabber. To her, old patriarch! Pap! (p. 346)

However, this blessed white milk is held within a figure of the black witch. The hag, an old woman with "shrunken paps," bears "white milk, not hers" in a jug (p. 12). The image might seem to render the old woman empty and pathetic, but not when taken in context with the host of images of hags, dark Circes selling virgins, and witch-like figures ruling throughout *Ulysses*. They are parallel images of the continuous cycle, of the new moon holding in her arms the old moon to come and vice versa (p. 575).

Images of a "wandering crone," an "Old and secret...witch on her toadstool" (p. 12), a "burnished caldron" and "Old hag with the yellow teeth" (pp. 36; 42), to a "shefiend" (p. 39), or a "crone" and "virago" ruling "nighttown" (p. 351), go on and on in the text. These Circe-ish

hags rule over the realm of transfiguration, for they are the surfacing and
re-surfacing images of the witch-queen of the underworld. Through her
realm heroes must typically pass and then emerge reborn. Their presence
in Dublin is significant, for it is in a moribund state whence it needs
regeneration.

Poignantly interspersed in the epic are images of the strange and
potent "weird sisters" and the "witchroasting" of Shakespeare's *Macbeth*,
a drama of a kingdom's hellish interlude and hardwon restoration (pp. 11;
168). Two such weird sisters pronounce a harsh judgement on Ireland as
they sit atop Dublin, perceiving it to be a dying mockery of a promised
land and spitting plum pits down upon it (pp. 121–22). These figures rule
"The witching hour of night" and its transformative Nighttown episode,
too (p. 364), an episode replete with laughing witches whom Bloom, in
Shakespearean allusion, pronounces too "weird" for words (pp. 374; 488).

Importantly, their creative nightmare constitutes Bloom's ritual
passage, as a heroic character, through the "hells gates" of the underworld
(p. 367). The souls of the dead like Paddy Dignam raise their ashen face
"moonwards," toward the realm whence these weird sisters hail, and bay
like dogs (p. 385). All dead souls belong to them. In the "stagnant pools
in the waning moon" lie the "faded flowerwater"s of virgins. In short,
images of virgins and witches, of fresh and decaying life, of promise and
despair, of white and black, are constantly interconnected throughout the
text.

Daedaelus's mother in particular embodies this duality. Many critics
have noted the ambivalence the young poet feels towards his mother, a
flowing source of love but also of devouring power. Her name, "May"
Goulding, associates her with the youthful maidens of the "May" moon,
in whose glow lovers bask (p. 137), but her dead ghost haunts the poet
throughout the epic and associates her with the nighthags of the epic who
belong to Hekate's demonic realm.

Many times, Joyce mixes the potency of black magic with images of
virgins in pretty "yellow shoes" (p. 339). These pastel beauties possess
underneath a power to bewitch. "Why have women such eyes of
witchery?" Bloom muses as he gazes on the maid Gerty MacDowell
(p. 286). It is the maids' "Devils ...Dark devilish" element that rises up
while they're in menses (p. 302)—an image tying white virgins, black
devils, and red menses simultaneously.

From the mingling of these colors arises the opalescent brilliance of Joyce's heroic females, and males too. One picture of his Blessed Bride and her Groom encompasses ebony, silver, and reddish gold in a manner symbolic of regeneration: "black blessed virgin with the silver dress and the sun dancing 3 times on Easter Sunday" (pp. 625; 438). Here is the black and silver moon-bride dancing with a red or golden sun-king, an image of triple-colored joy. Here is the new estate sought from Dante to Charlotte Bronte, one so hard to achieve given the mingled joys, the sorrows and errors, of human life.

This idea of a triad Joyce also applies not only to colors but to women. The Shakespearean "witchroasting" that alludes to *Macbeth*'s three weird sisters (p. 168) figures again when Leopold Bloom returns home one night evilly drunk to find "three women" who "didnt' near roast him, it's a queer story, the old one, Bloom's wife, and Mrs O'Dowd that kept the hotel" (p. 251). Or, "Three wise virgins" await Bloom in Nighttown (p. 425), and the black virgin, with her sun-groom, dances "3 times" in Molly's dreams (p. 625).

Zack Bowen's discerning eye has noted that Molly Bloom serves as a goddess in charge of inspiration, assisted, like Dante's Beatrice, by three women: (1) Mrs. Breen, who, like the Blessed Virgin, provides compassion; (2) Gerty MacDowell, whose realm, like Rachel's, is the contemplative life; and (3) Martha Clifford, who provides Saint Lucia's divine light and inspiration ("Young woman...To aid gentleman in literary work" [ch. 8]) (pp. 122–23). These wonderfully evocative images of triplicity go on and on in the text, imbuing the women with yet one more symbolc dimension.

The moon-bride dances threefold, perhaps to triple her power to bewitch her sun-groom, to thrice puissantly entice him to her, so that their union may herald a true apocalypse.

Sign and Countersign: The Union of Locks and Keys in *Ulysses*

Unlocking the Feminine: From Diana to Venus. Virginity, the harmonic containment of the forces of nature, has many representations in literature and art, from the walled and locked garden to the well-thorned white rose of Diana and Mary. Lust has its symbols, too, from the sensual and open garden to the perfumed red rose of Venus. For mortals, a balance between the ideal of virginity and the reality of lust lies in the tradition of "chaste love" and "chaste marriage," a construct Joyce applies to his Ulysses-Penelope scheme: "Twenty years he dallied there between conjugial love and its chaste delights and scortatory love and its foul pleasures" (p. 165).

Like references are present throughout the text: "...as her loving eyes behold her babe...the fruit of their lawful embraces" (p. 343). Ultimately, Leopold Bloom searches in *Ulysses* for the key which will unlock the garden of his lawful wife. That goal, their famous quest for "connubial communion," will give the final word to the epic. The struggle of Leopold and Molly, to unlock earthly delights, in the most viable manner, is not only a central one in the text, but one for which the construct of a Diana-hybrid is critical.

The image of the Dianesque nymph pinned over Molly's bed is one typical and key image of this theme, for the nymph's is locked-up sexuality, which can only herald human tragedy, sterility, and the separation of the sexes. Bloom admires the beauty of the nymph and saves her from the "cheap pink paper" pages of a magazine devoted to "stale smut" (pp. 444–45). He carries her off to his home and lawful wife, Molly Bloom, framing the nymph in "oak and tinsel" above their "marriage couch" (p. 445). In retaliation for this, the nymph comes alive in the Circe episode to condemn Bloom's act as an infamous one against her "virgin sward" (p. 448). She clings to her ethereal ideas of the feminine, sighing "O, infamy!" and covering her face in shame for having had to witness the goings-on in the Blooms' marital bed.

Unlike the Nymph, forever imprisoned in her girlish state, Molly is victorious in successfully unlocking her own sexuality. One of her initial movements in the epic is from her youth and the ethereal realm of Diana to womanhood and the realm of Venus, then beyond.[7] For example, in her soliloquy, she recalls that she and her "girl" friend Hester indulged in childish joys like nymphs as they innocently frolicked and slept together (p. 622). This youthful Molly wore a white rose, a white blouse, and a white ricestraw hat, which are all "newness" (pp. 625; 642).

Bloom arises from the innocent bed where she and Hester slumber in each other's arms, and she walks to the window to see Captain Grove. Their eyes exchange a sexually charged glance, and Molly blooms in "excitement like a rose," the red rose I assume. In a mirror, Bloom "hardly recognised" herself in "the change" (pp. 622; 643). Her journey as a woman has begun.

Her quest is revealed to be an intricately complicated one, for the act of unlocking feminine fecundity has a spiritual, as well as sexual, context in *Ulysses*. Joyce shapes his Diana-hybrid, "Marion" Bloom, as a type of Mary—especially in her role as Moon of the Church. The purpose of this role of Mary Joyce points to in the image: "...on the quiet church whence there streamed forth at times upon the stillness the voice of prayer to her who is in her pure radiance a beacon ever to the stormtossed heart of man, Mary, star of the sea" (p. 284). This image of a radiant beacon in the night for mortals indicates that Mary, as the Moon of the Church, is an illuminating Bride whose light guides Christian wayfarers, traditionally typed as male, on the shadowy earth; her soulful mysteries they seek to unlock, and her soulful bliss they seek to wed. To "unlock" Marion's state, then, can be read as a spiritual as well as a physical act, as a psychosexual triumph.

Joyce continues to develop this theme in his epic, rendering the figure of Molly Bloom, and her journey through life, more and more complex. Mary is also titled the Moon of the Church because she intercedes between mortals and God, just as the moon is the planet that occupies that intermediary space between the earth and heavens. Joyce alludes to this tradition of Mary as intermediary in the "Nausicaa" episode:

> Through the open window of the church the fragrant incense was wafted and with it the fragrant names of her who was conceived without stain of original sin, spiritual vessel, pray for us, honourable vessel, pray for us, vessel of singular devotion, pray for us, mystical rose.... the great saint Bernard said in his famous prayer of Mary, the most pious Virgin's intercessory power that it was not recorded in any age that those who implored her powerful protection were ever abandoned by her (p. 292).

Later, Joyce ties imagery of an intermediary power, one which unlocks otherworld realms to men, to Molly Bloom, whose voice is a gift that bestows immortal bliss on mortal ears. As the epic's secular counterpart of Mary, Molly's music excites and blesses human life:

> [Bloom] infinitely preferred the sacred music of the catholic church to anything the opposite shop could offer in that line.... He also yielded to none in

his admiration of Rossini's *Stabat Mater*, a work simply abounding in immortal numbers, in which his wife, Madam Marion Tweedy, made a hit, a veritable sensation, he might safely say, greatly adding to her other laurels and putting the others totally in the shade, in the jesuit fathers' church in Upper Gardiner street, the sacred edifice being thronged to the doors to hear her with virtuosos, or *virtuosi* rather. There was the unanimous opinion that there was none to come up to her and suffice it to say in a place of worship for music of a sacred character there was a generally voiced desire for an encore (p. 540).

Sacred music is spoken of as a "mooncarole" (p. 229), a word that evokes the idea of the moon's power of inspiration and transformation. This motif is repeated in the text, for many of its women, who are "glimpses of the moon," possess this magical kind of music. Even the music belonging to the sirens of the epic, those "sweet murderers of men," possesses the power of transfiguring, for their music lures mortals to trespass out of their realm into an otherworld one (p. 541). The sirens' spell-binding voices entice and unlock for humans another sphere.

Importantly, music also belongs to Socratic midwives, whose image appears in *Ulysses*. Those midwives traditionally are a model for guiding men to the higher spheres of wisdom. The young poet Daedaelus wonders if Shakespeare "like Socrates, he had a midwife to mother" (p. 166). This reference to Socratic midwifery not only establishes Joyce's knowledge of that idea, and that he linked midwifery to the birth of male genius, but an examination of this Socratic idea demonstrates the unity, in the mytheme of Artemis, of the images of music, birth, wisdom, and unlocking knowledge for male worshippers:

In Plato's *Theaetetus*, Socrates is said to be proud of the midwifery of his mother, using her success in bringing forth the fruits of human labor as a high model for his philosophy, and Plato continues to offer to his pupil Theaetetus a detailed explanation of the art of Socratic midwifery as a model for his own art. Artemis was responsible for this laborious art, and her midwives sang incantations, gave drugs, and were the cleverest of match-makers, for those in charge of the care and harvesting of fruits must also know what sort of seed should be put into which sort of earth.

Ultimately, Plato pronounces that the Socratic art is no less than the "art of midwifery" and the "gift of midwifery" that Socrates and his mother received from God. Plato concludes that true philosophy has the same characteristics as those of real midwifery, except that the philosopher attends to men, not women, and he watches over their minds in childbirth, not bodies (pp. 12–13; 109). In this light, the midwives of Diana are, in Socratic tradition, prototypes of the Western world's later concept of a Luna-Ecclesia who midwives the minds of male poets. Thus, in this Socratic idea lies one key to mortal bliss, pivoting on image of women singing magical incantations to bring forth new blessings. In this context can Joyce's images of midwifery and music surrounding Molly Bloom be read.

Critically, however, Molly Bloom's spirit and art are like Jane Eyre's, in that they are not only inspirational to men. Her poetry is equally creative to construct images and express feelings of her own inner life, a fact best evidenced in her soliloquy, a beautiful pattern of words that she weaves in her mind to image her inmost self. This factor points to Molly Bloom as a Diana-hero who, like others, is engaged in a long quest of self-realization.

In *Ulysses*, a *gestalt* arises from the myriad images of the moon, music, midwives, Artemis, Molly, the Bride, Mary, Luna-Ecclesia—and this is Joyce's *Femininum*. Many critics have noted that to unlock that secret is to attain paradise, and Bonnie Kime Scott has particularly observed that Joyce presents his *Femininum* as a state against which are posed the "male-centered" values of his sterile Ireland. The *Femininum* constitutes "a corresponding Utopian vision of a world shifted toward female values, a kind of androgynous world balance." This idea evokes and demands "one of the most profound and persistent questions asked in this book, and especially in the final chapters" (p. 6). If the Apocalypse shall be realized in *Ulysses*, in the form of a terrestrial paradise, it shall certainly—and only—come when the Groom successfully enters into harmony with the state of the *Femininum*.

The union of the Bride and Groom is central to the epic, for it can unlock the terrestrial paradise; it can herald the apocalypse. Leopold Bloom searches not for the sake of his key itself, but for the union this points to: "Locks and keys!" (p. 238). Both Leopold Bloom and Stephen Daedaelus are frustrated because they cannot achieve this intercourse. They are "the...keyless couple" who, in the epic's final pages, seek entrance to Molly Bloom's house and inspiring presence (p. 546). When Daedaelus later leaves this house, his exit is depicted in images of keys and locks that are so symbolical they conjure up an image of a female womb, one which the male can finally enter and exit in a free manner:

> How did the centripetal remainer afford egress to the centrifugal departer?
> By inserting the barrel of an arruginated male key in the hole of an unstable female lock, obtaining a purchase on the bow of the key and turning its wards from right to left, withdrawing a bolt from its staple, pulling inward spasmodically an obsolescent unhinged door and revealing an aperture for free egress and free ingress (pp. 577-78).

In sum, Molly Bloom, as the epic's fullest embodiment of the *Femininum*, can be read as Joyce's secular counterpart of the Cosmic Soul, for she is the queen of her "virgin Dublin" (p. 154). Like Diana of the Crossways, Molly Bloom is the mistress of that liminal point (her home) from which heroes ingress and egress, with much ado paid to locks and keys, to unions that can open and harmonize.

Hieros Gamos: The Revelation in 20th Century Ireland. The sacred wedding, the *hieros gamos*, of the sun god and moon goddess heralds the beginning of a new domain. And so the union of a male hero of the sun and a female hero of the moon offers the possibility of a terrestrial paradise in *Ulysses*. For this end its two heroes, the poetic Daedaelus and the scientific Bloom, are as carefully tied to the archetype of the sun god, the "Universal Husband" (p. 343) as women in the epic are tied to the moon goddess.

Musing on Daedaelus, Marion Bloom images first women, then the radiant moon, as the lodestar of male poets: "I always liked poetry...they all write about some woman in their poetry well I suppose he wont find many like me where softly sighs of love the light guitar where poetry is in the air the blue sea and the moon shining so beautifully coming back on the nightboat" (p. 637). She then connects Daedaelus the poet, and men in general, with the sun: "hes young those fine young men I could see down in Margate strand bathingplace from the side of the rock standing up in the sun naked like a God or something and then plunging into the sea with them why aren't all men like that thered be some consolation for a woman like that lovely little statue he bought...theres real beauty and poetry for you I often felt I wanted to kiss him all over" (p. 638).

Leopold Bloom is immediately linked with imagery of the sun. His name derives from the lion, the heraldic animal of the sun-king. Bloom begins his morning stroll in the sun, deliberately crossing to the "bright side" (p. 46) so that he may walk "in the track of the sun" (p. 47). Joyce even makes Bloom self-conscious of his origin, for he reads *Was Jesus a Sun Myth* (p. 396), then proceeds to link himself with Jesus when he informs Dubliners, "Christ was a jew like me" (p. 280). And, during his strolls through Dublin, Bloom is attracted to images of women and the moon: "A mother watches me from her doorway. She calls her children home in their dark language. High wall: beyond strings twanged. Night sky, moon, violet, colour of Molly's new garters..." (p. 47).

One way that Leopold Bloom consummates his union with the moon is to ingest it. Joyce's moon is imaged as "Pineapple rock, lemon platt, butter scotch," terms themselves connected with a "sugarsticky girl" (pp. 124; 137; 223; 396). All three would be desirably "eaten" in their golden sweetness, and such symbolism is constant in the epic. Mary's festival is linked with sweet "caramel," and the nuns celebrate it with "butter" that the youthful bride Molly ingests into herself (pp. 127; 152). Later, she shares this act with Leopold: "Softly she gave me in my mouth the seedcake warm and chewed.... Joy: I ate it: joy" (p. 144).

Molly's act of sharing, especially of sharing food, the vital essence of human life, is a highly sexual act, and it is the essence of the *hieros gamos* in *Ulysses*, for the married state is equated with overcoming the ineluctable modality of being—whether that modality be male, female, or something else. That is the ideal goal. When our mortal state ends, so shall the ineluctable modality of men and women: "but that in the economy of heaven, foretold by Hamlet, there are no more marriages, glorified man, an androgynous angel, being a wife unto himself" (p. 175). The mutual eating of Leopold and Molly Bloom hints at this state; it is one act, however limited, through which the two separate sexes may come to share their vitality while on this earth.

In a peculiarly modern irony, however, Joyce's Groom and traditional Savior, Christus-Bloom, cannot successfully produce a male heir. Just as the Reverend Arthur Dimmesdale leaves behind only a happy female bride, his daughter Pearl, who functions as a physical projection of the woman Hester Prynne, so Leopold Bloom will only leave behind a female bride, the child Milly, who is in the main a projection of Marion Bloom.

Moreover, as an image of Marion, Milly is a poignant reminder to her father of the absence of a son, one who would be created in his image: "sir Leopold that had of his body no manchild for an heir looked upon him his friend's son and was shut up in sorrow for his forepassed happiness" (p. 320). Joyce stresses this theme repeatedly: "the bridenight .... light shall flood the world.... She is the bride of darkness, a daughter of night. She dare not bear the sunnygold babe of day. No, Leopold. Name and memory solace thee not. That youthful illusion of thy strength was taken from thee—and in vain. No son of thy loins is by thee" (p. 338). Bloom seeks to adopt the young Stephen Daedaelus, but this union is left as tenuous as the Blooms' earthly marriage, a kind of the *hieros gamos* that is inescapably flawed in this world.

On this level, comedic succession in *Ulysses* belongs, on this earth, to the females, to Molly and her projection Milly, and in this Joyce shifts his culture's dominant androcentricity back toward a balance with the eternal feminine, just as Hawthorne shifted his world's perspective, of Puritan fathers, back toward the feminine through the heroic characters of Hester Prynne and Pearl.

Both texts end with the women, Molly Bloom and Hester Prynne, envisioning images of apocalypse. Molly's creative visions focus on love as the transforming factor: "love is sighing I am dying still if he wrote it I suppose thered be some truth in it true or no it fills up your whole day and life always something to think about every moment and see it all round you like a new world" (p. 624).

Molly Bloom as Infinite Poesis: The Moon Goddess as Eternal Spinstress in *Ulysses*

Marion Bloom, like most heroes modelled on the archetype of Diana, is a spinstress. Images of weaving begin early in the text. Stephen Daedaelus ruminates on life and time...: "Weave, weaver of the wind" (p. 21), and this weaving is soon associated with the moon and its goddess:

> To no end gathered; vainly then released, forth flowing, wending back: loom
> of the moon. Weary too in sight of lovers, lascivious men, a naked woman
> shining in her courts, she draws a toil of waters (p. 41).

This "loom of the moon" indicates Joyce possessed the idea of the
moon goddess as spinster, and other images in *Ulysses* support this. Joyce
applies his weaving motif more than once to his "mother Church"
(p. 319): "A long look from dark eyes, a riddling sentence to be woven
and woven on the church's looms" (p. 22). And his Mother Church is,
by analogue, Mary in his text.

This theme is critical to appreciating Molly Bloom's poetic powers as
a Diana-hero, for her main act, the creation of her soliloquy, is a weaving
of myriad images in her mind. The mythical idea of the moon goddess
as a creative spinner Briffault documents in "The Moon as Spinstress and
patroness of Feminine Occupations." Feminine duties such as spinning
and weaving were from time immemorial assigned to the moon (II,
pp. 624–28). The task of spinning, combined with the moon as a measure
of time, created the myth of the moon goddess as the undying "spinster"
of the heavens. She wove an ever-unfinished web of time and destiny.

Thus, nearly every configuration of a moon goddess—Artemis, Athene,
Minerva, the Nymphs, the Triple Fates—is a weaver and spinner. Even the
underworld Persephone is a weaver of shrouds (Briffault II, pp. 625–28).
The idea is catholic, and it is a main symbol of the moon goddess's
power of poesis. She weaves new patterns, and she does so eternally. This
is why her web is ever *unfinished*. In many accounts, the moon deity
frequently unravels by night (the symbol of her waning) what she weaves
by day (the symbol of her waxing). That is the exact act performed by
Penelope in Homer's *Odyssey*. Both she and Molly Bloom are arch-
weavers.

Moreover, Briffault notes this motif is responsible for the Blessed
Virgin's distaff and those of Teutonic or Nordic goddesses such as Frija,
a spinstress whose distaff was Orion (II, pp. 624–25). Mary, as the Moon
of the Church, is a symbol of the renewing powers of Christianity, and
her distaff is one key to this, for it is her tool to continue making the
ever-woven designs of ancient goddesses, her designs being woven anew
"on the church's looms" (p. 22).

Especially, the etymological roots of "moon" (*men*) link the idea of the moon not only to the idea of measuring time (*ma*) but to the idea of measuring as "knowing" (*mati-h*) in the sense of the study and acquisition of the parameters of wisdom and the mind (Neumann, p. 211–212). Much study points to the moon as a rich symbol from ancient times as the seminal reference for the creation and measurement of time and knowledge, of which her image as a Spinstress is one poetic manifestation.

Joyce would have found manifest precedents for this motif in Romantic literature, especially the works of Goethe and Shelley, two poets who influenced him. *Ulysses* itself hints at this. When Daedaelus precariously steers his way between Scylla and Charybdis, he turns to Goethe's "judgements" which "are so true. True in the larger analysis" (pp. 151; 161). Throughout Goethe's poetry, images of woman, weaving, physical creation, and looms of eternity co-exist, as in "The Spinner" or "Antepirrhema," a hymn to a "Weaver Woman's masterpiece." Equally important is Shelley's "The Witch of Atlas." Many critics single out Shelley's "Witch of Atlas" as unique to his poetry because its theme is solely the delight of making poetry. The maker of poetry is the moon-bathed Witch, and she "make"s by the act of weaving. In fact, Shelley's Witch weaves the Romantic veil:

> Which when the lady knew, she took her spindle
> And twined three threads of fleecy mist, and three
> Long lines of light....
> And with these threads a subtle veil she wove—
> A shadow for the splendour of her love.   (XIII)

This veil is strikingly similar to the veil of Joyce's "everlasting bride" of revelations, and both point back to the same myth, for the veils of Shelley's and Joyce's women are made—are spun and wound and coiled—to be a symbol of the Apocalypse:

> How serene does she now arise, a queen among the Pleiades, in the penultimate antelucan hour, shod in sandals of bright gold, coifed with a veil of what do you call it gossamer. It floats, it flows about her starborn flesh and loose it streams, emerald, sapphire, mauve and heliotrope, sustained on currents of the cold interstellar wind, winding, coiling, simply swirling, writhing in the skies a

mysterious writing till, after a myriad metamorphoses of symbol, it blazes, Alpha, a ruby and triangled sign upon the forehead of Taurus (p. 338).

The motif of spinning gains even greater significance in *Ulysses* when the patterns spun on the moon's loom are employed not only as an emblem for apocalypse but as a metaphor for the creation of art and life as well. Joyce's young poet-hero meditates this:

> As we, or mother Dana, weave and unweave our bodies, Stephen said, from day to day, their molecules shuttled to and fro, so does the artist weave and unweave his image. And as the mole on my right breast is where it was when I was born, though all my body has been woven of new stuff time after time, so through the ghost of the unquiet father the image of the unliving son looks forth. In the intense instant of imagination... (pp. 159–60).

From this, one can argue that the artistry of Molly Bloom's soliloquy, in which she makes the epic's final "Yes," is rooted in Joyce's motif of the "loom of the moon," for her monologue is patterned as the mysterious interweavings of a woman's mind (Tolomeo, pp. 439–54). Indeed, all of Molly Bloom's artistry, such as her music, Joyce associates in some manner with the idea of spinning: "...the accompanist wove music slow" (p. 231).

If one proceeds with this idea, what is *Ulysses* but Joyce's intricate pattern of interwoven images and characters? And if, as shown, the loom of the moon goddess is one symbol for Joycean art, then what is Molly Bloom but a projection of Joyce as an artist? In this context, Molly Bloom must be a Joycean artist as much as any other "male" hero in the text. True to the archetype of a Diana-hero, Molly Bloom is an artist striving to image paradise in her mind just as Jane Eyre or Hester Prynne so strive.

The singular nature of this kind of female artistry is once again portrayed by Shelley's "Witch of Atlas." The weaving Witch of Atlas possesses the "strange art" of creating a "living Image" (XXXV) and the "moonlight splendour" of her creations is "of intensest rime." In this, it is the highest creation of a poet, male or female, who strives for that Joycean "intense instant of imagination."

The loom of a Diana-type makes poetry. The "intensest" light of her tapestries can even "[dim] the burning brand" of the firmament:

All day the wizard lady sate aloof,
  ...Or broidering the pictured poesy
Of some high tale upon her growing woof,
    Which the sweet splendour of her smiles
        could dye
In hues outshining Heaven—and ever she
Added some grace to the wrought poesy. ("Witch of Atlas," XXVI)

Lunacy and Melody: The "Wrought Poesy" of Prophecy. Poetry is that "intensest rime" that turns words into symphonies. In *Ulysses*, Molly Bloom and females reign in the realm of music, of weaving melodies: "High wall: beyond strings twanged. Night sky, moon, violet, colour of Molly's new garters. Strings. Listen. A girl playing one of those instruments what do you call them: dulcimers. I pass" (p. 47). Molly is a gifted singer, and ultimately, the music of women points to paradise because, like their creative spinning, it derives from the mytheme of the moon goddess and her harmonious spheres.

In this manner, Molly Bloom reigns in the epic as both a creative figure and an inspiration to creativity. She not only sings, but her songs move those who hear it to new acts. The creative power of her music crosses the threshold from art into life. Her "music" is "a form of art for which Bloom, as a pure amateur, possessed the greatest love" (p. 539), and the joyful melody she makes at one concert later inspires her and her groom to more creative activity: "Happy. Happy. That was the night...." (p. 128). The poesis implied in the passage is the making of Rudy. Music is paralleled with the art of making new life through the figure of Molly Bloom.

Joyce links inspiring music to the sphere of the triune moon goddess not only by having it arise from his Diana-hero but from identifying it directly as a "mooncarole":

> It was the only language.... Walking, you know, Ben, in the moonlight with those earthquake hats. Blending their voices. God, such music, Ben. Heard as a boy. Cross Ringabella haven mooncarole (p. 229).

In fact, images of Molly, a goddess, triplicity, and music are conflated: "Body of white woman, a flute alive. Blow gentle. Loud. Three holes, all women. Goddess I didn't see" (p. 234). Molly Bloom is a human incarnation of a goddess's ethereal music, a melodious Diana-hero for a discordant Dublin.

Moreover, there exists a literary tradition of the music of the moon goddess being the source and agent for apocalyptic poesis. The "hymn of nine times nine" is one that "Poets oft have sung in rhyme," especially Elizabethan poets, like Drayton, who were guided and inspired by Diana's moonlight and mystical numbers. To triple the powers of the Triple Dian, to reach the height of "nine," was to arrive at her mystical numbers, and that was harmonious poetry at its best.[8]

Of this sacred tradition, of Diana, her music, and its poetic powers, Molly Bloom is a renewal and living symbol transplanted into the modern world. Ellman constructs a two-step argument that relates to this line of theory. First, he writes that "Scylla and Charybdis" end the first half of the epic on the note of art in nature, and Molly Bloom ends the second half of the epic by demonstrating nature is art, meaning that both deliberate and spontaneous creation are cojoined in Molly Bloom.

Secondly, Ellman clarifies that her figure then joins with Leopold Bloom's and Daedaelus' to create a tri-unity of poets. All three create individually artistic moments out of their lives (pp. 110–11). Moreover, Bloom and Daedaelus ultimately turn to and claim for themselves women's gossip, letters, dance, and music to gain forms for their artistic expression (p. 206). By deduction, then, Triple Dian, who is Joyce's seminal model for women and their gifts in *Ulysses*, is a main signifier of poetry in the text. From this, one can make a reasonable argument that her triune configuration is one of the patterns from which Joyce derives his tri-unity of poets.

Reinforcing this theory is the fact that Leopold and Daedaelus also subsume the moon goddess's art of spinning—spinning words—and the culmination of this fine art in the epic is Molly Bloom's creation of her soliloquy.[9] In sum, Molly Bloom is not only a poetic Diana-hero in the text, but to a certain extent the archetype of Diana is seminal to the figures of the other two poets as well, a theory conforming to the well-established presence of androgynous motifs in Joyce's texts. It also conforms to the heroism and artistry given the strong Hester Prynne by Nathaniel Hawthorne, whose male characters likewise turn to the feminine form of weaving and embroidery as a source of inspiration.

Repeatedly, Joyce ties poetry and prophecy to images of the moon goddess. From her sphere it derives, whether her poets be female, like Molly, or male, like Daedaelus. From the first time that Daedaelus declares his desire to move from "the fading prophecies" in library books to his own live words to renew modern Ireland (p. 33), his new prophecy is configured in images of the inspiring realm of Diana: "to the wood of madness, his mane foaming in the moon, his eyeballs stars" (p. 33). Also, Bloom imagines "selenographical charts" that map "the lake of dreams," and he connects these visions with the lunatic powers of moon and her women, they who "render insane" (p. 576). "Insane" is used in the sense of the "Lunacie," that state of fervid inspiration that the poet Drayton, among many, so ardently desired.

Ultimately, of the three poets in *Ulysses*, Molly Bloom gives the final prophecy, of terrestrial paradise: "Yes." As Carl Jung notes, "...it is Molly Bloom...who has the last word in her unpunctuated monologue, putting a blessed close to the hellish shrieking dissonances with a harmonious final chord" (p. 127). From Molly, who is the living body of music, the church, the moon, and poetic harmony, comes the final blessing, the Word.

Joyce also imbues her "Yes" with celestial imagery. Leopold, in his morning walk, meditates on "Yes," on the sun, the moon, and their celestial union in an eclipse. This becomes a type of his union with Molly, for his meditations soon blend into images of their own marriage, of Molly, the moon, and again on "Yes," which will be Molly's word of affirmation:

> He faced about and, standing between the awnings, held out his right hand at arm's length toward the sun. Wanted to try that often. Yes: completely. The tip of his little finger blotted out the sun's disk. Must be the focus where the rays cross. If I had black glasses. Interesting. There was a lot of talk about those sunspots when we were in Lombard street west. Looking up from the back garden. Terrific explosions they are. There will be a total eclipse this year: autumn some time.
>
> Now that I come to think of it that ball falls at Greenwich time....
>
> Wait. The full moon was the night we were Sunday fortnight exactly there is a new moon. Walking down by the Tolka. Not bad for a Fairview moon. She was humming. The young May moon she's beaming, love. He other side of her. Elbow, arm. He. Glowworm's la-amp is gleaming, love. Touch. Fingers. Asking. Answer. Yes (pp. 136–37).

When Bloom muses again on the creative marriage of the Bride and the Groom, he does so in grammatical terms, i.e. those of writing and words, which lead to fertile poetry:

> ...(parsed as masculine subject, monosyllabic onomatopoeic transitive verb with direct feminine object) from the active voice into its correlative aorist preterite proposition (parsed as feminine subject, auxiliary verb and quasimonosyllabic onomatopoeic past participle with complementary masculine agent) in the passive voice: the continued product of seminators by generation: the continual production of semen by distillation..." (p. 604).[10]

Bloom engages in these thoughts preliminary to entering his own marriage bed. There is Molly, who will now produce the final Word of the epic. She commences by contemplating if she should write her own book, inspired by her male muse: "...if I only could remember the I half of the things and write a book out of it the works of Master Poldy yes..." (p. 621). Her comedic authorship and its "yes" is an appropriate beginning to her final and all-encompassing "Yes."

The Word is a fitting end to her role in *Ulysses*, for, as Scott demonstrates, from its first pages Molly evinces an interest in words, an interest both spiritual and sexual. She asks the definition of "metempsychosis," and she constructs her own puns, especially those based on names, those words which represent a human's identity. Two examples are Bloom-bloomers or Mr. deKock, nicknamed for "going around with his tube from one woman to another" (p. 192).

Molly Bloom's poetic nature is indicated by her other plans and declarations, too. She meditates trying her hand artistically, an artistic hand inspired by a male muse, especially his phallus: "I tried to draw a picture of it before I tore it up" (p. 620). She also remembers, "I always liked poetry when I was a girl first I thought he was a poet like lord Byron...." (p. 637), and that is one reason she married her groom. Leopold reminded her of Byron, he gave her as a gift a volume of Byron's poems (p. 612), and he proclaimed to her, in the spirit of Keatsian Romanticism, "...everything connected with your glorious Body everything underlined that comes from it is a thing of beauty and of joy for ever" (p. 634).[11]

Indeed, Molly abdicates her love of the worldly Boylan for her love of spiritual Bloom: "...Hugh the ignoramus that doesnt know poetry from a cabbage" (p. 638). She realizes that Boylan's sexual powers are purely animal, devoid of the spiritual creativity she cherishes:

> ...the candle I lit that evening in Whitefriars street chapel for the month of May see it brought its luck though hed scoff if he heard because he never goes to church mass or meeting he says your soul you have no soul inside only grey matter because he doesnt know what it is to have one yes when I lit the lamp because he must have come 3 or 4 times with that tremendous big red brute of a thing he has (p. 611).

She asks her lover Boylan to try to raise himself to poetic heights, an act would that make him another male muse for her personal apocalypse:

> ...I wish somebody would write me a loveletter his wasnt much and I told him he could write what he liked yours ever Hugh Boylan...still if he wrote it I suppose thered be some truth in it true or no it fills up your whole day and life always something to think about every moment and see it all round you like a new world (p. 624).

But she can only achieve that "new world" in union with her true husband, Leopold. Together, the two try, however futilely, for a terrestrial paradise, and for a moment the idea comes true. It comes in the meeting of their souls, when to his proposal Molly says "yes": "...the greatest earthly happiness answer to a gentlemans proposal affirmatively" (p. 624).

In this moment, Molly leads Bloom: "I gave him all the pleasure I could leading him on till he asked me to say yes" (p. 643). She guides Leopold, just as she tries to guide Boylan and she plans to guide Daedaelus, into the inspiringly "mad" act of uniting with her spirit of creative affirmation:

> ...I asked him with my eyes to ask again yes and then he asked me would I yes to say yes my mountain flower and first I put my arms around him yes and drew him down to me so he could feel my breasts all perfume yes and his heart was going like mad and yes I said yes I will Yes (p. 644).

Ellman confirms that Molly Bloom's soul is impressive in its positive artistry. He considers her to be the "lyrical efflorescence" that brings creativity to the "dry, impersonal, and pseudoscientific order" of Dublin. He notes that hers is the only episode that has no specific hour, no o'clock, because she is lying on her side, an "8," the number of eternity and infinity, and in her episode the ruins of time and space and the mansions of eternity finally co-exist (p. 105). Her spirit confirms the opposite of Buck Mulligan's denying spirit "No," and though her own battle between "Yes" and "No" may be lengthy, its victory is foreshadowed in its own construction of "8" sentences (p. 106).[12]

On yet another level, Molly's "8" is the long-awaited and much-needed shattering of the male modes of discourse, with their rational, "linear" patterning of knowledge. This makes Molly Bloom's monologue a temporal, and radically feminine, re-ordering of a male-centered rational world—one in which Paradise could never be regained (Unkeless, p. 183).

Joyce's predecessors, the Romantics and Victorians, knew well that regaining paradise is on-going quest, one that will be the task of generations of poets to come. And, Bowen has noted that Molly's "Yes" is one affirmation of a vital spirit that validates this on-going process. Her affirmation is the essential feeling of comedy, of continuous and joyous renewal... (p. 15). One key to apocalyptic poetry in *Ulysses*, then, resides in the feminine, in the Dianesque, heroic voice.

❧ FOUR

ISABEL ARCHER: THE HERO OF TRAGEDY

"Who is this rare creature, and what is she?"

What happens when the poet's vision of a new Diana-hero clashes with the existing Old World? Henry James offered to his fictional world a new, fine, and troubled Diana-hero, Isabel Archer. She emerges a woman heroic in her nature and designs, and a woman stifled in both by a world that does not allow free expression for her gifts. Archer is a figure splendid and fresh among a host of cynical and worn-out ones.

Archer, however, is also stifled in her purpose to invent a new self and New World because of an element inherent in the traditional myth of Diana, the unconquerable chastity of the moon goddess. Chastity signified the moon goddess's purity from the earthly world and its lustful humans, but to experience life fully, and to give birth to a grander life for her self, Archer must purge from her old self this chastity and enter the modern world in all its sordid realities.

In a typical Jamesian paradox, Archer must remain chaste to be heroic in the midst of a sordid world, yet she must also cease to cling so fiercely to her chastity that it removes her from the real world. If not, the result will be, as it initially is for Archer, a stillborn child and a barren marriage. Archer begins as a dynamic hero in a paradoxical position in a tragically flawed world. Her success lies in her overcoming both challenges.

The Heroic Tragedy of Isabel Archer as a Diana-Figure

And the Creator uttered His decree:
'Whoever in the future bears thy name,
Wise, beautiful and courteous shall be,
And virtue cherish as her constant aim,
Renowned in rhyme, honoured in history,
It will be chronicled, and with its fame

Parnassus, Pindus, Helicon will ring,
"Isabella, Isabella" echoing.'   (Ariosto *OF*, XXIX, 28–29)[1]

Her Restless Nature. Henry James first identifies Isabel Archer as a Diana-hero through her name, "Archer." The maiden goddess Diana roamed the woods as huntress of the green chase. Well known were her fatal bow and arrows. Further, Archer is singled out as a figure from Titian, with whom Diana was a favorite subject. In describing Isabel's coming to England and his home, Ralph Touchett states, "Suddenly I received a Titian, by the post, to hang on my wall—a Greek bas-relief to stick over my chimney-piece" (I, p. 63).[2] Titian depicted Diana most often as Goddess of the Chase; she is a tall queen who bears a shimmering crescent as her crown and carries a sling of her fatal bow and arrows, in *Diana and Actaeon, Diana and Callisto,* or *Titian's Daughter, Lavinia, as Diana, Goddess of the Chase.*

Archer's physique befits a type of the maiden goddess Diana. She has the "light grey eyes" of a sky goddess, and they exhibit a pure "shining candour" (I, p. 143). Like the silvery moon, her "silvery eyes shone a moment in the dusk" (I, p. 134). She also is "slim and charming" (I, p. 27) as befits one modelled on the supple queen of the green chase. She is "spare, and ponderably light, and proveably tall; ...the willowy one" (I, p. 50). Her mind as well as her body moves "more quickly" than others' (I, p. 53). She is the "quickly-moving, clear-voiced heroine" who is natural and lively to the point that she reminds one "of flowing water" (I, p. 57). She is so "young and free in her movement that her very pliancy" seems to mock others (I, p. 118). Archer is "fond of a walk and had a swift length of step" (II, p. 342), she is "free of step" (II, p. 361)...the images go on and on. She is like "a free greyhound" (I, p. 37). She fits well the pattern of the sleek goddess of the green chase.

The inclination to step freely, however, creates difficulties for the Diana-type in her modern, civilized world. Through medieval and even Renaissance literature, the ideal was the wandering knight, male or female, and she was often a Diana-hero, be it Spenser's Britomart or Ariosto's Bradamante. But in modern literature, there are no longer fairylands in which male or female knights can wander and quest after heroic adventures. The modern female hero is trapped in layers of social conventions, from petticoats and whalebone stays to tea parties and constricted feminine roles.

Her wander-lust and free spirit can work both for and against her. Initially, James portrays his Diana-hero Archer as one severely-tried and socially-duped in her wanderings. The shrewd Madame Merle observes that Archer is of "a rather roving disposition" (I, p. 227) and she uses this against her, beginning her machinations that will end with Archer transported to Italian places where a false husband awaits.

Isabel Archer ends up in a prison, the Farnese Palace whose name implies a fortress and whose facade can conjure up images of dungeons (p. 307; 307 n.). Her quest on this level indicates the unique line of metaphoric development that Henry James elected to take with his Diana-hero. Charlotte Bronte assigned Jane Eyre a quest through a series of prisons until Eyre discovers the raw paradise of Ferndean. Nathaniel Hawthorne places Hester Prynne in a prison at the outset of her trials; her struggles end when she leaves the greater world to return to her cottage, a space of small parameters that is both self-imposed and willed by her larger culture. Henry James launches Isabel Archer on her quest as she delights in her perception of her state as a fortunate one of complete physical, mental, and financial freedom, only to find that she has been snared in a dungeon by an evil husband and her own ignorance.

Herein the ending of *The Portrait of a Lady* has more power than other endings. The Diana-hero has still not found a sacred "space" for herself in our world. She is only painfully aware of the enormous task this will present for her. This lack of closure in the novel leaves both Isabel Archer and the reader with the profound question of her fate. This is one manner in which Henry James makes the quest itself the main, on-going, and unresolved source of heroic action for Isabel Archer and source of serious contemplation for the reader.

Throughout the text, Henry James indicates that the questing Archer's singularly roving and rootless nature in particular makes her vulnerable to her tragedy. She can be taken up by any passing adventure—or taken in by any passing adventurer. For the entire first volume of *The Portrait of a Lady*, Archer wanders "about as if the world belonged to [her]." She does so simply because it is in her "power" to do so (II, p. 261).

James hints that Archer's risk-loving and roving nature is admirable but will precipitate her fall, for he ties it first to drinking, then to gambling:

> Isabel travelled rapidly and recklessly; she was like a thirsty person draining
> cup after cup (II, p. 274).

Draining cup after cup makes one intoxicated, whether it be on hard
liquor or the "free exploration of life," and this makes one foolish
(I, p. 101). We discover that Archer's father "was known to have gambled
freely" (I, p. 40), and a gambler is a person addicted to risks—just as a
drinker is addicted to cups. Evidently, Isabel inherited her fast-paced and
risk-loving nature from her gambling father, and in the end, she gambles
her happiness and her fortune away on a blindly deluded bet on the loser
Gilbert Osmond.

The text reinforces the idea of Archer as a reckless gambler. Her
nature harbors "a dozen capricious forces" (I, p. 41). Stackpole wisely
cautions her, "You're a creature of risks!" (I, p. 146), and she admonishes
Archer that her new-found fortune, which gives Archer an ability to
indulge her desires, will "certainly confirm your dangerous tendencies"
(I, p. 187). Rosier, a childhood friend of Archer's, wonders apprehen-
sively at the dangerous element in her: "He took a great interest in Isabel
and remembered perfectly the walk at Neufchatel, when she would persist
in going so near the edge. He seemed to recognise this same tendency in
the subversive enquiry" (I, p. 186).

Naively, like all gamblers who believe they will win the next day at
the next gaming table, Archer loves her travels because they feed a
constant desire in her, especially the one to "leave the past behind her
and...to begin afresh" (I, p. 39). Simply, she loves reckless action; she
loves to imagine the world "as a place...of irresistible action" (I, p. 54).

There is also no doubt, however, that James depicts Archer's energetic
nature as a unique, healthy, and heroic one amid the stagnant civilization
of Rome. He praises her spirit in comparison to that of women who are
mere creatures of this society, those social *belles* who sit and wait "in
attitudes more or less gracefully passive, for a man to come that way and
furnish them with a destiny. Isabel's originality was that she gave one an
impression of having intentions of her own" (I, p. 64). Her will to
"positive exertion" and her ability "To 'do'" shall, when they come under
the rein of a matured wisdom, aid Archer's salvation from the snares into
which she has so recklessly fallen (II, p. 348). In short, her identity as a

free-spirited and supple-limbed Diana-hero creates both her heroism and her tragedy, in James's subtle hands.

Her Grand Spirit in a Trivial World. Both Archer's heroism and tragedy are grand because they are rooted in an ideal Dianesque youth, innocence, and superiority. Archer walks "in no small shimmering splendour" (II, p. 276); she possesses an immortal "flame-like spirit" (I, p. 54). She contains inside "spiritual gems" and "jewels" of revelatory splendour (I, p. 163). She has a "mystical smile" (II, p. 319), and she has a "radiance," or "even a slight exultation," as she utters "truthful rapture"s (I, p. 151; II, p. 254). Her truths are no less than "sacred" (I, p. 240). Of worldly things her celestial mind knows nothing. She honestly declares to Lydia Touchett, "...but I don't know anything about money" (I, p. 35).

This element of grandness in Isabel's nature can, like her reckless streak, work for and against her. Ralph admires how she seems always "to be soaring far up in the blue—to be sailing in the bright light, over the heads of men" (II, p. 291). In his last days, she becomes to him no less than a beautiful "angel of death" ministering at his bedside (II, p. 477). But average male suitors, wary of Archer's noble mind and her reputation for intellectual pursuits, are frightened that she exists in "the cloudy envelope of a goddess in an epic" (I, p. 41). They deem her celestial nature "cold and dry" (I, p. 55). Archer certainly does have the ability, of a celestially chaste Diana-type, to turn an ethereally "cold" smile even on her good friend Henrietta Stackpole (I, p. 91).

Supporting this idea is imagery of the Virgin Mary, which also surrounds Archer, making her a figure so coolly pure that she cannot accept and balance within herself any worldly desires and elements, those typically represented by Venus. Archer is a "Cimabue Madonna!" (I, p. 182). The convent-bred Pansy prays to Archer as if she were "praying to the Madonna," and this "Madonna" answers the child "with unusual frigidity."

Ironically, Archer realizes that her ethereal nature and ideals will always leave her coldly alone on this warm and imperfect earth: "She often wondered if she ever had been, or ever could be, intimate with any one. She had an ideal of friendship.... But she often reminded herself that there were essential reasons why one's ideal could never become concrete" (I, p. 163).

Worse, Archer's attempts to reach correct judgments of earthly beings is hopelessly erring. It usually increases her predicaments. Her blindness to real flaws and her total ignorance of the worldliness in others leads her to reveal her "spiritual gems" to the vulgar Madame Merle (I, p. 163), who instantly perceives how easily the naive Archer can be handled. "You appear to have the vaguest ideas about your earthly possessions" (I, p. 176) Merle says. She then proceeds to appropriate Archer's "earthly possessions" for the use and abuse of herself, her sordid ex-lover Gilbert Osmond, and their daughter, who is an innocent herself but one had by Merle and Osmond in their backstairs manner.

In further irony, Osmond, a shrewd art collector, desires to add Archer to his collection precisely because she is an ideal figure. The Diana-hero possesses a "lustre" unknown to commoner women (II, p. 309). Once in his worldly trap, Archer, who could once soar, temporarily hovers, a "poor winged spirit" (II, p. 340).

This also works as a literary irony. The soul of Archer's namesake, Ariosto's Isabella, was "flown to heaven" in untainted bliss (*OF*, XXX, 17). In the modern world, a heroine cannot be whisked to the skies. When Isabel Archer lands firmly in the "base, ignoble world" of Gilbert Osmond (II, p. 360), her wings are clipped, and she wanders, without hope of celestial aid, in a "labyrinth" of "repulsive" and "ugly possibilities." Her fate is not to be a blissful ascension to the Renaissance heavens, but a permanent struggle on the decayed Continent.[3]

It is one of the text's most consistent ironies that Archer's high ideals always make her mistakes the more tragic. Archer initially imagines that the chaste love she feels for Osmond is mutual and that the two exist in a special "strange pale rosiness." She believes this in a "large decorated sitting-room" in a hotel that is "ugly to distress" with its flamboyant frames. Its naked muses and cherubs offend in "false colours" and "sham splendour." The bright-eyed and youthful Isabel cannot perceive how "vulgar" the worldly scene surrounding her is, nor how appropriate it is for Osmond and his love (II, pp. 261). She insists that Osmond is a celestial rose like herself, not the worldly rose his name indicates him to be, not the "faded rose-bud" Ralph warns her that he is (I, p. 291).

It is not until she has "completely lost her way" in the "ugly possibilities" of her marriage that she realizes her husband is an evil person whose touch will "wither" and "blight" anything special (II, pp. 355–56). Then, our Diana-hero grows "weary" with the world and its tin men who blight all that is natural (II, p. 411). Her heroic type, awake and stunned, issues a "cry for help" (II, p. 389). However, her strength and chastity will give her the ability to acknowledge, painfully, her errors, and hold onto her better self.

Isabel will confront in the main two worldly forces: flesh and money. Especially embodying these elements are Gilbert Osmond, his ex-consort Madame Merle, and his sister the Countess. Every one of the three engages in adulterous relationships and prizes money. Archer becomes involved with them when she receives a worldly inheritance: piles of money. Ralph Touchett convinced his father to leave Archer a fortune for "She wishes to be free, and your bequest will make her free" (I, p. 160). The older and wiser father warns Ralph that this will make Archer bait for "fortune-hunters" (I, p. 162), just as Henrietta Stackpole intuits that the fortune will be "a curse in disguise" to the naive Archer, specially to "ruin" Archer by exposing her "on the moral side" (I, p. 187). Even the corrupt but shrewd Countess cries, "Ah, my dear,...why did you ever inherit money?" (II, p. 455). The pile of money, in short, tied this green and fresh Diana-type to the social world.[4]

In *The Portrait of a Lady*, James reinforces his literary experiment, of trying the soul of a pure maid who is sold to the world, through the predicament of Pansy. Archer censors Osmond's scheme to marry Pansy to the wealthy Lord Warburton: "She cares for an other person, and it's cruel to attempt to bribe her by magnificent offers to give him up" (II, p. 388). But Osmond has no more scruples in so marrying Pansy than he did in marrying Archer. He flatly states his view of his child, "I set a great price on my daughter" (II, p. 318).

Further, James gave to Archer the name of "Isabel," a name within literary tradition, from Ariosto to Keats, that points toward this theme. Archer's predecessor Isabella was captured by pirates who are forerunners of Osmond:

> They keep me here a virgin well I know,
> Thinking that I will fetch a higher price.

...That to a merchant I shall soon be sold,
Then to a Sultan in exchange for gold   (*OF*, XIII, 31).

James "traps" his maids in this pattern. Isabel Archer and Pansy Osmond are trapped in the Farnese Palace, whose name "implies a fortress" (II, p. 307 n.). Ned Rosier, the true lover of Pansy, perceives this prison-like atmosphere of Farnese Palace, a bit extremely perhaps, but certainly not without justness:

> In a palace, too, little Pansy lived—a palace by Roman measure, but a dungeon to poor Rosier's apprehensive mind. It seemed to him of evil omen that the young lady he wished to marry, and whose fastidious father he doubted to his ability to conciliate, should be immured in a kind of domestic fortress, a pile which bore a stern old Roman name, which smelt of historic deeds, of crime and craft and violence... (II, p. 307).

This is an especially cruel irony for Archer, derived from the free-spirited goddess of the chase. Archer's final perseverance, then, when she awakes to find herself in a prison, is all the more heroic and singular. Unlike Isabella, she endures her fate on earth, and, unlike Pansy, she will triumph, not succumb.

One reason is that Isabel Archer is, like Jane Eyre, a dynamic hybrid figure, one composed of elements from both the pagan Diana and the Christian Mary. She is like Titian's Diana and Cimabue's Madonna (I, p. 63; 182). The easily deafeated Pansy Osmond is a passive Mary-type, one like the pretty but deficient Mary Ingram in Charlotte Bronte's *Jane Eyre*. Pansy has none of Isabel Archer's Greek forces and passions. Pansy has been exclusively reared in a Convent, a place "not like [this] world" (I, p. 199). When the sisters turn their product over to Gilbert Osmond and Madame Merle, the latter archly dismisses them with the words, "*Je vous salue, mesdames*", which are a twist on "*Je vous salue, Marie*," or "Hail, Mary" (I, p. 202; 202n.). The words identify the Convent as the realm of Mary. There Pansy has been schooled in humility and submission.

Ironically, Gilbert Osmond intentionally saw to this so that he might coerce his virginal daughter into marrying the highest bidder. When discussing his wish that Pansy marry the wealth Lord Warburton, and not the man she loves, Ned Rosier, Osmond states, "It's what I educated her for. It was all for this—that when such a case should come up she should do what I prefer" (II, p. 315).

Pansy does, but Archer cannot as easily accept her fate. Archer actively struggles to make the best of her life without conceding defeat. She resolutely determines "to make her peace with the world—to put her spiritual affairs in order" (II, p. 405). In the height of her grand soul, she even comes to feel "compassion" for the world-chained and thus "poor Madame Merle" (II, p. 432). Madame Merle ends conceding her defeat to Osmond, "You've not only dried up my tears; you've dried up my soul.... You're *very* bad." (II, p. 434). She ends admiring the final victory of Archer, whose "moral fountains" are forever "flowing" (I: 81).

In James's subtle sleight of hand, even more bravery is added to his Diana-hero. Ariosto's Isabella, when cast about by the world's rude forces, had one desire:

> The maiden answered frankly, without guile,
> That with God's help she had resolved to reach
> Some holy convent, to escape the vile
> And foolish world, and to perform good works   (*OF*, XXVIII, 99).

But that escape, like Isabella's later celestial ascension, is no longer viable in the modern world. The holy convent has become in the hands of Gilbert Osmond a "great penal establishment" (II, p. 460-62). And, to this prison Isabel Archer temporarily comes to offer help and flight to Pansy.

Moreover, once awake and rebelling, Archer is willing to cast aside her entire worldly fortune: "She wondered whether, since he had wanted her money, her money would now satisfy him. Would he take her money and let her go?" (II, p. 432). She draws on internal resources alone, on her forces stronger than the worldly ones of her foes:

> Osmond was as lofty as ever, but his wife would not be an easy victim. The Countess was not very exact at measurements, but it seemed to her that if Isabel should draw herself up she would be the taller spirit of the two. What she wanted to learn now was whether Isabel had drawn herself up; it would give her immense pleasure to see Osmond overtopped (II, p. 376).

Her Character Type. In the main, four facets inherent in Archer's identity as a chaste Diana-hero are key to her final victory. These traits operate dually because they are responsible for Archer's earlier mistakes as well as her final victory. These are (1) her innocence, (2) her imagination, (3) her Romantic heritage, and (4) her character, that of a celestial and pure spirit incarnated in human form and trapped in a trivial social world.

First, Archer's innocence insists on projecting onto all persons, even sordid ones, her "inflated ideals" (I, p. 54). This aids her fall into Osmond and Merle's hands. However, her "inflated ideals" also connect her to the best of idyllic visions, the Garden of Eden. Archer takes pleasure in imaging her own fresh and green innocence:

> Her nature had, in her conceit, a certain garden-like quality, a suggestion of perfume and murmuring boughs, of shady bowers and lengthening vistas, which made her feel that introspection was, after all, an exercise in the open air, and that a visit to the recesses of one's spirit was harmless when one returned from it with a lapful of roses (I, p. 56).[5]

Isabel indulges in these speculations in the shelter of the appropriately named "Gardencourt," a "sacred" realm (II, p. 414). Gardencourt is the "much-embracing refuge" to which the wearied Isabel returns, later, to replenish her wearied soul:

> She had gone forth in her strength; she would come back in her weakness, and if the place had been a rest to her before, it would be a sanctuary now (I, p. 465).

When enmeshed in the social world, there is much folly in this Diana-hero's blind persistence in her garden-green innocence. In fact, to continue basking in her idyllic bliss, Archer is willfully ignorant: "With all her love of knowledge she had a natural shrinking from raising curtains and looking into unlighted corners. The love of knowledge coexisted in her mind with the finest capacity for ignorance" (I, p. 173). This folly, coupled with her inherently "plain mind" (I, p. 215), causes an incredibly slow process of revelations of the baseness around her, revelations which will become all the more profound and disturbing for their retarded unveiling.

In the midst of these tragic revelations, however, Archer's innocence keeps her heroically true:

> But there were certain things she could never take in. To begin with, they were hideously unclean. She was not a daughter of the Puritans, but for all that

she believed in such a thing as chastity and even as decency. It would appear that Osmond was far from doing anything of the sort; some of his traditions made her push back her skirts. Did all women have lovers? Did they all lie and even the best have their price? (II, p. 362)

Eventually, Archer's innocent state, which lacks corrupt desires, triumphs when it infuriates and oftentimes humiliates the petty spirit of Osmond. The Countess may lament that Isabel has "so many scruples, so many reasons, so many ties ....a beastly pure mind," and she may even cry in exasperation, "I never saw a woman with such a pure mind!" (II, pp. 449–50). But, these sentiments, coming from a woman whose "spiritual principle" rattles and tumbles about like "a little loose nut...inside of her" (II, p. 375) condemn more the Countess than Isabel.

The second facet inherent in Archer's character as a Diana-hero is imagination, an imagination as green and active as the nature of its goddess, Diana. Archer possesses a "nobleness of imagination" (I, p. 54), and a love of knowledge so "strong" that it has "a fertilising quality" in her mind (I, p. 31). A dual gift, however, her imagination can go the extreme of being "ridiculously active; when the door was not open it jumped out of the window."

This wild imagination, coupled with Archer's gambling streak, leads to dangerous results. Her imagination initially "inspired her with a sentiment of high, or rare respect" for the sterling qualities of Caspar Goodwood (I, p. 42), but, joined with her reckless nature, it also causes her to abandon Goodwood, for when she receives her new fortune, she becomes intoxicated with the idea that she now has a course of absolute "freedom" in the world (I, p. 193). Her imagined ideal of complete freedom is a delusion, par excellence, for any mortal in the real world, with all its trappings and complications.

In a further Jamesian twist, Osmond marries Archer partly "because she was the most imaginative woman he had known" (II, p. 357). He proclaims, "You have an imagination that startles me!" (II, p. 262). And it is Archer's Edenic imagination that goes "forward to meet" Osmond's proposal. It even decks out this "perfect nonentity" with its own glorious trappings (II, p. 279).

In the next twist, Archer realizes that her prized imagination brought her to her troubled state: "...during those months she had imagined a world of things that had no substance. She had a more wondrous vision of him, fed through charmed senses and oh such a stirred fancy!—she had not read him right" (II, p. 357).

Then, James's pen, more subtle then ever, has that imagination allow Archer to grasp the enormity of Osmond's fiendishness while simultaneously holding her back from disavowing him. Archer perceives that Osmond is the snake in Eden—and that he is her husband, taken at a sacred altar. The latter "weighed upon her imagination...; constantly present to her mind were all the traditionary decencies and sanctities of marriage. The idea of violating them filled her with shame as well as with dread, for on giving herself away she had lost sight of this contingency in the perfect belief that her husband's intentions were as generous as her own" (II, p. 386).

James repeatedly refers to the almost-paralyzing force of her imagination, as well as Osmond's sly appreciation of this. He plays on it adeptly when he argues the sanctity of their marriage to persuade Archer to renounce her trip to England to see her dying cousin Ralph Touchett:

> ...he had the power, in an extraordinary degree, of making her feel this need. There was something in her imagination he could always appeal to against her judgement (II, p. 445).

In the last analysis, however, that imagination sets Archer right. It not only allows her to grasp the sinister nature of Osmond and hold firm to her own morals, it also allows her to recognize and pay proper homage to kindred spirits. She comes to appreciate and love the "mystery" of Ralph's "wisdom" (II, p. 364), for example, and his is a kindred wisdom in that it was purchased at a great price, like hers. Archer's imagination even allows her to be true, in crisis, to the desperate Pansy: "...her imagination was hushed with horror at the idea of taking advantage of the little girl" (II, p. 269).

Indeed, that her mistakes were made through her own "generous" imagination and spirit means that they likely will not hurt her "for more than a little" (II, p. 479). When Archer is tested with the temptation of fleeing her misery with her lover Goodwood, her imagination, still active but now more seasoned, comes to her rescue, for with it she can see the full horror of an adulterous relationship. It makes her choose the "very straight path" instead (II, p. 490).

In sum, her imagination, like her dogmatic innocence, aids her fall, but it also leads to whatever salvation she will find for herself—and make for others. To Archer, the Countess hopes aloud: "...we're dreadfully fallen, I think, and perhaps you'll pick us up. I have great confidence in you" (II, p. 300).

Both her innocence and imagination spring partly from the third facet inherent in her identity as a Diana-hero: her Romantic element. Like most modern Diana-heroes such as Jane Eyre or Molly Bloom, Archer has some roots in Romantic poetry. James states that "romanticism" is the color of her childhood, and the one home Archer knows in childhood, her grandmother's, is "romantic" (I, p. 32). Her imagination douses in "romantic" colors her wayward travels as a child with her father and his shady employees (I, p. 40). When arriving at Gardencourt, Archer brashly announces to Ralph Touchett that she has "brought a great deal" of the romantic to his prosaic old mansion (I, pp. 50–51).

In typical Jamesian irony, this romanticizing makes Archer hold back from Goodwood, the man who truly and deeply loves her, because "He was not romantically, he was much rather obscurely, handsome" (I, p. 42). Goodwood's solid exterior and demeanor do not fit Archer's naive illusions of rainbowesque romanticism.

Archer's romanticism is also dangerous because she is a hero of a modern novel, not a Romantic poem. Her romanticism can only be archaic and misplaced in her world.[6] Archer's modern friend, Stackpole, rails to her about the dangers of romanticism:

> The peril for you is that you live too much in the world of your own dreams. You're not enough in contact with reality—with the toiling, striving, suffering, I may even say sinning, world that surrounds you. You're too fastidious; you've too many graceful illusions. Your newly-acquired thousands will shut you up more and more to the society of a few selfish and heartless people who will be interested in keeping them up....
>
> Well...you think you can lead a romantic life, that you can live by pleasing yourself and pleasing others. You'll find you're mistaken. Whatever life you lead you must put your soul in it—to make any sort of success of it; and from the moment you do that it ceases to be romance, I assure you: it becomes grim reality! (I, p. 188)

Stackpole's words prove prophetic when Archer is enticed into the house of Osmond by his collection of "romantic objects" (I, p. 225). Her romanticism belongs in a museum, in short, and it so ill prepares her for her world that it lands her in Osmond's museum, an interesting romantic object for his cynical study. Osmond also soundly defeats the "young love" of Pansy and Rosier, a love that Archer admired as the "romantic form" (II, p. 366). Romanticism is a high-minded but archaic luxury for James's Diana-hero to indulge in his modern world.

The fourth facet of Archer's identity, her character as a human incarnation of the goddess Diana, is equally dangerous amid the everyday trivialities and broad corruption of the modern world. Estimably, she is, like Jane Eyre, an original, a social renegade of sorts. She possesses absolutely no traces of being "in the least stupidly conventional" (I, p. 60). She is "exceptional" (I, p. 243), and she very likely has "a genius" of some kind (I, p. 48). In fact, everything of the conventional world is an imposition on Archer and her Dianesque spirit:

> I don't know whether I succeed in expressing myself, but I know that nothing else expresses me. Nothing that belongs to me is any measure of me; everything's on the contrary a limit, a barrier, and a perfectly arbitrary one. Certainly the clothes which, as you say, I choose to wear, don't express me; and heaven forbid they should!... they're imposed upon me by society (I, p. 175).

Archer's objection hints at her celestial naivete, which can be quite misplaced. Archer's model, Diana, was the pagan goddess so pure that she was the only one whom the Masters of the Golden Age could, without censure, depict bathing in naked splendour (MacCurdy, "Bathing Nude," pp. 160–61). In fact, pictures of Diana's glorious nakedness were embellished to become an emblem no less than a "second Eden" of natural innocence (I, p. 166). But this heavenly innocence has become a foregone conclusion in the mundane and sordid world, and to Archer's protests that clothes hide the original wonders of her glorious self, the experienced Merle urges her to "take the worldly view sometimes" (I, p. 176).

Archer stoutly refuses Merle's earthly wisdom. She insists, typical of a Diana-hero, "I'm very fond of my liberty" (I, p. 30). Indeed, as a child, Isabel's grand and superior spirit caused her to leave school when "she had protested against its laws." This event gives her "the pain of exclusion," perhaps, but also "the elation of liberty" (I, p. 33). It also left her with even less of an education—precisely what she needs to comprehend the world.

Her superior ideas and nature eventually lead the Diana-hero into other errors. With her new fortune, Archer blissfully imagines her future to present untrammelled opportunities for a superior life, one blessed with a union "of great knowledge with great liberty." When Osmond begins to close his "rigid system" about her, she pleads in a high-souled manner for "the cause of freedom, of doing as they chose, of not caring for the aspect and denomination of their life—the cause of other instincts and longings, of quite another ideal" (II, p. 361).

Especially, her superiority leads to pride (I, pp. 55, 165, 195). Archer entertains "a general idea that people were right when they treated her as if she were rather superior" (I, p. 53). Such blind pride eases her fall into the snares of Merle and Osmond, practiced players upon her pride. She is "flattered" by their homage (I, p. 168), and when Osmond declares that she is the most important woman in the world, Isabel decides this is true. She decides to fill the role "with a certain grace" (II, p. 264).

In fact, Isabel Archer, filled with her own celestial image of her self, is too fond of her own way (I, p. 36). She is blatantly "presumptuous" (I, p. 52) and "a rank egoist" (I, p. 56). Archer rejects Caspar Goodwood and his love because his powers challenge her "sense of freedom" and threaten "diminished liberty" (I, pp. 104–05). The superficial—and sly—Osmond never presents to Archer the threatening prospect of not always having her own way. Ironically, Goodwood alone, from true motives and clean intentions, would have given Archer what he promised and she wanted: perfect independence in their marriage (I, p. 142). But as the shrewd Madame Merle perceives, Archer, in egoistic response, only enjoys the "power" she has over the powerful Goodwood (I, p. 176); she is vigorous in resisting his own potent spirit.

Just as pride went before the fall of a Greek hero, so it goes before the fall of the heroic Archer, out of Goodwood's true-hearted realm and into Osmond's sinister one. Only after much buffeting is Archer's rank ego pierced at the end of the novel: "Then she wondered if it were vain and stupid to think so well of herself" (II, p. 466).

With Jamesian subtlety, however, Archer's high pride, like her high imagination, innocence, and romanticism, will aid her in rescuing herself from the very snares into which those traits precipitated her fall, for her pride pricks her to struggle against her adversaries "to the end" (II, p. 466).

Moreover, her pride, when mortified, brings shame, and with this comes maturity and the resolution not to err again. She decides not to abdicate the sacred form of marriage, albeit with Osmond, for an adulterous union with Goodwood, and she explains to Stackpole that she is being considerate of herself, not others, when she does so:

> I don't know what great unhappiness might bring me to; but it seems to me I shall always be ashamed. One must accept one's deeds. I married him before all the world; I was perfectly free; it was impossible to do anything more deliberate. One can't change that way (II, p. 407).

Archer once contemplated, in the isolation and loneliness of her pride, if she were not too superior, too much of a "cold, hard, priggish person" (I, p. 102). Yet, her high pride and ideals will end holding up supremely the frail moral architecture of a decadent European world. In *The Portrait of a Lady*, the Diana-hero has found her natural mission, and it is a hard one whose challenge only she has the rare capacities to meet.

The Chaste Diana-Hero: Her Intimate Relations with Women

The Fate of Women. The goddess Diana was the protector of women, especially maidens; moreover, in her chaste splendour and her vigorous chase, Diana embodied the free-spirited female. In a literary work, therefore, a Diana-hero's status as a woman in her society and her relation to other women reveals much on this question. In *The Portrait of a Lady*, this question is immediately raised. There are two heroic female types, Isabel Archer and Henrietta Stackpole, the latter serving as a comparative model to the Diana-hero, for Stackpole strives to "make" a new world, in her own way, as much as Archer does in hers.

One of the first acts of these two "sister-spirit"s (I, p. 88) is to resist the traditional idea of marriage as the defining role for women in their society:

Henrietta, for Isabel, was chiefly a proof that a woman might suffice to herself and be happy.... even if one had not the journalistic talent and a genius for guessing, as Henrietta said, what the public was going to want, one was not therefore to conclude that one had no vocation, no beneficent aptitude of any sort, and resign one's self to being frivolous and hollow. Isabel was stoutly determined not to be hollow.... she held that a woman ought to be able to live to herself, in the absence of exceptional flimsiness, and that it was perfectly possible to be happy without the society of a more or less coarse-minded person of another sex (I, p. 55).

The reward for this belief of Isabel Archer and her friend Henrietta Stackpole is a lack of the usual bevy of fatuous suitors, a situation more to their credit than against it. In general, as women from the New World, both Archer and Stackpole are typed positively as free, heroic, and "self-sufficient American" girls (I, p. 195). Stackpole champions American women as "the companions of freemen" (I, p. 89), ones in contrast to the Old World figures of Madame Merle, the frail Pansy Osmond, or the corrupted Countess. The New World, both literally and figuratively, lies in the figures and the visions of Stackpole and Archer.

However, the resources of even the bravest American women are sorely tried in the World. When Goodwood proposes to see the married Archer in Italy, Stackpole confronts him:

"You won't hurt her, perhaps. But will you help her?— that's the real issue."
"Is she in need of help?" he asked slowly, with a penetrating look.
"Most women always are," said Henrietta... (II, p. 384).

Here is more irony. The Diana-hero, one fitting neatly the pattern of the fierce and chaste goddess, repeatedly needs help. So do her charges. Archer finds Pansy, "a childish martyr decked out for sacrifice" by Osmond, and Archer and Pansy have no "hope to avert" this sacrifice (II, p. 391). Diana saved Iphigenia, decked out for sacrifice by her father, but Archer shall not lift Pansy from the fires. There are no heavenly miracles to console the women mired in James's modern scenario. Isabel can do no more than stay by Pansy's side through the ordeal and guide her as much as possible.

Whatever can be salvaged of their lives depends on Archer's strength. The "vanquished" Pansy clings to Isabel's dress and cries not to be deserted: "I'll do everything they want. Only if you're here I shall do it more easily." Archer promises not to desert her, and they enter into a "silent embrace, like two sisters" (II, p. 462–63). The modern Diana-hero has to work to find a limited salvation for her sisterhood.

The theme of sisterhood is developed more with Archer's maturer "sister," Henrietta Stackpole. Ironically, she not only rushes to help Archer, but to urge the Diana-hero to help herself. When Stackpole learns from the Countess just how dire is Archer's situation, she decides "Isabel ought to make a stand." She sets out for Rome the next morning to accomplish this task (II, p. 378–80).

Archer intuits that Stackpole travels so far solely to aid her: "Henrietta...had after all a better reason for coming to Rome than that she cared for it so little. Her friend easily recognised it, and with it the worth of the other's fidelity. She had crossed the stormy ocean in midwinter because she had guessed that Isabel was sad" (II, p. 406). This sisterhood leads to salvation, too: "She had a sudden perception that she should be helped. She rejoiced Henrietta had come...." (II, p. 466). In this sense, Stackpole has striven, and successfully contributed, to "shaping" Archer's final triumph.

Of the men in the novel, Osmond is the foe of women *par excellence*. He uses all women: his lover Merle, his wife Archer, his sister the Countess, and his daughter Pansy. He condemns any independent activity of Archer, such as her travels, because he does not think "a woman ought to do that" (II, p. 261). He wants Archer "to have nothing of her own but her pretty appearance" (II, p. 359). Archer finally realizes the type of man she ignorantly chose: "The real offence, as she ultimately perceived, was her having a mind of her own at all. Her mind was to be his—attached to his own like a small garden-plot to a deer-park .... It would be a pretty piece of property for a proprietor already far-reaching" (II, p. 362). In her naivete, the Diana-hero chose the one man who strives to turn her green chase into his personal property.

On the other side, Osmond soon realizes in anguish that he has married a woman of heroic stature, one who can "turn the hot light of her disdain upon his own conception of things." This is a "danger" of which he had not even conceived. He comes to feel "hatred" intensely for her (II, p. 362), burning at her "freedom of mind" so much that he wishes to, literally, lock Archer in her room (II, pp. 363; 386). He threatens Archer with "revenge" if she disobeys him (II, p. 445). His reaction to the free-spirited Diana-hero is, in short, to immure her in a prison of his own design, as he has so immured his daughter.

Osmond views women as "plastic." Even his own daughter is an object to be molded to his worldly desires (II, p. 298–99). Osmond plays "theoretic tricks on the delicate organism of his daughter" (II, p. 442), and he educates Pansy for submission (II, p. 315). His feelings toward her are best revealed by his comment: "I set a great price on my daughter" (II, p. 318). The price is entirely material, as when he tries to force her into a marriage with Lord Warburton. In sum, both Archer and Pansy he cold-bloodedly manipulates into "unholy marriages" for his personal gain (II, p. 308). Truly a satanic creature, Osmond has deviously trapped a chaste Diana-hero and a sweet Mary-type in his worldly castle.

Thus James places his Diana-hero in a problematic situation. Ultimately she must rely only upon her own heroic nature, and that is her final act in the novel. When Goodwood urges her to escape with the cry "...a woman deliberately made to suffer is justified in anything in life," Archer wavers for a moment: "She had wanted help, and here was help" (II, p. 488–89). But with his passionate kiss, his "act of possession" that is meant to bring her into an adulterous liaison with him, Archer finds anew her inner resolve, particularly not to run away from a marriage of her own resolve. She darts from the spot, into a difficult but, one assumes, a better future, one in which she shall overcome, not flee, her regretful mistakes, one in which she shall try to regain whatever limited honor and freedom she can shape for herself in her world (II, pp. 489–90).

Lastly, Henry James hints that there is something inherently tragic for the golden feminine in his world:

Please be careful how you treat that precious object....

Madame Merle's plea hints of *The Golden Bowl*, forever broken in that future work of Henry James. In *The Portrait of a Lady*, Madame Merle's valued china is cracked, an emblem of her life. Osmond claims his unruly wife makes his life a tragedy, and Merle replies, "The tragedy's for me!" She takes the cracked object into her hands and wails, "Have I been so vile all for nothing?" (II, pp. 436–37).

Merle, however, rises to achieve "a quiet noble pathos" (II, p. 459), especially in her choice to do "a kind of proud penance" in her exile to America (II, p. 464). Even the most cracked female soul in James's novel is capable of heroism at moments. Pansy, in her convent-prison, timidly issues "heroic remarks" on her plight (II, p. 441), and within these limits she "became the heroine of a tragedy" (II, p. 443).

The self-serving Aunt Lydia finds tragedy, too, in suffering. When Ralph Touchett is dying, Archer discovers his mother, Aunt Lydia, looking bright, but older, with thin lips that "seemed a repository of latent meanings." Touchett dies, and Lydia experiences her own sad revelation: "Isabel could perceive, however, how it had come over her dimly that she had failed of something, that she saw herself in the future as an old woman without memories. Her little sharp face looked tragical" (II, p. 473).

The only woman in the novel who evades tragedy is Stackpole. Her last name, coupled with phallic images of her as a "steel pen" (II, p. 409), hint that she is shaped as the least stereotypically feminine woman, the most androgynous, in *The Portrait of a Lady*. Her liberated lifestyle and her career as a journalist, a profession that had been traditionally much the domain of men, strengthen this theory.

It is James's women who are the most feminine, those who are his golden "bowl" or his round and "precious" coffee cup are the ones whose fates are inescapably cracked. But this, precisely, leads to any redemption they can discover in their milieu, for the women's capacity to experience and survive tragedy points to their capacity to experience transformation.

The Duet of Poets. Isabel Archer, like Jane Eyre and other Diana-heroes, is very much a shaper, a "poet" in the original sense, one who will attempt to "make" serious transformations in her world. Her direct connections to art I address below, but an excellent preface to this theme is Archer's intimate relation with another woman artist—an evilly plotting sister. Archer's hardest trial arises when her spirit confronts that of Madame Merle, whose abuses her own power to shape.

Merle "makes" Archer's marriage, and that may be an act of bad poetry, but it is an act of poetry nonetheless. Henry James so describes the art of arranging marriages and Merle's limited but great role in the union of Isabel Archer and Gilbert Osmond:

> "There were people who had the match-making passion, like the votaries of art for art; but Madame Merle, great artist that she was, was scarcely one of these. She thought too ill of marriage, too ill even of life; she had desired that particular marriage but had not desired others" (II, p. 432).

Archer concedes that Merle has become "a powerful agent in her destiny" (II, p. 428), and one can assume that Henry James had enough finesse with the English language to use "agent" in its full meaning, denoting one with the power to act and make things happen. In fact, speaking of Merle's skill in making Archer's marriage, James not only identifies her as a "great artist" (II, p. 432), but he gives to Merle the same art that Nathaniel Hawthorne gives to the adulterous but artistic and voluptuous Hester Prynne: "...she was usually employed upon wonderful tasks of rich embroidery, cushions, curtains, decorations for the chimneypiece; an art in which her bold, free invention was as noted as the agility of her needle" (I, p. 167). Both Prynne and Merle are gifted women and artists.

James cautions that Merle's art is not to be trusted for the reason that she takes her art too lightly: "Of painting she was devotedly fond, and made no more of brushing in a sketch than of pulling off her gloves" (I, p. 166). A statement like that, coming from the pen of a painstaking artist like Henry James, is damning. Moreover, Merle misuses her artistic talents to achieve worldly ends. She is devoted mainly to a social end for her arts, and to the social arts themselves. Her "delicate kindness" to her friend Archer artfully masques devious designs (II, p. 275). Whereas Archer is a Titian come alive, Merle's abused art degenerates until it is a lifeless imitation of the real thing, until it is like "a sentence in a copybook." The one piece of art which Merle possesses, a precious coffee-cup, is cracked, and Merle's bad art helps to crack the golden bowl of Archer's life (II, pp. 436–37). Indeed, Madame Merle is envious of Archer's poetic powers, her powers to "make," for Archer's are so much greater than hers. She confesses of Osmond "No; it's the idea of the good I may do for you. It's that...that made me so jealous of Isabel. I want it to be my *work*" (I, p. 436).

James adds another twist to the relation between his two artists, Merle and Archer, a twist touching on the idea of goddesses, poetry, and motherhood. Textual allusions indicate that Merle not only derives her heroic powers from her associations with two goddesses, but her motives spring from this, too. Merle's models are mother goddesses, and Merle "makes" Archer's marriage to help her daughter Pansy. Merle and her powers, connected to these mother goddesses, also stand in direct contrast to the childless Diana-hero Archer and all that she represents.

Archer herself intuits that Merle is like a classical bust of Juno or Niobe (I, p. 154), Juno being the goddess who reigns over human marriages and Niobe the one who grieves eternally for her children.[7] The relation of Merle and Archer fits these symbolic allusions pointedly. The marriage that Merle "made" for Archer takes place in June, the month belonging to Juno (II, p. 327). And, Isabel describes Rome, into which Merle's machinations have lured her in her marriage, as "the Niobe of Nations" (I, p. 242). For her bad poetry, Merle will eventually be exiled from Rome, thus losing her child to Archer, just as Niobe lost her children to Diana. Such parallels between the figures and actions of Merle, as a living idea of Juno and Niobe, and Archer, as an embodiment of Diana, are consistently fitting, even striking.

Archetypally, Niobe embodies the darker powers of the moon. Originally a local configuration of the moon goddess, Niobe sits three days, signifying the time when the moon is "dead," at the tomb of the dead, her children. In complement, the "fair" goddess Leto, and her children, Apollo and Diana, embody the lighter side of the moon and its powers—brighter but less potent in that they are the less fertile (Kerenyi, pp. 61–78). In this vein, Merle can be read as a manifestation of the dark but fruitful powers of the waning moon, and Archer as a manifestation of the fairer but chillier ones.

Supporting this idea are the images surrounding Osmond. He is Merle's ex-lover and the father of Pansy. He is, on this level, as dark and fruitful as Merle. Moreover, Henry James uses moon imagery for the revelation of Osmond's identity to Archer:

> He was not changed; he had not disguised himself, during the year of his
> courtship, any more than she. But she had seen only half his nature then, as one

saw the disk of the moon when it was paretly masked by the shadow of the earth.
She saw the full moon now—she saw the whole man (II, p. 357).

This allusion, coupled with Isabel's maiden residence at "Palazzo Crescentini," leads to the theory that Osmond is typed as a god of the dark moon, just as Merle, his old lover, is typed as a goddess of dark moon, and Archer as a goddess of the bright new crescent. In the end, the new moon holds the old in her arms, when Archer embraces Merle's old life—her ex-lover, her daughter, and her Rome, in her innocent new arms.[8] The combination of Merle's dark poetry and Archer's fairer powers has been to give new life to the old estate.

The inheritor of this new estate is Pansy; she is the future bride just as Pearl, on another level, was Nathaniel Hawthorne's bride, albeit a more hopeful one. The best hope for Pansy comes from what Isabel Archer has helped to "make" her, through her friendship and guidance.

In a humorous play of allusion to "Pansy," Isabel Archer describes her role as a grand "rose" to her diminutive step-daughter to Lord Warburton:

Your society must have been a great benefit to her. You've talked to her, advised her, helped her to develop.
Ah yes, if she isn't the rose she has lived near it (II, p. 368).

"Pansy" is a mildly sweet bloom compared to Archer, and she announces that Archer shall be her "model." Archer responds with both kindness and a prophetic foreboding—Pansy will indeed have need of a Diana-hero's model guidance and protection (II, p. 299). In the final analysis, the virgin Pansy loves and follows Archer "as if she were her own mother" (II, p. 303), just as the nymphs of Diana's train admired her.

Archer pays a significant price for being this Diana-hero, the "guardian angel" (II, p. 400) of maids and future brides, for her role becomes one of sacrifice. She endures in her marriage partly out of a desire to help Pansy. In ages past, Diana rescued maidens from sacrifice to Agamemnon's fires or Alpheus's lust. In James's world, Archer helps but does not rescue Pansy from the evil precincts of Osmond, and she does so at the cost of remaining herself in those polluted grounds, for a time at least.

The mild Pansy can find limited comedy in this sphere, for she will always "cling" to a hero and go along with worldly designs as best she may (II, p. 349), and she benefits from being "shaped" by Archer's influence. The pure-bred Archer, however, shall stand and act alone, discovering high tragedy.

The Diana-Hero: Her Intimate Relations with Men

For Isabel Archer, there are four possible grooms: Ralph Touchett, Lord Warburton, Caspar Goodwood, and Gilbert Osmond. Touchett, her cousin, is in one manner very similar to Archer but in another equally dissimilar. The healthy Archer embarks the world over while the ill and dying Touchett reclines in "mere spectatorship at the game of life." He enjoys watching Archer because she, an active Diana-hero with a reckless gambling streak, always strives to keep "the game in [her] hands" (I, pp. 132–33).

His role as an ailing spectator, however, proves damnable when combined with his own gambling streak, the trait of strongest kinship between him and Archer. When Touchett's father argues that Archer's inheritance will make her bait for fortune-hunters, Ralph coolly replies, "Decidedly. That's a risk.... and I'm prepared to take it" (I, p. 162). Touchett gamed away his cousin's future, and Madame Merle is the first to appreciate this. She informs Archer: "He imparted to you that extra lustre which was required to make you a brilliant match. At bottom it's him you've to thank" (II, p. 464).

In irony, Merle is victorious in her game to abuse Ralph Touchett's gamble on his cousin, for she is a cheater who assesses how honest he is: "However, one feels that he's a gentleman and would never say anything underhand about one. *Cartes sur table....* I'm not afraid of him" (I, p. 173). The dishonesty of Merle and Osmond also temporarily defeats Isabel Archer, who comes to perceive that their secret designs made her life "resemble an attempt to play whist with an imperfect pack of cards..." (II, p. 465).

Later, when Ralph realizes his error, he wails, "I believe I ruined you" (II, p. 478). The cry is all the more reprehensible when one recalls that "Ralph" means "Counsel"—a role he has completely abdicated toward his young cousin for the sake of a good game. The "good game" turned out to be doubly risky because his kin, Isabel Archer, is equally a reckless gambler.

In the end, Touchett assumes, and feels to his heart, the full liability for his error:

> Ralph remembered what he had said to his father about wishing to put it into
> her power to meet the requirements of her imagination. He had done so, and the
> girl has taken full advantage of the luxury. Ralph felt sick; he felt ashamed
> (II, p. 294).

If Touchett is an irresponsible spectator and gambler, he is also a loving cousin and idealist, and in this sense also he shares a true kinship with Isabel Archer. His clean "nature" exists, like Archer's, in "antipathy" to the worldly Madame Merle's (I, p. 173). The light of his spirit is to Archer, snared by the dark moon god Osmond, "a lamp in the darkness" (II, p. 363).

Touchett ends as Archer's "brother" (II, p. 363). As her "brother" and a light to her, he may be read as an ailing Apollo-type. His flickering light succors Archer in a critical moment during her blighted marriage to Osmond with his black designs. With Touchett, Archer joins "supremely together" in their germane love and in the truth of their fates, and she bids him farewell, "Oh my brother!" (II, p. 477–79).

The next in her orbit is Lord Warburton. He would be an ideal match for a Diana-hero, for he is a vigorous man of the chase. He comes into the novel all "booted and spurred," and he frequently bears an "implement of the chase," his "hunting-crop." Warburton clutches "dog-skin gloves"—a further tie to a Diana-hero like Archer, modelled on the goddess of the hunt, her hounds and her prey (I, pp. 100–01). Archer attracts dogs, and she is herself titled a "grey hound" (I, pp. 25–27; 37). Warburton is as "brilliant" as she, too (I, pp. 19). His person brings to Archer's nostrils the odors of "strange gardens, what charged airs"—more confirmation that he would be ideal partner for Isabel and her Edenic spirit (I, p. 100).

Isabel Archer refuses not only Lord Warburton, but Caspar Goodwood, another suitor whose name evokes images of the green and Edenic world, and she does so for the mediocre Gilbert Osmond. This raises "the idea of the paradox of the fortunate fall" (Humpherys), for Archer's error plunges her into a tragic mode, whence derives much greater wisdom and self-perception for her. She leaves behind the blessed Gardencourt to enter the sinister world of Farnese Palace.

Archer so errs with Lord Warburton and Caspar Goodwood in her wealth of naivete and egoism combined. She fears Goodwood's strength will hinder her own, and she fears her fellow hunter, Warburton, too, when his strong presence makes her feel like a "wild, caught creature in a vast cage" (I, p. 100). Her self-willed ignorance, of their truly liberal natures, allows her to persist in her delusion of an absolutely free life, a delusion both frigid and foolish.

Archer's rejection of Lord Warburton renders him despondent. Archer mourns before a statue of the Dying Gladiator, emblematic of Warburton, in an Italian museum. This "lion of the collection" has become an "attributive victim" of the erring judgement of our Diana-hero (II, p. 256–57). In her cold will and self-absorbed designs, Archer, a pattern of the singular goddess of the green chase, wounds a true hero. In the end, as Touchett ends an ailing Apollo-type, the knightly Lord Warburton is similarly afflicted, a Dying Gladiator. James reserves tragedy for noble male types, too, in his troubled modern arena.

The last name of Caspar Goodwood indicates that he would be another excellent consort for Archer, derived from the goddess of the green chase. Goodwood is also a true knight. When Henrietta Stackpole tells him that Archer is in need of help, he immediately decides to go to the aid of Archer and Stackpole:

> ...she was a lady travelling alone; it was his duty to put himself out for her. There could be no two questions about that; it was a perfectly clear necessity. He looked extremely grave for some moments and then said, wholly without the flourish of gallantry but in a tone of extreme distinctness, "Of course if you're going tomorrow I'll go too, as I may be of assistance to you" (II, p. 385).

Upon arriving in Rome, Goodwood tries to do whatever "service" Archer requests of him (II, p. 412). Goodwood has such a gallant and knightly spirit that he even treats Osmond generously: "His host had won in the open field a great advantage over him, and Goodwood had too strong a sense of fair play to have been moved to underrate him on that account" (II, p. 421). Never does Goodwood forget the "laws of knighthood" (*Ariosto*, XXIII, 97).

Moreover, Goodwood harbors poetic powers, the necessary and glorious complement to Archer's. His passion has so much of its own truth and poetry that its words "dropped deep into her soul" (II, pp. 486–87). Like Archer, a Titian come alive in the text, and indeed like all well-crafted works, Goodwood is "very original" (II, p. 412). In this, he is, like Archer, "artless" in the worldly sense of the word only (I, p. 166). He and Archer lack the false, social "art" of the devious Madame Merle and Gilbert Osmond (I, p. 286).

But our Diana-hero is dogmatically chaste. She flees the fierce poetry of Caspar Goodwood. Ever willful, and true to the spirit of the huntress Diana, Archer perversely takes up her "best weapons" against him (I, p. 137). She delights when her "sharpness" wounds the knightly Goodwood (I, p. 138), and on this error James writes that Archer's words sound an "infernal note, and it is not on record that her motive for discharging such a shaft had been of the clearest" (I, p. 140).

Later, Archer comes to see not only the "serious harm" she has done Goodwood (II, p. 404), but that "no one had ever been so close to her" as him (II, p. 486). She perceives that no man has ever loved her as truly as he does (II, p. 488), and had she married "Goodwood," she would have "been a woman more blest" (II, p. 472).

Finally, Archer marries the "perfect nonentity" Osmond (II, p. 279). In a world full of suitors like Goodwood and Warburton, men who possess the generous spirit of medieval knights, Archer falls into the hands of the man who possesses the medieval spirit of Machiavelli.[9] His favorite reading subjects are Machiavelli, the poet—but wastrel—Metastasio, and the poet—and convent-flower—Vittoria Colonna, who, after her husband's death, renounced the world. In other words, she sacrificed herself for the male (I, p. 223), an act which Osmond highly esteems.

Shrewdly, Osmond intuits that Archer is capable of sacrificing herself for him if he can make her believe that she is marrying "to please herself" (II, p. 294). This will satisfy her ideal of disinterested, and thus true, love. As such it will satisfy her pride, her sense of power and ownership:

> The finest—in the sense of being the subtlest—manly organism she had ever known had become her property, and the recognition of her having but to put out her hands and take it had been originally a sort of act of devotion (II, p. 358).

Archer self-gloriously imagines that she is humbly taking up Osmond. She discovers that she has reached for the snake because Osmond, as a god of the dark moon, will prove to have a truly serpentine nature. Like a snake, he charmed her. His consort Merle lies to Archer that Osmond is not a "professional charmer" (I, p. 210), but that is precisely the serpentine designer he turns out to be.

In fact, Touchett perceives that Osmond, like a snake, is a "perversity" that has bitten Archer (II, p. 331). He is the "serpent" in the Edenic garden which is her nature (II, p. 360). His touch poisons her life.

Moreover, "Osmond" identifies him with this world, and that alone makes him an unfit husband for the idealistic Diana-hero. The piece of art Osmond cherishes witnesses his devotion to this world, for it depicts Antinous and the Faun. Antinous, a fair Egyptian youth, was associated with lusty nature and catalyzed a cult (II, p. 258), making him a figure tied more closely to physical desire than ideal love. The Faun reinforces this idea. Henry James implies the falsity of Osmond further when he describes Osmond and his voice as "fine" as the art in an Uffizi gallery, adding that it's strange so "fine" a voice "somehow wasn't sweet" (I, p. 213).

Osmond serves one god, the god of "propriety" (II, p. 265). His only true genius is for "upholstery" (II, p. 324). In short, Osmond is "an obscure American dilettante" (I, p. 234), "a sterile dilettante!" (II, p. 292), and a "vulgar adventurer" (II, p. 432). Mrs. Touchett proclaims of Osmond that, in the final analysis, there is "nothing *of* him" (II, p. 282). No surprise that his garden is as narrow and dilettantish as he is (I, p. 195).

Moreover, images of evil surround the figure of Osmond. His own sister admits that he wields a "poisoned" point, one especially "dangerous" in "chemical combination" with Merle (I, pp. 229–30). She specifies that he is "capable of everything" (II, p. 416), and he himself wishes "it to be known that he shrank from nothing"—including the imprisonment of his own daughter Pansy (II, p. 443). Osmond is "sordid" and "sinister" (II, p. 286).

As the wielder of a "poisoned" point, of a demonic arrow of his own devising, Osmond is a black parody of and counterpart to the figure of "Archer." He is, indeed, a dark moon for her fair one. He is "evil" in his will to "malignantly...put the lights out one by one" until his blackness engulfs her (II, pp. 355–57). He is, indeed, modelled to a certain extent on the image of the dying moon, for he is Archer's nemesis, the dark shadow that eternally threatens to engulf the shining crescent.

The Queen of Tragedy

From Diana-type to Diana-hero. Traversing this realm of darkness makes a long and arduous passage to heroism for Isabel Archer, and this Diana-hero is both fearless and fearful. As a young Diana-type at the start of *The Portrait of a Lady*, Archer seems fearless. She spends her time in dreams of "beauty and bravery and magnanimity" (I, p. 54).

When her trials commence, Archer never loses her bravery, and others respect this courage. Pansy states of Archer, "She's not afraid of anyone" (II, p. 326). The Countess, a clever woman, does not put Archer on "her guard" against Merle and Osmond because she perceives that Archer will never be an "easy victim" for them. She intuits "that her brother had found his match" and looks forward to seeing him "overtopped" (II, p. 376).

Eventually, Osmond launches his nasty attacks on Archer only to discover that she humiliates him (II, p. 352). When she obeys any of his directions, she does so to the letter because she knows that "doing so appeared to reduce them to the absurd" (II, p. 369). Osmond knows this, too. Merle accuses him of making Archer afraid, to which he replies, "Isabel's not afraid of me, and it's not what I wish" (II, p. 435). Indeed, he wishes Archer not to be full of fears but to be empty of strength—a more sinister wish. If she had no "ideas" of her own (I, p. 244), she would be incapable of "defying" him in any sort (II, p. 447). She would be incapable of resolution and heroics.

In her worst moments, she keeps her courageous faith:

> "Deep in her soul—deeper than any appetite for renunciation—was the sense that life would be her business for a long time to come. And at moments there was something inspiring, almost enlivening, in the conviction. It was a proof of strength—it was a proof she should some day be happy again" (II, p. 466).

In Jamesian irony, however, his Diana-hero is also plagued by certain fears, ones inherent in her nature and ones that specifically cause her tragic errors. Archer, a chaste Diana-type, fears any act of possession by men. Archer can impose rosy visions of her own imagination upon the nonentity Osmond, but she is cold to a better man, such as Warburton, "from a certain fear" of his own strength (I, p. 78).

The passion of the "manly" Goodwood terrifies her: "...she was afraid of her visitor. She was ashamed of her fear" (II, pp. 277; 280). Another passionate meeting with Goodwood brings Archer to her knees after he departs, and it does so before the "looming...big four-posted bed." Before this monument of physical intimacy, the chaste Diana-type Archer hides her face (I, p. 144). When Goodwood later comes to carry her away from the evil Osmond, Archer shrinks from the force of his love: "It wrapped about her; it lifted her off her feet, while the very taste of it, as of something potent, acrid and strange, forced open her set teeth" (II, p. 488).

The frigid Archer's fears run so deep that even the professionally charming and placating Osmond does touch them at rare moments. Contemplating their future together, Isabel studies "—the sense of something within herself, deep down, that she supposed to be inspired and trustful passion. It was there like a large sum stored in a bank—which there was a terror in having to begin to spend. If she touched it, it would all come out" (II, p. 263).

In irony, new fears then hinder Archer breaking openly with her husband. The bonds of marriage are sacred. If she disavows these "tremendous vows," ones she uttered "at the altar" (II, p. 449), she would feel "a confusion of regrets, a complication of fears" (II, p. 340). In this state of confusion, the horror of her married life rises before her with an "architectural vastness" (II, p. 465) and renders her temporarily "like a creature in pain" (II, p. 489).

Her fears and her fearlessness then meet to form an interesting crisis. She is "heart-broken" (II, p. 487) but not spirit-broken. When her husband censures her for going to England to see the dying Touchett, she answers, "That's very little; that's nothing. I might do much more" (II, p. 447). But, when Stackpole, Goodwood, and Touchett urge her to do "much more," Archer refuses. She is wounded, but still persistent in her ideals, ones which she fears living beneath, and ones which keep her in fearful situations.

A vein of heroic tragedy from Greek drama, also full of fearful and tragic situations, informs Archer's fate. Isabel Archer's last name constantly reminds one that she descends from the goddess of the chase, the huntress slaying creatures and trespassers, from prize stags to Acteon. "Archer" becomes "like a winged creature held back" (II, p. 323). In this bleak moment, James writes the one sentence that crystallizes Archer's flaw: she is "...in her embarrassment rather wide of the mark" (II, p. 394).

The Diana-hero "Archer" is shooting wide of the mark. *Hamartia*, to miss the mark, is the tragic flaw Greek dramatists assigned to a hero. So, Archer's shooting wide of the mark points to the roots of her tragedy. In that bleak moment, when the Diana-hero misses her mark, she feels "mortally cold" (II, p. 401). Her tragic humanity has fully settled upon her.

Thus, like the heroism of ancient Greek characters, Isabel Archer's heroism also derives from a creative sorrow, one initiated by her own deliberate act, in this case her marriage. This act which shall move her from *pathos* to *mathos*, from suffering to the truth of that suffering, its significance. In her chosen married home, Archer exists in the "incredulous terror...of her dwelling" (II, p. 360). Covered with darkness, she finds it hard not to lose sight of her bright ideals: "...there were days when the world looked black and she asked herself with some sharpness what it was that she was pretending to live for" (II, p. 337). However, her resolute spirit does not fail her: "...if life was difficult it would not make it easier to confess herself beaten" (II, p. 338). Finally, when Archer has endured her "hellish" life (II, p. 469), James spills a drop of comedy into her dark drama; she feels the light of some future happiness dawning inside herself once more (II, p. 466); her future redemption and liberation is assured.

For her tragic struggles and creative sorrow Archer, like tragic Greek heroes, deserves "pity" and "charity" (I, p. 95; II, p. 426). James applies to her situation such words, filled with dramatic significance, and they are key to understanding the rich—and Grecian—nature of her heroism and her redemption. When Henrietta Stackpole comments on the tragic irony of Archer, our Diana-hero, snared "in a mesh of fine threads" (II, p. 446), Isabel counters her with allusions to drama, its comedy and its tragedy.

This conversation paints Archer's wounded condition in terms that create sharp irony for a Diana-hero, a female modelled on the goddess of the chase. She discovers that she has been the prey, the vulnerable deer, in the worldly realm:

> "I want to be alone," said Isabel.
> "You won't be that so long as you've so much company at home."
> "Ah, they're part of the comedy. You others are spectators."
> "Do you call it a comedy, Isabel Archer?" Henrietta rather grimly asked.
> "The tragedy then if you like. You're all looking at me; it makes me uncomfortable."
> Henrietta engaged in this act for a while. "You're like the stricken deer, seeking the innermost shade. Oh, you do give me such a sense of helplessness!" she broke out.
> "I'm not at all helpless. There are many things I mean to do" (II, p. 417).

Her creative sorrow has prompted firmer resolutions, an act opening the way to her heroic apotheosis. Henry James writes that Archer will never again feel a "superficial" wound. She has traversed beyond this "inferior stage" to a superior one (II, p. 467). She has survived her ordeals, emerging in a wiser if sadder state.

From Revelations to Regeneration. Hints of revelations surround Archer throughout the text, revelations that shall realize her personal apocalypse. Dogmatically she tries to keep them at bay. When she meets Osmond, this trait in her surfaces: "For the present she abstained from provoking further revelations" (I, p. 228). She persists in this manner well into her marriage, yet she will, eventually, have to penetrate the secret workings of "nature, providence, fortune, of the eternal mystery of things" (II, p. 339).

One of her first glimmers comes upon beholding Merle and her husband together:

> But the thing made an image, lasting only a moment, like a sudden flicker of light. Their relative positions, their absorbed mutual gaze, struck her as something detected. But it was all over by the time she had fairly seen it (II, p. 343).

When the light is finally so bright that it can not be ignored any longer, Archer realizes that she has in the past only seen parts, never wholes, and this has led her very often to have "mistaken a part for the whole." She meditates the revealed nature of her consort, and she does so in terms that, ironically, alloy him with her own nature as a Diana-hero: "But she had seen only half his nature then, as one saw the disk of the moon when it was partly masked by the shadow of the earth. She saw the full moon now—she saw the whole man" (II, p. 357). The revelation is fitting to her own growth, for it catapults her from Diana-type to Diana-hero, from, metaphorically speaking, the innocent stage of the crescent to the matured stage of the full moon.

Following, she begins to perceive dimly the dark and hidden powers of Merle. However, Archer, a chaste Diana-hero, is ultimately incapable of fathoming worldly wickedness on her own. She must be aided by an agent of decadence, the Countess Gemini. The Countess cagily guesses that Archer has come for this purpose: "*Ca me depasse*, if you don't mind my saying so, the things, all round you, that you've appeared to succeed in not knowing. It's a sort of assistance—aid to innocent ignorance—that I've always been a bad hand at rendering." The "exultant" Countess offers Archer the "revelation" of her brother and Merle's past adultery and their deceit with their child's identity (II, pp. 449-51).

Henry James plants in the description of Archer's new experience a word that falls into the text's pattern of allusions to the moon:

> Now that she was in the secret, now that she knew something that so much concerned her and the eclipse of which had made life resemble an attempt to play whist with an imperfect pack of cards, the truth of things, their mutual reactions, their meaning, and for the most part their horror, rose before her with a kind of architectural vastness (II, pp. 465).

The term "eclipse" points toward a rebirth for Archer, for the moon emerges anew from that moment of dark apocalypse. In this new stage, in her new arms Archer shall hold the old life of the dark Merle: her daughter, her lover, and her working knowledge of evil. The term "eclipse" also calls to mind Archer's previous revelation of Osmond as a "full moon," which revelation was precipitated by her move from the Palazzo "Crescentini" into the world of experience.

The text reinforces the theory that by passing from her residence at "Crescentini" and the "eclipse" stage of her innocent maidenhood, into the realm of that shadowed full moon, Gilbert Osmond, Archer has emerged from a symbolic death into another life:

> She had moments indeed in her journey from Rome which were almost as good as being dead.... Not only the time of her folly, but the time of her repentance was far.... She saw herself, in the distant years, still in the attitude of a woman who had her life to live, and these intimations contradicted the spirit of the present hour....
>
> Deep in her soul—deeper than any appetite for renunciation—was the sense that life would be her business for a long time to come.... it was a proof that she should be happy again (II, pp. 465–66).

This promise of her future ascension is strengthened by Archer's proceeding to wax over the figure of Madame Merle. Archer's words banish Merle to America (II, p. 464). Soon after this, Touchett senses and confirms her renewal from her mortification:

> "I feel very old," said Isabel.
> "You'll grow young again." (II, p. 479).

Ritually, successfully, the Diana-hero has completed her apocalyptic cycle. Nearly every grand symbol in the work hints at this idea of cyclical regeneration. As one instance, Archer's new state, one sadder but wiser, is signified by her ability to see the ghost of Gardencourt. Gardencourt, a seeming Eden, hides the dead within itself. This is fitting for the Diana-hero Archer, in her youthful and Edenic state, for her emblem is the bright crescent that typically holds the black and waning moon within.

Moreover, Touchett, Archer's "brother" who introduces her to the existence of the ghost at Gardencourt, soon passes into the realm of the dead himself. He is her best guide to those regions. When Archer initially asks Touchett to be her guide to the realm of ghosts, he refuses, knowing that she has not yet suffered enough (I, p. 52). Her later revelations of the Merle and Osmond join with his death to encompass the fullness of sorrow for her. At this point, Archer experiences the ghost, but the dead, again, is held in an image of rebirth, the dawn:

> He had told her, the first evening she ever spent at Gardencourt, that if she should live to suffer enough she might some day see the ghost with which the old

house was duly provided. She apparently had fulfilled the necessary condition; for the next morning, in the cold, faint dawn, she knew that a spirit was standing by her bed (II, p. 479).

The Uniquely Troubled Modern Hero. The language, theme, and roles of *The Portrait of a Lady* consistently identify Archer as the hero in a drama. "Spectator" Touchett is eager to watch her performance: "He wanted to see what she would make of her husband—or what her husband would make of her. This was only the first act of the drama, and he was determined to sit out the performance" (II, p. 332). Archer, witnessing Osmond's deception, employs similar terms: "She remembered perfectly the first sign he had given of it—it had been like the bell that was to ring up the curtain upon the real drama of their life" (II, p. 359).

Strikingly, Archer, the hero of the novel, has no active heirs as of yet, her son having died (II, p. 305), and her marital inheritance consisting of the passive Pansy. This is troubling because Archer embodies the archetype of the two chaste goddesses of the Western world, Diana and Mary. The art in the novel emblems these archetypes for the reader in the descriptions of Titian, Ghirlandaio, or Correggio, who painted the Virgin "kneeling down before the sacred infant, who lies in a litter of straw, and clapping her hands to him while he delightedly laughs and crows.... the most beautiful picture in the world" (II, p. 382).

No such joyous birth shall come from the novel's Virgin, Isabel Archer, a hint that the modern world has become sterile. None of the "harmonious" life and blessed birth captured by Correggio informs James's scene. The only birth comes from Merle, linked with the "Medicean Venus" (II, p. 383) and with the type of Niobe, who suffers over her children. Merle's fertility is far divorced from bliss or chastity. There are, simply, no heroic fruits of a chaste marriage in *The Portrait of a Lady.*

We are left with a potential of a future birth, but in a manner as open-ended as Archer's future (II, p. 305).[10] Thus, the only success established clearly in the course of the novel is Archer's heroism itself, and she is a troubled hero in this sterile modern world.

In her youth, Archer entertained a magnanimous desire to suffer trials to attain true heroism: "Sometimes she went so far as to wish that she might find herself some day in a difficult position, so that she should have the pleasure of being as heroic as the occasion demanded" (I, p. 54). It is the experienced and worldly poet Merle who judges Archer's coming apotheosis. She tells Archer that "every gain's a loss of some kind," prophetic of Archer's loss of innocence that brings about the gain of experience. Merle though also judges accurately of Archer and her future struggle in the corrupted world, "It may pull you about horribly, but I defy it to break you up" (I, p. 164).

In fact, Archer's trial often clarifies for her what she wished for—her own grandeur and power:

> [The words] made a comparison between Osmond and herself, recalled the fact that she had once held this coveted treasure in her hand and felt herself rich enough to let it fall. A momentary exultation took possession of her—a horrible delight in having wounded him; for his face instantly told her that none of the force of her exclamation was lost (II, p. 396).

In the end, the main image Archer retains of her adversary, the serpentine Osmond, is his "fall": "He was going down—down; the vision of such a fall made her almost giddy: that was the only pain. He was too strange, too different; he didn't touch her." In this moment, she rises victorious: "Isabel slowly got up; standing there in her white cloak, which covered her to her feet, she might have represented the angel of disdain, first cousin to that of pity" (II, p. 402).

Her natural heroism raises her above the bad poet Merle, too, offering some hope, however limited, of future successes in Archer's life and realm. When Archer challenges Merle, the latter censures Archer: "Now don't be heroic.... Ah then, you take it heroically!" (II, p. 429-30). But that is exactly how the singular Diana-hero takes life, as Merle will discover, with her banishment.

The Diana-Hero and Art: Roman Ruins

> Rome is your handiwork; in your safe-keeping
> The Trojan band reached an Etruscan haven,
> ....Rain on the race of Romulus wealth, offspring,
> Honours of every kind.   (Horace, *Phoebe silvarumque potens Diana*)

Old Rome is Diana's handiwork, Old Rome is Diana's city, and New Rome is Mary's. Isabel Archer, a Diana-hybrid, rightfully assumes her role as keeper of the Old and New Rome in *The Portrait of a Lady*. She ascends to her position in modern Rome after her marriage to a decadent Old Roman, Gilbert Osmond, a marriage arranged by a woman who shares his Old Roman nature, Madame Merle.

One image of this process in the novel is art. Art—or, at times, the noted absence of it—is one key to unlocking the symbolism of every locale, of every person's real nature, and of every proposed marriage. For instance, Lord Warburton woos Archer partially through giving her a tour of his private art gallery (I, p. 117). He is a collector of art and fine objects. Osmond similarly woos Archer by guiding her through his own lesser but still impressive collection (I, p. 225). Rosier, another collector, loves Pansy for being a precious object. These collectors are distanced or defeated—not engaged successfully—in the challenges of life.

Only Goodwood, who loves Archer with the deepest and truest passion, is "artlessly" plain and simple, allied only to life itself. He cannot even recall various pictures (I, p. 107; II, p. 382). The idea rises again with Henrietta Stackpole. She is another true and active friend of Archer's, and she is so full of human energy that she is bored and uncomfortable in the Victoria and Albert Museum. She wants to rush off to engage with the living genius of England (I, p. 125).

A person's true worth is reflected through his or her art also. Merle is a collector, too. Her most precious is cracked, and in her "false position," she is pronounced to be as unoriginal as a "sentence in a copybook" (II, p. 436). This contrasts to the finer crafting of a true gentleman, Bantling, who is "as clear as the style of a good prospectus" (II, p. 470). Ralph Touchett appreciates art and people together, as when he contemplates Archer as the "finest work of art" (I, p. 63), and the intelligent and honest Henrietta Stackpole is not that interested in art, perhaps, but she loves the tenderness of Correggio's Virgin (II, p. 382).

Archer appreciates art, particularly of the great masters like Titian or Correggio, but she is, like Goodwood, truer to life than art. Interestingly, her immature attitude toward life is reflected, by Henry James, in her erring judgement of art. And evidence surfaces of her flawed artistic judgement in the text. Archer is blind to the fact that Lord Warburton is like the marble and noble lion before the statute of the Dying Gladiator and that Gilbert Osmond is the symbol of Antinous and the Faun come alive (II, pp. 256–58). Osmond produces silly art in the form of a "little sonnet" (II, p. 259), and Archer generously believes that it is a "piece of correct" verse. Her lack of perception continues when Osmond declares his love for her in a hotel lobby whose fake art, of paintings and cherubs, is "ugly to distress" (II, p. 261). Such a setting contrasts to the love of Warburton, declared amid the genuine art in his own private gallery and the Italian Museum.

Brownstein has delineated the "terribly unconscious irony" with which Isabel, when she is tempted by her new fortune, acts as a collector and mis–sees Osmond as a desirable object, an original and fine organism. She is blind to the significance of Osmond's copying a copy of an antique coin—an act underscoring his distance from real art—or that, like his medallions, his preferred objects, Osmond is cold and hard. In short, when Archer acts on her own "purely aesthetic"—and, I would add, widely erring—view of Osmond, she goes quite wrong in her real life (pp. 259–60).

For James, however, there is always another turn of the screw. The collector Osmond considers his daughter and his wife as objects of art for his own display. His artistic taste can be as false as his life. He can have "very bad" taste (II, p. 313). But this calculating creature is far less subject to error in judging his wife's worth for his collection than she is in judging him.[11] Osmond shrewdly studies Archer as a piece of good art come alive:

> She looked up from her book. "What you despise most in the world is bad, is stupid art."
> "Possibly. But yours seems to me very clear and very good" (II, p. 261).

In the end, Archer's live and forceful nature is "finer than the finest work of art" (I, p. 63). She has the chaste soul that artists ardently seek to capture in their finest works. She is a living figure of Titian (I, p. 63), of Cimabue's Madonna (I, p. 182), Benini's or Terpsichore's dancing nymphs, the Greek's muse of song and dance (II, p. 287), Ghirlandaio's medieval maidens (I, p. 222), and Correggio's Virgin (II, p. 382).

Importantly, this sum of artwork points to Roman art. Archer's figure is tied intimately with the ideal of Italian artists—Titian, Cimabue,

Bernini, Ghirlandaio, and Correggio. In this context can one assess in the most meaningful manner Henry James labelling of Archer's trip to Rome as a "pilgrimage" and his declaration that it is a foregone conclusion she will be a "Rome-lover" (I, p. 242). She is its art embodied, come alive. This context deepens with another Jamesian twist: once Archer makes her pilgrimage, she experiences a "spiritual shudder" (II, p. 481), for there she finds—and temporarily embraces—the false art of Osmond and the cracked art of Merle.

In short, Archer, a cool and chaste human incarnation of the Virgin goddesses, the Diana of Titian and the Mary of Correggio, has arrived to find her Rome in a spiritual and artistic crisis. The celestially naive Archer is snared in this Rome, particularly by "Rome Revisited," a piece of empty art Osmond pens for her (II, p. 259). The living embodiment of Roman art, Archer has stumbled, literally and figuratively, upon her natural mission, to regenerate her eternal city.

Archer at first creates this image of her pilgrimage to Rome:

> —so it pleased her to qualify these too few days in Rome, which she might musingly have likened to the figure of some small princess of one of the ages of dress overmuffled in a mantle of state and dragging a train that it took pages of historians to hold up—that this felicity was coming to an end (II, p. 262).

This image of an overmuffled princess with a dragging train is accurate for Rome, an overcivilized ancient city. Ironically, Archer is blind that this image is also accurate for her. She will end up dragging the entire train of Roman history in the form of her marriage, fostered by the squalid motives of two Old Romans. James is being keen *par excellence* when he specifies that Archer has come to live, with Osmond, "in the very heart of Rome" (II, p. 307).

The text contains a seed of comedy within the tragedy. James hints that his Diana-hero's mission to Rome will be successful over time. The "vague eternal rumour" that Rome sounds in her ear keeps Archer's "imagination awake" (I, p. 212). To its "deep appeal" she responds naturally, and in its eternal beauty Archer comes to know not only tragic humanity but many days that are her "happiest.... The sense of the terrible human past was heavy to her, but that of something altogether contemporary would suddenly give it wings that it could wave in the blue. Her consciousness was so mixed that she scarcely knew where the different parts of it would lead her, and she went about in a repressed ecstasy of contemplation" (I, p. 245).

The comedy lies in the "contemporary" moment, the New Rome and its possibilities, ones that are bright opposites of the dark tragedies held in the long history of Old Rome. The idea is alluded to elsewhere in the text. Henrietta Stackpole is struck by the similarities between the busy and bustling ancient Rome and the busy and bustling New York, Washington, and American cities in general (I, pp. 245; 251). Thus, Rome, the "Eternal City," exists parallel to the new cities of America (II, p. 374), and its contemporary spirit is full of promise. In this light is America seen as a new type of Rome, and from there the new Diana-hero hails, a type of New Roman.

Further, Touchett informs Archer that "Rome...confessed to the psychological moment." In this sense, James's experiment, of transplanting the Diana-hero from the New World into the Old World, from the "New Roman" to the "Old Roman," can be read on one level as a study of the "psychological moment" of Archer as the new—the contemporary—agent of redemption for the tired spirit of Rome. The conflict between her "high spirit" (I, p. 27) and Rome's low spirit clarifies the "psychological moment" of our age, a "critical" one (I, p. 70). Perhaps herein lies one "key to modern criticism" for which heroic Jamesian characters search (I, p. 44). Isabel Archer's error came when "the key to her cabinet of jewels" not to a true spouse or friend but to Madame Merle and Gilbert Osmond (p. 163). This catapults the fresh Diana-hero into the realm of decadent Old Rome.

Henry James details this key "moment" well. Immediate upon Archer's arrival in the Eternal City, he describes both the disjunction and the continuity between the spirits of the fresh Diana-hero and those of the declining Old World: "From the Roman past to Isabel Archer's future was a long stride, but her imagination had taken it in a single flight and now hovered in slow circles over the nearer and richer field" (I, p. 246).

Archer's heroism, then, lies partly in her mind's ability to stride the vast expanse of two worlds, old and new, in one moment of imagination. She realizes the fullest potential of this kind of heroism, with its vast, imaginative capacity, when she inherits all of the sordid past of Merle and

Osmond, essentially the ruins of Old Rome, absorbs its message of human tragedy, then determines to proceed onward with it into a brighter future.

Constantly, the images of Roman art and Archer's modern mission— her drama—conflate. She turns from her revelation of Merle's extreme falsity to a parallel revelation in Roman art of eternal human suffering and tragedy:

> She had long before this taken old Rome into her confidence, for in a world of ruins the ruin of her happiness seemed a less unnatural catastrophe. She rested her weariness upon things that had crumbled for centuries and yet still were upright; she dropped her secret sadness into the silence of lonely places, where its very modern quality detached itself and grew objective, so that as she sat in a sun-warmed angle on a winter's day, or stood in a mouldy church to which no one came, she could almost smile at it and think of its smallness. Small it was, in the large Roman record, and her haunting sense of the continuity of the human lot easily carried her from the less to the greater. She had become deeply, tenderly acquainted with Rome; it interfused and moderated her passion. But she had grown to think of it chiefly as the place where people had suffered. This was what came to her in the starved churches, where the marble columns, transferred from pagan ruins, seemed to offer her a companionship in endurance and the musty incense to be a compound of long-unanswered prayers (II, pp. 430–31).

When Archer sees in these Roman ruins a symbol of tragedy and of endurance, she has gained a perspective on her individual drama, and it relates to her condition as a hero. Rome, with both its grand art and its terrible human past, shows her "history is full of the destruction of precious things" (II, p. 466), and in James's text, "precious things," like Merle's coffee cup or Titian's and Corregio's art, frequently emblem the female being. Roman art, however, also reflects and assures that Archer's spirit, though afflicted, can endure.

In this Roman moment, the artist Henry James collapses time and space, conflates past history and modern moments, in the figure of Isabel Archer. He does so not only in the tradition of the art of ancient Rome and of the Italian Renaissance, images that find an emblem and are subsumed in the creation of the contemporary Archer, but he does so in the tradition of literature as well. In her trials and her quest, Isabel Archer has become a continuing "type" of sad and beautiful feminine heroics striving and wandering through the ages:

And the Creator uttered His decree:
"Whoever in the future bears thy name,
Wise, beautiful and courteous shall be,
And virtue cherish as her constant aim,
Renowned in rhyme, honoured in history,
It will be chronicled, and with its fame
Parnassus, Pindus, Helicon will ring,
'Isabella, Isabella,' echoing."   (Ariosto, *OF*, XXIX, 28-29)

FIVE

GWENDOLEN HARLETH: THE SPLENDID, SAD-HEARTED HERO

"An uncommonly fine girl, a perfect Diana..."

George Eliot's vision of a tragic world, and her desire to re-vision a comedic new one, were, perhaps, even stronger than Henry James's. Indeed, from George Eliot did Henry James take the troubled but dynamic idea of his hero, for the literary model of Isabel Archer was Gwendolen Harleth. Specially intriguing is the unique line of metaphoric development that each author, from George Eliot to Henry James, took with his or her own Diana-hero. That reveals much about each author's attitude toward his or her creation and subsequently about each author's ideas on female heroics in our modern world.[1]

Harleth's figure neatly fits the pattern of a tragic Diana-hero, one whose roots also run deep in Greek tragedy, especially, I believe, in Aesychlean tragedy. Harleth loves, from the first pages of *Daniel Deronda*, to appear in "Greek dress" (pp. 44; 47).[2] But she, like Archer, shall discover that giving birth to a glorious new self is not facile within the realities of the sordid world into which her own egoism plunges her. Her naive idea, and nature, also undergo a tragic purging and re-invention, to allow for the emergence of a better self, one capable of shaping a wiser life.

Gwendolen Harleth as a Diana-Hero

"Gwendolyn" means "White Crescent," which identifies Harleth with the moon. Eliot's epithets for Harleth confirm this: "An uncommonly fine girl, a perfect Diana" (p. 136), or "Why, you will see the fair gambler, the Leubronn Diana" (p. 272). Traditional imagery of a Diana-type surrounds Harleth. Her physique is like that of the "perfect Diana" of the green chase. She is a "wood-nymph" (p. 122) and a "delicate-limbed sylph" with the "full height of a graceful figure" (pp. 5; 31). She has a "perfect movement" to "her fine form" (p. 89). She has a "rare grace of movement and bearing, and a certain daring" (p. 42), and her "face and form" are "noble" (p. 98). These details accumulate as the novel goes on.

Harleth's radiant youth specially conforms to the model of the maiden huntress of the green chase. Harleth is "quite young" (p. 21). She is in the bloom of a "charming maidenhood"; she is repeatedly "a fair maiden" (p. 30). Her face is "beaming with young pleasure in which there were no malign rays of discontent" (p. 85). She has a "deer-like shyness" (p. 580).

Harleth is associated with hunting and horses.[3] She herself is like "a young race-horse" and a "high-mettled racer" (pp. 19; 25; 85). Full of "animal stimulus," Gwendolyn Harleth longs to join the Wessex hunt (p. 57). A horse is the one item she insists upon having at Offendene, and it is the greatest gift she receives from Grandcourt (pp. 27; 108).

George Eliot ties these images of hunting to Harleth's nature, making her a Diana-type as willful and blissfully egotistic as Isabel Archer. Hunting in Harleth's milieu is the sport of the aristocracy, one of their "symbols of command and luxury" (p. 258). While engaged in this sport, Harleth feels more than ever her Diana-hood: "Gwendolen on her spirited little chestnut was up with the best, and felt as secure as an immortal goddess" (pp. 58–59).

In general, the maiden Harleth, as much a rank egoist as the young Isabel Archer, imagines she can wield an "omnipotence" in her life as a "goddess" (p. 470). She possesses the "command" of a "queen" (p. 93) and dreams of herself as a "princess in exile" and a "queen in exile" (p. 32–33). She believes "that the world was not equal to the demands of her fine organism" (p. 66), and she condescendingly responds to other mortals with a "queenly...air" of "royal permissiveness" (p. 519). Harleth feels hard her fate as a "queen disthroned." One reason she marries the aristocrat Grandcourt is to realize her own "divine right to rule" (pp. 245–46; 346).[4]

Like Isabel "Archer," Harleth is an archer, one whose aim will also go widely amiss during the course of the novel. She becomes a member of the Archery Club (p. 26), and she boasts that her "arrows will pierce" Grandcourt before anyone else's can (p. 79). The "Archery Hall" is like a pagan Greek creation, with "an arcade in front" showing the "white temple against the greenery" (p. 83). During the competition, Harleth's shooting temporarily shows admirable precision, and she makes "three hits running in the gold" (p. 89). Her archery outfit, "white cashmere with its border of pale green" sets "off her form to the utmost" (pp. 96; 123), a form like that of the Greek Diana, goddess of the white moon and green chase.

Lastly, Harleth has the free and fierce spirit of a Diana-type. She has a "native force" of "fire and will" (pp. 18; 64), and "a certain daring" and "rebellious" tendency that make her "assert her freedom by doing" impulsive acts (p. 43). She possesses a "fearlessness in active exercises," "high spirits," and "a defiant spirit" (pp. 47; 112). Every one in the novel wonders at Harleth's "force" (p. 589).

Harleth's figure bequeathed many other fierce traits to Henry James's Isabel Archer, most importantly the gambling streak, one tingeing Harleth with the demonic at Leubronn (p. 138). This combines with Harleth's celestial "illusions" about herself to create a woefully inaccurate and self-pleasing conception of a winning self, a lucky future, and an appropriately servile husband (pp. 252; 299; 511). All of this spells future tragedy for the Diana-hero. She shall become the "splendid sad-hearted creature" of the modern world (p. 501).

Harleth's rashness and illusions result in a marriage as woeful as Archer's. She marries a husband as shrewd and sinister as Osmond, one possessing the same manipulative power to reduce his wife, at moments, to the state of a dumb, weak, and helpless animal, overcome by her own fears and inclination to shrink from the experience of real evil (pp. 363–64; 377; 505). Her husband, like Osmond, uses his Machiavellian techniques to create a "prison" for his wife (pp. 504; 510; 594; 718 n.).

Four traits that Harleth in particular possesses, and bequeaths to Archer, determine their similar fate: (1) rootlessness, (2) willful ignorance, (3) icy chastity, and (4) Romantic illusions.

Both Harleth and Archer are orphans in the sense they have deceased and weak fathers, and they move around a lot in "roving" childhoods (pp. 13; 17). George Eliot stresses the effect of a childhood spent in visits at different residences: there is a lack of "blessed persistence in which affection can take root" (p. 16). Harleth has the dubious blessing of being a wayfaring and "dowerless beauty" (p. 109), and she is one addicted to her own desires—especially reckless gambling. The novel charts her mortifying travels through life.[5] This takes on deeper significance when one remembers that the initiate-hero in tragedy traditionally suffers from "wanderings, exhausting rushing to and fros, and anxious, interminable journeys through the darkness" —especially Aesychlean tragedy (Fagles, p. 72).

Second, Harleth's tragedy is precipitated from her willed ignorance: "She had a *naive* delight in her fortunate self" (p. 13). When considering marriage, Harleth likes her idea that "everything is to be as I like," full of "imagined freedom" for herself (pp. 25; 262). She indulges this "ignorantly rash" streak (pp. 346; 520) until her marriage forces her "into an amazed perception of her former ignorance." Her subsequent grasp of her husband's morbid nature creates in her one of her first genuine fears, that of "what their life with each other might turn into" (p. 365).

Thirdly, the willed ignorance of Harleth exists in collusion with her willed chastity. She desires to remain, literally and figuratively, untouched. Her frigidity is pronounced. She sleeps on a "pretty little white couch" (pp. 21; 262), significant of maidenhood, the state that Gwendolen does not want to grow beyond. She clings fiercely to the "little...couch" and its untouched snowy ideal of maidenhood. She is a "glacier" (p. 581), who "...objected, with a sort of physical repulsion, to being directly made love to" (p. 57). She dislikes men (pp. 117; 259), claiming that she hates them because they are in general a bad sort (p. 130).

Harleth seeks to perpetuate her frigidity in the married state by wedding Grandcourt, the one man whose coldly evil glance can freeze her (p. 622). Further, she wishes for to remain childless in her marriage (p. 265).

George Eliot clarifies that the obstinate frigidity of Harleth, like that of Hippolytus, is erring, indeed neurotic. When her cousin Rex makes love to Harleth, she is filled with disgust. She wants to "curl up and harden like a sea-anemone at the touch of a finger." She bursts out, "I hate it!" Her mother finds her in a state of mourning, her hair falling over her figure like an elegiac garment. Harleth, weeping, confesses her inability to "love anybody" (p. 68). Eliot concludes that this kind of rigid chastity can end "...in that mild form of lunatic asylum, a nunnery" (p. 508).

Fourthly, Harleth's chastity, her snowy ideals and illusions, are partially rooted in the grand ideas of Romantic poetry, ones preferable to the banal realities of modern prose. Eliot weaves allusions to "romance" throughout Harleth's portrait. Her roving disposition and impetuous gambling spring from and in turn encourage her "romantic superstitions" (p. 13). Harleth accepts the modest Offendene because she can imagine it to be "romantic," the home of fallen royalty (p. 19). This is a grand idea, but it is one, like others, that does not prepare her for the frustration of living in the actual world and its devolved form of "genteel romance":

> She rejoiced to feel herself exceptional; but her horizon was that of genteel romance where the heroine's soul poured out in her journal is full of vague power, originality, and general rebellion, while her life moves strictly in the sphere of fashion;... Here is a restraint which nature and society have provided on the pursuit of striking adventure; so that a soul burning with a sense of what the universe is not, and ready to take all existence as fuel, is nevertheless held captive by the ordinary wirework of social forms and does nothing particular (p. 43).

Harleth appears to be a "Lamia" (p. 7), but her fate as one is "pathetically incomplete: she is not to win the scholar from the power of reason and the wise old tutor. Instead, she is to find herself in the serpentine toils of Grandcourt, often described in reptilian images" (Hardy, p. 886). The magic spell that a Lamia was able to cast in Romantic poetry has vanished in the modern world.

Eliot qualifies that "poetry and romance" are in themselves good things. They are considered a way of "erroneous thinking" only by dull gentlemen and ladies. Especially, these elements are fine in a person like Deronda, for he possesses a "calm and somewhat self-repressed exterior" that can regulate his fervor in a way that Harleth with her impetuous nature can not regulate her impulsive romanticism (p. 245).

But Harleth especially puts her romantic element in service to her ego, not to the noble cause of poetry or of the human condition. The first threat to her romantic illusions is Sawyer's Cottage. When forced to abide there, she feels a "general disenchantment" and can't see any more "magic" in her world (pp. 245–46). Eliot proceeds increasingly to mimic the self-flattering romantic vistas that Harleth wants to be her realm. She describes Harleth's joy in Grandcourt's admiration to a slave's who is proud to be first-bought, therefore "mythical" in his success (p. 84). As Harleth comes to perceive the reality of her fate, she is full of "egoistic disappointment and irritation." The new "vision of herself on the common level" mortifies her (p. 223).

In fact, so romantically and egotistically delusive is the maiden Harleth that her natural force is at moments overcome by "world-nausea." She has no wish "to live" and sinks into "sick motivelessness." Eliot then chastises Harleth for ignoring

> ...the sweetness of labour and fulfilled claims; the interest of inward and outward activity; the impersonal delights of life as a perpetual discovery; the dues of courage, fortitude, industry, which is mere baseness not to pay towards the common burthen; the supreme worth of the teacher's vocation;—these, even if they had been eloquently preached to her, could have been no more than faintly apprehended doctrines:... poor Gwendolen had never dissociated happiness from personal pre-eminence and *eclat* (pp. 231–32).

George Eliot further implants into the text this theme of romantic illusions versus everyday disenchantments by continually opposing the terms "ideal" and "real." She comments on her countrymen and women: "We English are a miscellaneous people.... our prevailing expression is not that of a lively, impassioned race, preoccupied with the ideal and carrying the real as a mere make-weight" (pp. 85–86).

That "lively, impassioned race" may be, among others, the Greek, whence derives the model for our Diana-hero Harleth. Her origins in that "lively, impassioned race" render her a displaced person in Victorian England. When Gwendolen blithely aspires to heroics, her mother reminds her that she is afraid to be alone at night. Harleth impatiently replies, "I am not talking about reality, mamma" (p. 44). She is talking of her "ideal" image of herself, an image of a female winner engaged in daring heroics (p. 50). She finds annoying any "encounter with reality" (p. 131), and she likes to believe herself so "exceptional" a creature that she doubts she can ever remain long in "ordinary circumstances" (p. 17).

Sadly, Gwendolen is genuinely of an active and gifted nature, one that should find more avenues to express its genius. Eliot notes that "Gwendolen and her equivocal fate moved as busy images of what was amiss in the world" (p. 534), and this is one of many reminders that the lack of opportunities for Gwendolen to realize her heroic goals lies as much in her constricting society as in her rash nature.

The "Active" Principle

The Diana-type Harleth becomes, slowly, a Diana-hero partly due to the active streak of her nature. Ironically, however, the Diana-type simultaneously needs to temper this active principle, her will to action, to realize herself as a Diana-hero. Harleth begins by declaring, "I only feel myself strong and happy" (p. 93). Eliot sums up her case: "...her will was peremptory" (p. 12). There is something admirable in Harleth's active spirit, all "fire and will" (p. 18), but she abuses this gift to ensure that "other people" can not "interfere" with her own desires (p. 22). She delights to feel the "white reins in her hands," to "exercise her power" (pp. 253–54).

So, Harleth's active principle is initially devoted to serve her youthfully egoistic will. She kisses her image in the mirror, a "cold glass" that reflects her icy egoism, and she announces that she shall refuse to believe in sorrow for her gifted, lively self. With her beauty, luck, and power, Harleth is sure she will triumph over all sorrow; she has enough "force to crush it, to deny it, or run away from it" (p. 13). The concepts of acceptance, compromise, and redemptive suffering are missing from Harleth's maiden mind.

Especially, Harleth's ego makes her susceptible to the flattery and machinations of Grandcourt, a hunter who pursues his prey cagily. He induces a state of egoistic "exultation" in Harleth by letting her indulge a belief in her power to rule him (pp. 100–01). She falls into his snare in the "intoxication of youthful egoism" (p. 299). She convinces herself that her marriage would consist of "easy homage" from Grandcourt, and she will delight in her play "at reigning" (pp. 259; 266).

Later, with horror, she realizes the truth: "the cord which united her with this lover and which she had hitherto held by the hand, was now being flung over her neck" (p. 299). The subsequent clash of Harleth's peremptory will with Grandcourt's perverse wilfulness (p. 267) leads the two into a contest of wills, sick wills that are perversely intent on asserting their mastery at all costs (Bonaparte, p. 98). Both are equally "—ah, piteous...in the need to dominate!" (p. 256).

Harleth basks in the perverse battle: "Aha! he is very proud. But so am I. We shall match each other" (p. 264). She considers it impossible that she cannot win "indefinite power" over him (p. 265), and she envisions the coming day when she will "mount the chariot and drive the plunging horses herself" in their marriage (p. 115). Harleth, a type of the goddess of the chase, indulges her worse inclinations to love power for herself and subjugation for her prey.

Grandcourt admires Harleth for this spirit, for he perceives she exists in the same sphere as his prized hounds and pet dogs. He views her as a worthy acquisition in his "*cortege* of egoism" (p. 237), just as Gilbert Osmond considered Isabel Archer a worthy objet d'art for his collection. Grandcourt will like to use a "long whip" to flog his dogs and his wife (pp. 299). He will enjoy the spectacle of our Diana-hero, Harleth, stricken like a wounded deer, just as Osmond will so desire to see Archer.

Harleth will be so "stricken." At last, she realizes that she has mounted a chariot with horses going "at full speed" and with her husband, not her, holding "the reins" (pp. 276–77; 283). His supreme triumph is his Machiavellian ability to lead his gifted wife "captive"; it adds "to the piquancy of despotism" (p. 575).

Thus, Harleth, derived from the image of the free-spirited goddess of the chase, finds herself in a cruel prison, her horrid marriage, and she was catapulted there, like Isabel Archer, from the very elements in her nature that make her a Diana-type. Her indulgence of her own peremptive will aids her fall into Grandcourt's snares, as does her for gambling. In both her sport at the Leubronn resort and in her marriage to Grandcourt, Harleth is a "pretty gambler" (p. 138).

The very first time we see Eliot's "Leubronn Diana," she is "occupied in gambling." Indeed, she is in "the passion of gambling" (pp. 3–4). She finds solace in "the excitement of play" (p. 6), for gambling may offer a "narrow monotony of action" (p. 5), but it is action nonetheless, and for our spirited Diana-hero that is a relief from the limits of the mundane: "It is a refuge from dullness," she proclaims (p. 352). Harleth dreams of being the "heroine of the gaming-table" (p. 231).

Eliot indicates the tragedy inherent in a gaming spirit through Harleth's fate at the roulette-table: She passes quickly from being a "winner" to having her stakes completely "gone" (p. 6). This impoverished state not only foreshadows the illusions and disillusions of Harleth's reckless marriage with Grandcourt, but this initial loss foreshadows the impoverished state that makes Harleth so vulnerable to the wealthy Grandcourt's proposal, for Harleth's family becomes poor after the advisors of Grapnell & Co. foolishly believe they are "reigning in the realm of luck" (p. 132); they rashly gamble on assets, losing and rendering their investors "totally ruined" (p. 10). Harleth's response to her family's loss is to take another gamble. She pawns the necklace her father gave her to earn more stakes (p. 13).

In a perverse manner, Harleth's free spirit, which in itself is admirable, is exacerbated by and in turn exacerbates her gambling streak. She decides to take a wide channel on the horse Criterion: "...if I chose to risk breaking my neck, I should like to be at liberty to do it" (p. 111). Harleth's mind then jumps from the risk she takes on Criterion to the risk she takes with Grandcourt, the man who gave her the horse as a gift (p. 111). That their marriage arises a mere "three weeks" after they meet reinforces that it is a terrifically high gamble (p. 124).

Eliot further uses gambling as an image to embellish her theme that the fate of Harleth, the near ruin of a heroic type, is a symbol of what is amiss in the world.[6] Gwendolen's uncle, the Christian Rector, misguides his young charge on this point. He knows of Grandcourt's immoral past and abdication of social and marital duties toward Lydia Glasher and their four children, but he blithely labels this immoral past as an act of "gambling" on Grandcourt's part, then excuses Grandcourt because he left off this episode before he totally ruined himself (p. 77). The Rector, who should be Gwendolen's Christian guide, a much-needed one given her pagan roots and inclinations, thus condones gambling—if one quits the game while still ahead.

Another figure, who genuinely cares for and more successfully guides Harleth spiritually, perceives her marriage to spring from the same source as her "gambling" at Leubronn (p. 273). Daniel Deronda knows that Harleth gains wealth and status in her marriage, a gain that causes a severe loss to Lydia Glasher and her four children. Gwendolen thought that her playing so well materially at "the game of life" would be admirable (p. 299), but Deronda informs her how truly ugly such a game can be: "There are enough inevitable turns of fortune which force us to see that our gain is another's loss: —that is one of the ugly aspects of life" (p. 284).

The ugliness of peremptory wills and gambling goes even deeper. Deronda notes of Harleth, "Roulette was not a good setting for her; it brought out something of the demon" (p. 304). Later, he again perceives this element in her: "...there seemed to be at work within her the same demonic force that had possessed her when she took him in her resolute glance and turned away a loser from the gaming-table" (p. 348). The reader discovers that Harleth, at this moment, was plotting the murder of her husband. That is a gambler's rash solution to a rash bet, one lost wildly.

Wild games, then, of roulette and murder, take root and grow in Gwendolen's nature, willful and fierce. When her murderous plans strongly tempt her, she cries "God help me!" (p. 584), her wisest cry so far, one to a Judeo-Christian deity of patience and endurance. The pagan Harleth resists her demonic and reckless temptation to murder, and for the first time she finds herself happy that she has lost.

Her new freedom from her compulsion to win and to ride high is her first step toward redemption. She grows to accept the reversal of her material fortune when Grandcourt bequeaths his estate to Lydia Glasher and his sons. Harleth can now "bear to be poor" (p. 656). Then, her suffering doubles when she finds herself "the victim" of Deronda's happiness. Mirah Lapidoth will gain in marriage what Gwendolen Harleth will lose (p. 690). These are the worse turns for the former pretty gambler, but Harleth is at last prepared to accept and handle the downturn of the wheel. Her tragedy, like Archer's, becomes a paradoxical fortunate fall. Sadder but wiser, she ends with a promise to be better, hinting that she will begin to realize her inner powers in a manner more suited, perhaps, to comedic, not tragic, heroism.

Finally, Harleth's gambling nature is linked with insatiable thirst. Harleth is "intoxicated" with the feeling of "daring everything to win much" as she plays "at the game of life" (p. 299). A fellow gambler Mr. Lapidoth similarly feels "the thirst of the drunkard" (p. 678). The passion of the roulette table is a "flood-tide" threatening to overtake her (p. 6), and when deprived of her reign in the realm of luck, she experiences a "thirst" equal to that of a man in a desert (p. 256).

This hints once more that the elements that make Harleth a Diana-type also make her tragic, for Diana was queen of the moon, governess of

floods. The excerpt which opens Chapter 29 indicates that Eliot knew that
the moon controlled waters:

> Surely whoever speaks to me in the right voice,
>> him or her I shall follow,
> As the water follows the moon, silently,
>> with fluid steps anywhere around the globe.
>> —Walt Whitman (p. 275).

From this one can deduce that her Diana-hero is not governing her own
nature. Especially, in Chapter 29, Harleth conducts her wildest, out-of-
control gamble, the love-making between her and Grandcourt. Ultimately,
Harleth's uncontrollable thirst after her desires and her near death by
drowning in a flood of her own passions is a clear indictment of her
immature state, her youthful unwillingness to harness her own powers.

Further, Harleth's thirst and gambling, linked with the demonic, hint
that Harleth has not mastered the underworld side of her nature that
threatens to flood her fairer side. Like Jane Eyre, whose maddening
passions constantly threaten to flood her psyche, for Harleth the element
of darkness within threatens to gain full sway. Like a fury of the
underworld, she thirsts wildly for revenge and confesses her fatal designs
to Deronda: "I wanted to kill—it was as strong as thirst" (p. 593).
Harleth's punishment is symbolically correct: to inherit the *black* waters
of Gadsmere, of Grandcourt's shadowed and hidden old life, which, for
her, is to be subsumed literally into what had subsumed her metaphorically: powers that are dark and hidden.

In essence, just as Isabel Archer, who begins as a type of the crescent
moon goddess, comes to hold in her new arms the world of the old moon,
Madame Merle, so has the "White Crescent" Harleth come to embrace in
her young arms the dark inheritance of the once waning Lydia Glasher.
Both heroes of *The Portrait of a Lady* and *Daniel Deronda* realize their
fullest maturity when they have enacted the complete cycle of the moon
with an older, darker woman.

In Harleth's first grasp at her redemption, she asks Deronda for "a
glass of that fresh water" (p. 380). She is now "athirst toward the sound
of unseen waters" (p. 658), the "great waters" being the fluid body of the
world's spiritual knowledge (p. 426). Our Diana-hero, in the real world,
is coming to hold the reins on herself, to control the flood of her own

peremptory passions, so that she may ride the waters of life more nobly than before.

The "Fury" of Greek Drama

Diana was goddess of the waxing and the waning moon, of the Triple Fates who weave lives and cut their threads, of the serpents that rhythmically shed old skin for new, and thus are the cultic animal of the moon goddess and her Furies. All are symbols of a continual process of death and regeneration. They are so in Aesychlean drama (Fagles, p. 58), one important influence on the tragic scheme of *Daniel Deronda*.

According to Fagles, in *The Oresteia*, Clytemnestra is a grand hero modelled on the goddess Artemis.[7] Clytemnestra gives birth to the "serpent" who will murder her, and this murder then brings the Furies of Clytemnestra down upon her "serpent," Orestes. The forces of these Furies both mortify and electrify him. Thus, both Clytemnestra and Orestes suffer a "violent birth" which will eventually prove a "constructive regeneration" for their world. Moreover, Clytemnestra not only gave birth to the "serpent" but she summoned him through the Furies within her: "Fury brings him home at last,/the brooding mother Fury" (p. 89). Her figure unites the drama's emblems of birth, death, Furies, and regeneration, and her actions precipitate its final outcome.

In addition, her son must be baptized in her blood, making Clytemnestra both "diabolic and and deeply human...the murderess and the mother." She calls her son home "to suffer into truth—a mutual ordeal" (Fagles, p. 61). When she cries "Ai—you are the snake I bore," she is proclaiming that she has both created her fate and accepted it, and this makes her death cry into a birth cry as well. This makes her brutal destiny a creative sorrow: "The play is named for Agamemnon, but the tragic hero is the queen" (pp. 46; 64).

Harleth shares with Clytemnestra a death cry that becomes a birth cry. She, too, creates and accepts her brutal fate. She experiences both murderous and redemptive urges. The Furies haunt both her past and her future, and there exists the serpent within and without her.

From the first pages of the text, symbols of the Furies and their ancient cult swim about Harleth. Her nature derived from the regions of the Furies, Gwendolen is frequently linked to demons and said to be a witch (pp. 55; 63; 79; 304). There is a plethora of imagery of serpents, the Furies' heraldic animals. When Gwendolen first appears, she "has got herself up as a sort of serpent now, all green and silver, and winds her neck about a little more than usual." These sea-green robes and silver ornaments are her *"ensemble du serpent"* (p. 7). The next morning, Harleth "...walked on with her usual floating movement, every line in her figure and drapery falling in gentle curves attractive to all eyes except those which discerned in them too close a resemblance to the serpent, and objected to the revival of serpent-worship" (p. 13).

Appropriately, Harleth's consort, Grandcourt, is led on to their union by *fey* (p. 267), an allusion fusing the motifs of demon-haunting and snaky-headed Furies in the novel (Hardy, p. 893). And, just as Jane Eyre's mad passions and dark powers were embodied in Bertha Mason, a Fury and Rochester's first wife, so Harleth's nemesis is Grandcourt's past consort, Lydia Glasher. Glasher can be quite a Fury in her fierce passions and her dark magic, her powers also being tied to serpents, Hekate, the Furies, and to Harleth's coming death and regeneration, her creative sorrow.

Glasher resides at the "purgatorial Gadsmere" full of "evil spirits" who may soon be "hissing around [Harleth]with serpent tongues" (p. 651–52). She herself is a "viper" and a "Medusa," the serpent-haired goddess, and she uses her gifts as a "sorceress" to engender the mortification of Harleth (pp. 474; 517). She sinks her "fangs" into Harleth (p. 384), with the force of a "withheld sting" that has been "gathering venom" for years (pp. 288). Glasher, with her "hair perfectly black" and her "black" eyes (p. 121), typifies the waning moon goddess of black magic, the one whom the fair young moon "Gwendolen" must take fatally into her arms. When Glasher sends Harleth the "poisoned" diamonds, with her letter laying on the jewels like an "adder," she bestows upon the young bride her old "curse." Her act unleashes the Furies: "In some form or other the Furies had crossed [Grandcourt's] threshold" (p. 303).

In an ironic twist, in the end the humbled Gwendolen must shed her "heroine's skin to prove she is not the serpent she seemed" (Brownstein, p. 230). That Gwendolen can do so indicates her identity as a type of the serpentine moon goddess, one who can regenerate herself, from ancient times to modern.

Further, the creative sorrow of the Diana-hero, from the Greek Clytemnestra to British Harleth, springs from both their own fair and dark sides. Harleth is the maiden and the murderess as much as Clytemnestra is the mother and the murderess. Imagery of murder is prevalent about Harleth, especially that linked with the ritual hunt and sacrifice of prey. As a child, Gwendolen strangled her sister's canary. This is Gwen's first "infelonious murder" (p. 18). Anna Gascoigne senses this force in Harleth, speculating that her cousin is a like "wondrous and beautiful animal whose nature was a mystery, and who, for anything Anna knew, might have an appetite for devouring all the small creatures that were her own particular pets" (p. 53). Grandcourt, her consort, appropriately has his own murderous hand capable "of clinging round her neck and threatening to throttle her" (p. 366), a hand Harleth wishes to murder.

Harleth courted "danger" and her murderous husband for their own sake (p. 93), an act like Clytemnestra's summoning of her own Furies. Once caught in her furious marriage, Gwendolen enjoys dwelling on accidents that can happen to Grandcourt—because the alternative is heinous: "To dwell on the benignity of accident was a refuge from worse temptation" (p. 576). She becomes consumed with "vengeance" and finding a "dark vent for her rage." She dreams of murder, "of satisfied hatred," of finding "death under her hands," of finding the "white dead face" made with her own "murdering fingers." These are well-labelled "nightmares" (pp. 576–77), for they arise from the underworld passions in her of the Furies.

After Grandcourt's accident, Harleth confesses to Deronda that there had been "an evil spirit" working within her, that many times she has already been a "murderess" in thought (p. 591). She prayed "to have the forked lightning for a weapon to strike him dead" (p. 594). Her hand stays for one instant the rope for which the drowning Grandcourt cries; her mind cries back, "Die!" in her "momentary murderous will" (pp. 596; 598).

The image of the hunt in *Daniel Deronda*, as in the drama of Aesychlus, is symbolic of ritualistic killing and murderous wills, too. Harleth and Grandcourt love the hunt, and he comes to Harleth's neighborhood during the hunting season (p. 77). He is looking for new prey, and he finds it in Harleth as well as the foxes. Harleth senses and admires his love of hunting and its murderous tendencies in him: "I know he would have hunters and racers, and a London house and two country houses,—one with battlements and another with a veranda. And I feel sure that with a little murdering he might get a title" (p. 80).

As time progresses, Harleth finds herself more and more deeply snared in her marriage, and the ironic image of a Diana-hero tangled in toils and nets becomes repeated. Critically, it points to the heart of Aesychlean drama in *Daniel Deronda*. Nets are woven, and weaving comes under the domain of the moon goddess. The 'spinstress' Diana traditionally used nets in her murderous hunts. Clytemnestra, avenging the child-murder of Iphigenia, becomes a spinstress. She weaves blood-soaked tapestries for the "sacrifice" of her husband, an act of dark poesis, and she streams a "running weave of words" about her prey as she does so (Fagles, pp. 50–51). This poetry specially comes with the nature of a Fury: Clytemnestra is "the great artist of ritual," a stupendous ritual that "exhilarates herself with sacramental power—whipping the priestess [Cassandra] into fury" (pp. 32–34).

In this act, Clytemnestra realizes her powers as a Diana-hero: "As she re-enacts the trapping and the killing of the king, she impersonates Artemis the Huntress in effect" (Fagles, p. 40). Her marriage becomes an infernal union, "a death-pact" (p. 44), and that is also a description of the marriage of Diana-hero Harleth and Grandcourt, from which Harleth emerges to work toward a new life.

Moreover, Agamemnon is, like Grandcourt, a hunter. Symbols of nets and hunts surround him: "In the opening chorus Agamemnon is associated both with the hunt, that captures Troy and with its first extension, the bridal robes his attendants wind around his daughter as he kills her. The robes of ceremony and the nets of capture: the chorus stresses the second in its hymn of triumph; the nets of the Night have trapped the prize of Troy. But soon the nets of Clytemnestra trap the king.... And, as 'she winds about him coil after coil of her glittering rhetoric..., her words materialize in the gorgeous tapestries that lure him to his death" (Fagles, p. 50).

Aesychlean nets, be they of words or of cloth, are "hellish nets" exactly because they are the "mantles of the Furies" (Fagles, pp. 50–51).

When Clytemnestra unfurls the robes around her husband's body, he has no way to escape this murderous net or the murderous running weave of her words, and her gift of weaving words derives from the arch-spinners in The *Oresteia*, the Furies. "[I]n the weave of their binding-song—they shuttle, they suffer into higher states of awareness" (pp. 76–78). They are also the drama's greatest poets, for when they "turn their hunt into a dance," they turn murder into creative art. On this level does Harleth, like Clytemnestra, wait at home to murder her husband in the name of Artemis and the Furies. All are darkly poetic "mid-wives" who would birth action and weave tragic murders (pp. 28–29; 67).

Ultimately, the poetic power of the Furies helps to shape the new hero Orestes:

> The nets materialize in the black cloaks of the Furies and the hunting nets through which Orestes slips and which they lay aside. Both robes and nets will yield to a freely weaving play of image and enactment. The Furies' nets extend into their binding-songs that bind them to their victim, but Orestes is 'twined' in Athena's idol, too. His guilt and his innocence can never be disentangled, and neither can the Furies and the gods, the threads of the Fates and the grand design of Zeus. Their binding-song connects us all, mortals, and immortals, in a vast moral network (Fagles, p. 90).

This description can be applied to the revelation and the unfolding fate of the Diana-hero Harleth, too. She constantly falls into, then futilely tries to escape, the nets of her own impulsive doing, of her Machiavellian husband, and of society in general. Then, she is bound by both the murderous threads of the Fury Glasher and by the redemptive designs of the Judaic-Christian hero Deronda. This makes the two figures, Harleth and Deronda, interwoven in a "vast moral network." Eliot's emphasis on Deronda in the novel's title is yet another parallel the text of Aesychlus, who placed emphasis on the new law by making his drama's title the name of its new hero. In sum, the interweaving of the old and new in Eliot's novel follows the same pattern as it does in Aesychlus's drama: the progressively woven "fabric of society" (Fagles, p. 91).[8]

Critically, these images of nets and capture in *Daniel Deronda* are imbued with as much progressive moral force as they are in Aesychlus' drama. The first "fetters" Harleth will eventually feel will be "spiritual restraints," a leap forward from her youthful consciousness that considered religion of no more account than banking or arithmetic (p. 51). The "yoke" Grandcourt places around her neck gnaws at her guilty conscience, for it is the "yoke" of her "own wrong-doing," and Deronda counsels her that she needs desperately the refuge of "the higher, the religious life" (pp. 473; 386–87). The worst of her "entanglement in those fatal meshes" is its "inward torture" (p. 572). All these nets will effect the "bitterest mortification" of Harleth's soul (p. 384).

This theme points toward yet another intriguing parallel between the dramas and the heroes of Aesychlus and George Eliot when Eliot crafts Harleth as a pagan, especially an Aesychlean, Diana-hero, then juxtaposes her against the Judeo-Christian hero Deronda. In this, she makes her novel's action analogous to the movement of *The Oresteia*. That drama proceeds from the old law of the witches' powers and maternal cults, embodied in Clytemnestra and the "snaky-headed Furies," to the new law of Athenian and androcentric justice, embodied in Orestes (Fagles, pp. 58; 68). The drama of *Daniel Deronda* proceeds in a similar manner, from the old powers of pagan Greece, embodied in the glorious and fiercely-willed Gwendolen Harleth and Lydia Glasher, to the new law of the Judeo-Christian ethic, embodied in the wise and gentle Daniel Deronda.

Harleth's spiritual "mortification" (p. 384) becomes so complete that she gladly envisions their mutual death as a welcome end: "Let us go, then.... Perhaps we shall be drowned" (p. 582). Grandcourt is drowned literally, and Harleth is figuratively. She emerges from the horror an image of death: "—pale as one of the sheeted dead, shivering, with wet hair streaming, a wild amazed consciousness in her eyes, as if she had waked up in a world where some judgment was impending, and the beings she saw around were coming to seize her" (p. 587). Deronda, coming to rescue her, finds "the unhappy ghost of that Gwendolen Harleth whom Deronda had seen...at the gaming-table" long ago (p. 590). Harleth is "like one who had visited the spirit-world" (p. 652), "withered" (pp. 690–91).

But the Furies spin life as well as death (Fagles, p. 51), and Harleth will come to experience "that new terrible life lying on the other side of the deed which fulfills a criminal desire." The Judeo-Christian hero, Deronda, assures her that from her scourging, she will emerge "worthier than you have ever yet been—worthy to lead a life that may be a blessing." In the midst of her "great sorrow," Harleth feels "a gradual awakening to new thoughts" (pp. 599–600). Her experience is like that "Greek victory" which is the "triumph" over the barbarian latent in one's self (Fagles, p. 14). Deronda is moved by the spectacle, feeling "pity" for her, and that feeling fits the mode of Greek tragedy, too (p. 533). In sum, Harleth's painful series of mortifications and visions act as initiations into stronger states of consciousness, according well with the archetype of Greek tragedy, its "double thrust of shattering and confirmation" (Fagles, p. 20).

In Aesychlus' drama, the Furies incarnate the "paradox of woman," her power of murder and of birth. Their own transformation into the Eumenides is a triumph of the better graces within themselves (Fagles, p. 23). In Eliot's drama, Harleth's slow transformation from one of the Furies into one of the Eumenides is also a triumph of her better self, one promising future heroism from this Diana-type.

The Diana-Hero

Woman as Hero. Eliot clearly stresses her quest to restore the heroic stature to women throughout the text. She imbues this quest with sharp irony, too, by shackling to convention its Diana-hero, a figure like the goddess who was fierce but free, who protected woman, and who existed chastely with her following of female devotees.

During the first scene of Harleth, dramatically winning and losing at the gaming-tables, Eliot raises the issue: "...she had visions of being followed by a *cortege* who would worship her as a goddess of luck and watch her play as a directing augury. Such things had been known of male gamblers; why should not a woman have a like supremacy?" (p. 6). This may be an egotistical wish, but it is also the wish of a gifted woman, one who desires to be accorded as much homage for her passions as that given to men.

Those ambitions cause Harleth to rebel against the "domestic fetters" and "vexatious necessity" of her society's demands on her as a woman and as a wife (p. 30). Her rebellion is constant and constantly gender-specific. She complains to Grandcourt, "We women can't go in search of adventures—to find out the North-West Passage or the source of the Nile, or to hunt tigers in the East" (p. 113), and she protests to Rex: "Girls' lives are so stupid: they never do what they like.... —go to the North Pole, or ride steeplechases, or go to be a queen in the East like Lady Hester Stanhope (p. 56–57).

Harleth is as dynamic and strong in her character as she is willful and egotistical. When her family is ruined, she declares, "I could carry out some plan" to save them (p. 198). But her feminine education hasn't prepared her for any plans besides marrying well. In the midst of growing despair, Harleth realizes she is "no more cared for and protected than a myriad of other girls" (p. 201). Eliot identifies Harleth's dilemma "the higher crisis of her woman's fate" (p. 214).

Thus Harleth discovers herself held "captive" by the forms of "genteel romance" (p. 43) while her heroic passions belong more to the realm of Clytemnestra, Orestes, Prometheus, or Macbeth (p. 33). She announces to her mother:

> I think a higher voice is more tragic: it is more feminine; and the more feminine a woman is, the more tragic it seems when she does desperate actions.... As if all the great poetic criminals were not women! I think the men are poor cautious creatures (p. 44).

The term "poetic" is one of many pointers that Eliot gives to Harleth's nature an artistic capacity, however abused or misguided, like that Aesychlus gave to the Furies and Clytemnestra. In Harleth's world, however, her force and tools are inane. For amusement is this Diana-hero allowed to engage in the hunt and archery. Harleth is given "bows and arrows" for they are "the prettiest weapons in the world for feminine forms to play with" (p. 84).

Even to this mild amusement for Gwendolen the Rector Gascoigne objects: "...her uncle declaring that for his part he held that kind of violent exercise unseemly in a woman, and that whatever might be done in other parts of the country, no lady of good position followed the Wessex Hunt" (p. 57). He consoles Harleth by reminding her of the very social laws against which she chafes: "When you are married, it will be different; you may do whatever your husband sanctions" (p. 64). Upon her marriage, Harleth picks up the prettiest weapon indeed—a murder weapon, "small and sharp, like a willow leaf in a silver sheath" (p. 592).

It is the perfect weapon for a Diana-hero, a cold and hard piece of metal art that can signify her natural, and amoral, realm.

Eliot writes: "I like to mark the time, and connect the course of individual lives with the historic stream" (p. 74). She has, perfectly, by dropping a type of the free-spirited Greek Diana into the midst of nineteenth century England, then charting her trials. Her male hero, Daniel Deronda, sympathetically acknowledges that the "equivocal fate" of gifted, and potentially heroic, women like Harleth move "as busy images of what was amiss in the world" (p. 534).

In contrast, there is one Diana-hero in the novel whose fate is almost amiss, but it ends comedically, perhaps because this figure is a Diana-hybrid. The last name of Catherine "Arrowpoint" ties her to Diana, goddess of the green chase, but her first links her to Saint Catherine, whose wedding to Christ was a popular subject of art from the Renaissance on. Thus, Arrowpoint can be read as a hybrid Diana-bride.

A Christian-pagan hybrid such as Catherine Arrowpoint is neither a unique nor unusual creation in Eliot's highly symbolic texts. In *Middlemarch*, for instance, Dorothea Brooke is a heroic composite of the figures of St. Theresa, the Virgin Mary, Antigone, and Ariadne, as is her heroic lover, Ladislaw, a composite hero of Christ and Dionysus (Bonaparte, "*Middlemarch*," pp. 108; 110; 129; 133; 147). The theme is pervasive in Eliot's texts, as she discovers and explores the grandest ideas and characters in Western history.

The figures of Harleth and Arrowpoint reflect off each other in instructive ways. When Harleth appears at the Archery contest "as a slim figure floating along in white drapery," Arrowpoint is a sister image, "also dressed in white" (p. 35). Eliot employs imagery of the moon directly when she writes that Harleth's beauty is capable of "eclipsing" that of Catherine Arrowpoint's. So is Harleth's will, for Arrowpoint has none of Harleth's paganesque aspirations and ambitions. Nonetheless, Miss Arrowpoint is "one of the best archeresses" (p. 85), one as good as Harleth, if not better, and Arrowpoint will win the game of archery and of life, not an easy task for a woman in her time and place.

Especially, Arrowpoint may be heiress of "Quetcham Hall—worth seeing in point of art" (p. 26), but she is willing to renounce all her superior material possession of Quetcham for the truer gifts and love of her teacher and musician, Klesmer. Arrowpoint does not "miss the mark"—in the archery shoot or in her life. She lets fly a finely aimed arrow when she proposes marriage to Klesmer, and he accepts. When Klesmer declares the impossibility of their love, Arrowpoint replies with Dianesque bravery and initiative: "I am afraid of nothing but that we should miss the passing of our lives together" (p. 209).

In sum, Arrowpoint's high mind and spirit, touched by a Christian and saintlike devotion to ideal love and not to this world, combine with her family's fortune to create in her a hybrid Diana-bride for one of the novel's great artists, Klesmer. In the midst of women caught in tragedy, Arrowpoint's fate is a comedy, one she earns. It may be true that unlike the gifted Harleth, Arrowpoint will never aspire higher than her wedding and therefore never suffer. She will be limited to and satisfied in her sphere. But, clearly, the wealth she brings her groom is figurative as well as literal; her nature is as rich in its own way as is Harleth's; she brings to her world the gift of comedic heroism. Even two obtuse bystanders discern a symbolic element in her fine figure:

> But how remarkable well Miss Arrowpoint looks today! She would make quite a fine picture in that gold-coloured dress.... Well, perhaps a little too symbolical—too much like the figure of Wealth in an allegory (p. 87).

Lastly, the image of art in *Daniel Deronda* further clarifies the idea that Harleth, tragically, has no poetic outlet for her heroic powers. The literature and art of the era offers little in guidance or inspiration to the women. Harleth is frustrated that her society's popular art, that "genteel romance" which constrains heroines to effusively, and ineffectively, pour out their souls in journals. Harleth's lack of anything but a proper feminine education exacerbates this, for it amounts to a lack of consistent schooling in superior art. Harleth clearly suffers from a "dreary lack of ideas that might help her.... She was clearly an ill-educated, worldly girl" (p. 354).

The high art to which she has been exposed, however, does elicit certain yearnings. As a girl, she had figured in *tableaux vivants* at school, and from this she longs to assume Greek dress and to enact Greek scenes of "tragic intention" (p. 44). She has a severe trial to undergo before she can attain this height, and when she does so, it will be not in her genteel *tableaux vivants* but in real life.

However, her real tragedies correct her flaws that were sharply exposed in her earlier interpretations of drama. When her group stages a scene from Shakespeare, a maiden Harleth demands Leontes kneel and kiss the hem of her garment instead of embracing her. This egoistic revision of Shakespeare is a capsule of the youthful naivete that becomes mortified in her sinister marriage with Grandcourt (p. 48). Life, the state of our female hero, and art constantly interrelate in *Daniel Deronda*, just as they did significantly for the Diana-heroes in *Jane Eyre*, *The Scarlet Letter*, *Ulysses*, and *The Portrait of a Lady*.

Significantly, the mature artist Klesmer calls the youthful Harleth's pageant a "magnificent bit of *plastik*" (p. 49). This term indicates life as mere impersonation (Hardy, p. 888), one that largely serves an individual ego, much like the "plastic" view of art and life taken by the false Osmond in *The Portrait of a Lady*. The "perfect climax" to Harleth's piece of amateur *plastik* comes when she faints from terror. The piano panel flies open and reveals a dead white face, which will one day be her husband's drowned face and her own ghastly one (pp. 49; 577; 587; 597; Hardy, p. 901). In short, true art, art that is a mirror of Harleth's real life to come, interrupts Harleth's naive art.

In addition, pagan art, initially, is emblem of Harleth's noble nature: "Dressed in black without a single ornament, and with the warm whiteness of her skin set off between her light-brown coronet of hair and her square-cut bodice, she might have tempted an artist to try again the Roman trick of a statue in black, white, and tawny marble" (p. 214).

In sum, throughout Eliot's novel, the idea of art surfaces in a varied manner with Harleth. At moments, art offers itself, through the piano panel, for better and worse, to our Diana-hero. At other moments, the presence of art is sadly and pointedly lacking. Harleth is ignorant of high art, an ignorance willed not only by her headstrong inclinations that preoccupy her with gambling and wasteful activities, but through her world's encouragement of female naivete, of its woefully limited form of genteel romance. And through art, the image of Roman sculpture, Eliot reveals the true type of Harleth, and other characters, to us.

Religion and the Diana-Hero. In George Eliot's novel, the transition from old law to new law, the Aesychlean "cultural evolution" (Fagles, p. 73), traces the progress from pagan law to Christian. The Judeo-Christian hero, Daniel Deronda, at first irks the Greek Diana-hero, Gwendolen Harleth, because he views her "as a specimen of a lower order" (p. 6). He thinks he can best aid her as a "mentor" (p. 14), but he perceives the difficulty of this, for the difference between his ideas and Harleth's are "like a difference in native language" (p. 687). And so they are, metaphorically, the difference of Greek versus Hebrew. Each religion, paganism and Judeo-Christianity, was in its own time a "conceivable vesture of the world" (p. 306), and George Eliot marches out these two grand vestures of the Western world for a sharp comparison.

Harleth harbors both the glorious force and the reckless action of a pagan Diana-hero while Deronda perfects the wisdom and "reflective hesitation" that is one of the "demerits" of a meditative Christian soul (p. 153). His figure is clearly the morally superior. In his gentle goodness, he gently cautions Harleth, "—all reckless lives are injurious, pestilential" (p. 382).

Deronda, in accord with his role as "redeeming influence" (p. 273) of the new law, begins Harleth's salvation on the day he redeems for her the inheritance she impulsively pawns, her father's necklace. The young Harleth greets his influence with "resentment," but an older and wiser Harleth later turns to his "corrective presence" with more "love and trust" (p. 682). Now, Deronda's voice sounds to her as "the deep notes of a violoncello." His notes contrast to her husband's "toneless drawl," which points toward the inferiority of Grandcourt, a pagan hunter (p. 279).

The youthful and pagan Harleth gradually comes to know the "conscious error" of her behavior at the gaming-tables and in her marriage, and in her crisis Deronda wakens "something like a new soul" to replace "her former poise of crude self-confidence" (p. 280). She is progressing toward a better, new self, imploring him to continue "the rescue he had begun in that monitory redemption of the necklace" (p. 655):

> You must tell me then what to think and what to do; else why did you not let me go on doing as I liked, and not minding? If I had gone on gambling I might have won again, and I might have got not to care for anything else. You would not let me do that (p. 382).

Repeatedly, Harleth asks him to "enlighten my ignorance," and Deronda responds with patient counsel: "Take the present suffering as a painful letting in of light" (p. 388). His "words" and "tone" succeed in touching a "new spring in her" (p. 520). He fortifies her with the thought that her "violent shock" and "keen remorse" are enlarging her life (p. 377). It is this prospect of heroically struggling to gain a new life that makes Harleth's trial so worthwhile:

> But her remorse was the precious sign of a recoverable nature; it was the culmination of that self-disapproval which had been the awakening of a new life within her (p. 597).

It is precisely Harleth's "wonderfully mixed consciousness," both her pagan recklessness and her Christian remorse, that makes her struggle so dramatic (p. 595), for it makes complex and turbulent her "regenerative process" (p. 660). She is a pure Diana-hero, but one reared in a country and era that are Christian. This creates such conflict—and possibilities—for her. As a singular character in a society unalloyed to her natural realm, there is a fierce but dynamic duality in Gwendolen's situation.

Significantly, Harleth's other Christian instructor, the Rector Gascoigne, is good-natured but superficial. His conscience is easy on her marriage, and his instructions to her on it are easy also, because of the earthly consideration of Grandcourt's wealth (pp. 117–20). When the Rector fails to give Harleth the guidance needed on her possible marriage, it helps to precipitate her nightmarish marriage. Evidently, then, in Eliot's schemata, the progress of cultural evolution needs to be carried out carefully and actively.

In Harleth's worse crisis, Deronda's redeeming influence penetrates to Harleth's soul and manifests itself in her dreams:

> ...she had wild, contradictory fancies of what she might do with her freedom—that "running away" which she had already innumerable times seen to be a worse evil than any actual endurance, now finding new arguments as an escape from her worst self. Also, visionary relief on a par with the fancy of a prisoner that the night wind may blow down the wall of his prison and save him from desperate devices, insinuated itself as a better alternative, lawful to wish for.
>
> ... she felt herself escaping over the Mont Cenis, and wondering to find it warmer even in the moonlight on the snow, till suddenly she met Deronda, who told her to go back (pp. 578–79).

After Grandcourt drowns and Harleth seeks his aid, Deronda sits before her, like a saint with his "halo of superiority." She offers him her greatest confession (p. 595), and he advises her that the better half of her mixed consciousness gained ascendancy in the end, for she not only resisted all impulses to withhold the rope from Grandcourt, but she jumped into the water to save him. He takes her hands in his, and a "stream of renewed strength" passes from his soul into hers (p. 592). As his spirit enters hers, Harleth finally speaks of redemption: "...it was not my own knowledge, it was God's that had entered into me" (p. 593). At last, her life has passed from the "curse" of pagan furies and demons with Grandcourt to the "blessing" of Judeo-Christian angels (pp. 303; 599).

She has entered the realm of Deronda, the "terrible-browed angel" (p. 577), one bringing the laws of superior Judeo-Christian philosophy. In this success lies her heroism. The Diana-hero has passed from the old world to the new, where she shall survive anew. In evolving from that old state to a new and higher one, Harleth's soul undergoes "a whole heroic poem of resolve and endurance" (p. 604). The Diana-hero weathers her "tragic transformation," finding a new life "growing like a plant." She will end among "the best of women," one replete with "new powers" (pp. 656; 658-59).

The structure of *Daniel Deronda* indicates that this transformation is not only heroic, but it is on the level of a personal apocalypse. St. John's ideas are thematically central to Eliot's *Daniel Deronda*, "Book Six" being titled "Revelations" for instance (p. 434). As humanity as a whole moves toward revelation and apocalypse in St. John's text, so humans move individually in Eliot's text:

> ...to many among us neither heaven nor earth has any revelation till some personality touches theirs with a peculiar influence (p. 368).

Every individual's history in the text can be read on the symbolic level as "a chapter in Revelations" (p. 168). Mirah's story will be a "revelation" to Ezra Cohen, just as Cohen's story will be to Mirah (pp. 464; 496) and Mirah's love for Deronda will be a "a flash of revelation" (p. 625). For our Diana-hero, her earliest forebodings of tragedy take this form:

> Gwendolen felt an inward shock, but her immediate thought was, "It is come in time." It lay in her youthfulness that she was absorbed by the idea of the revelation to be made (p. 126).

Her revelations continue, increasing her suffering and her regeneration. The final and most painful "revelation," Deronda's exit to help his people, is also the greatest spur to her growth (p. 683). It forces her to survive on the resources of her own soul just born anew. Throughout the text, the Christian Deronda witnessed the "sad revelation of spiritual conflict" to the paganesque Harleth (p. 595), and that has transformed her at last.

Tragedy, Hamartia, and the Diana-Hero. The first time Deronda sees Harleth, she arrests his attention for she makes "the moment become dramatic" (p. 5). Thus the "drama" begins (p. 6). Persons who meet her observe that she "has some drama in her" (p. 137). Throughout the text, Eliot so identifies and charts Harleth's journey as a drama, specially a tragedy.

The naive Harleth imagines her drama will take the form of comedy, for she and her "happy nose" are too pretty to be fated for "tragedy" (p. 21). For fun, applause, and self-glory does Harleth want to appear in "Greek" dress and act a "tragic intention" or to bask publicly in the role of a great "poetic" criminal of some sort. Her youthful egotism plunges her into her tragic errors, however, ones she must suffer through to correct her "erroneous way of thinking" (pp. 44; 47).

Her main tragic error, her marriage, is titled a "subtly-varied drama" (p. 255). She and Grandcourt are antagonists battling for triumph over each other. Grandcourt is attracted to Harleth for the "drama" her nature offers, and he snares her by allowing her to "[play] at reigning" as a dramatic queen (p. 266). Harleth believes his alluring promise that in her marriage she will be "the heroine of an admired play without the pains of art" (p. 301).

When the wedding ceremony is over and her married life begins, however, she experiences "agony" (p. 594), one of the main emotions of tragedy. Her conscience becomes a "lava-lit track" (p. p. 661). Out of and in the midst of this "grief" comes Harleth's final cry, one of tragedy and its heroism:

Don't be afraid. I shall live. I mean to live.... I shall live. I shall be better (p. 692).

Hers is the high tragedy of the Greek kind in another manner, too. Aristotle's *hamartia*, "to miss the mark," is the flaw which heralds tragedy. Gwendolen Harleth, modelled on the goddess of the chase, of arrows and of prey, misses the mark as woefully as Isabel "Archer" will. Harleth misses for the same reason many Greek heroes do: Pride. An unredeemed Harleth brags, "There is nothing I enjoy more than taking aim—and hitting" (p. 26). She vaunts to her mother that no other maiden at the Archery contest will have even "a shadow of a chance" for Grandcourt against her (p. 79).

Eliot makes clear that her words, full of pride, point toward her tragedy with Grandcourt. When Harleth continues to crow to others at the contest, "If I am to aim, I can't help hitting," the Lord Brackenshaw cautions: "Ay, ay, that may be a fatal business for some people" (p. 88).

Harleth persists in glorying in her precise shot and victory. Significantly, she is eyeing the point of her arrow at that fatal moment she is introduced to her husband (p. 90). While conversing with him, Harleth assumes—in "dark" error—that a cold man might be the best husband, for he will be less likely to interfere with his wife. At this equally fatal moment, she discovers that she has lost "the gold arrow" of the Archery contest to another maiden (p. 94). In sharp contrast, one of Harleth's "great rivals" in archery, the humbler and kinder Diana-hybrid Catherine "Arrowpoint," will not miss the mark in either the contest or her marriage (p. 93).

At the end of Harleth's drama, her arrows, once tipped in the poison of Pride, are now dipped in tragedy's other great emotion, Pity. In this one instance, the "pity" is identified as Dantean pity, and this makes Harleth's progress shift from the realm of Greek tragedy to the Christian. This makes her heroic struggle once again like the cultural evolution of Aesychlean tragedy. In the scheme of Eliot's imagery, the fatal arrows of a Greek Diana-hero have been transformed into the regenerative arrows of Christian sentiment:

...her words of insistence that he "must remain near her—must not forsake her"—continually recurred to [Deronda] with the clearness and importunity of imagined sounds, such as Dante has said pierce us like arrows whose points carry the sharpness of pity (p. 533).

LILY BART: THE CREATIVE MARRIAGE OF THE DIANA-HERO

"...and she was alone in a place of darkness and pollution."

The ultimate act of poesis achieved by many Diana-heroes is the *hieros gamos*, the sacred marriage. It is the glorious wedding that signifies new life and a new domain. Edith Wharton's vision of the possibility—and impossibility—of this sacred wedding, for her gifted Diana-hero, is both a resplendent and disturbing revelation for her readers.

The idea of the *hieros gamos* occurs in both pagan and Christian myth and literature. This is a traditional goal of questors, and upon realizing it, the heroes find transcendental love and unity, ushering in a new era of life. The forms and numbers of the *hieros gamos* are as kaleidoscopic in Western literature as are the myriad shapes of its Diana-heroes. In *The Golden Ass*, Apuleius symbolically weds the spirit of the moon goddess, Isis, when, after a long and trying journey, he attains a crowning vision of her being. In the *Iliad*, it is the spectacular wedding of Zeus and Hera. In the Bible, to this goal allude the books of *Isaiah*, *The Canticles*, *Revelations*, and others when they call the worshipper to the Wedding. In Spenser's *The Faerie Queene*, Artegall journeys to be united with the chaste and glorious Britomart.

In the *Aeneid* and the *Odyssey*, the union is the absolute end of the quest, yet it takes place beyond the text. Aeneas completes his struggles and shall, as his reward, wed Lavinia to usher in the reign of a New Troy, and Ulysses endures to return to Penelope and restore their kingdom. In these instances, the wedding of the individual characters is a rich symbol for the reign of a new era within themselves and sometimes without, too.

In the wealth of its variety of forms and characters, the *hieros gamos* most often concerns the sun god and the moon goddess, for here is the union of two beings who are radiant symbols of the male and the female principles. Erich Neumann so well defined the meaning of this paradigm of the *hieros gamos* for its participants as a means of attaining a "wholeness" that comes from their "union of opposites":

> Then, the patriarchal sun-consciousness reunites with the earlier, more fundamental phase, and matriarchal consciousness, with its central symbol the moon, arises from the deep, imbued with the regenerating power of its primal waters, to celebrate the ancient *hieros gamos* of moon and sun on a new and higher plane, the plane of the human psyche (p. 228).

In Edith Wharton's *The House of Mirth*, the Diana-hero Lily Bart does achieve, simultaneously, a beautiful but ephemeral kind of the Sacred Wedding and subsequent Apocalypse for her psyche. Bart poetically creates the "Word" with Selden Lawrence, but she does so as she embraces him on her deathbed; she achieves an act of poesis in the throes of death.

When Selden Lawrence kneels at Lily Bart's deathbed, Wharton writes:

> It was this moment of love, this fleeting victory over themselves, which had kept them from atrophy and extinction;... He knelt by the bed and bent over her, draining their last moment to its lees; and in the silence there passed between them the word which made all clear (pp. 255–56). [1]

The two creating the "word" in silence is a hint to the symbolic import of that "word," for it remains an unspoken mystery. Wharton's poem "Artemis to Acteon" clarifies its symbolic import and points to her intentions in that scene. While making their silent "word," Bart and Lawrence "drain" their last moment "to its lees," an act that directly parallels that of Artemis and her lover in "Artemis to Acteon":

> For immortality is not to range
> Unlimited through vast Olympian days,
> Or sit in dull dominion over time;
> But this—to drink fate's utmost at a draught,
> Nor feel the wine grow stale upon the lip,
> To scale the summit of some soaring moment...
> Secure forever in the vaults of death!

Just as Artemis woos Acteon to drink fate's utmost at a draught with her, so Lily Bart attracts Lawrence to drain to the lees that moment in which they create the word. That is to find true immortality *as Wharton defines it.*

In that moment, Lily Bart moves beyond *pathos*, her suffering in squalid surroundings, to *mathos*, the significance of that suffering, its truth. Her suffering has turned into her creative agony. It becomes the labor needed for the discovery of the "word," however fleeting a moment that "victory" will be in the text's shabby world. When Bart passed from her Fifth Avenue manor to the dingy boarding house, she passed from the House of Mirth to the House of Mourning, and her physical poverty heralded psychic richness, for she ends inspiring the "word" with her beloved at the price of her own death. In the moment of destruction, she achieves creation. She realizes the New World, and she does so, purely, as a personal apocalypse.

Lily Bart as a Diana-Hero

Like many Diana-heroes, Lily Bart fits the archetype of a black-haired Bride (pp. 7; 10). She possesses the Bride's traditional powers of renewal (p. 153), Wharton especially linking her with the moon's typically refreshing symbols, the life-giving waters and tides. This imagery also signifies the bride's flow of love for her intended groom, for Bart's moods are a "current" drawing her toward Lawrence (p. 44), and their talks evoke in her "deep wells" of feeling (p. 57). Further, Wharton gives Bart a natural reign over other brides. At the "sylvan rites" of marriages Lily Bart stands, like Diana traditionally over her nymphs, much "taller than the other attendant virgins" (p. 69). This last image makes particularly poignant Bart's struggle to realize her own *hieros gamos*.

In every way, Lily Bart is as ineluctably superior as most gifted Diana-heroes are to other mortals. The "dinginess, the crudity of this average section of womanhood" makes Lawrence appreciate "how highly specialized" Bart is (p. 6). Beyond her gift of physical beauty, Lawrence admires the "deeper eloquence" of her nature and "the bravery of her words" which make her so "matchless" (p. 168).

Nearly every character in the book pays homage, openly or secretly, to Bart's superior being. Trenor is obsessed by her "divine" qualities (p. 94). Rosedale appreciates the "noble directness" by which Bart assumes "command" of any occasion, and he wants to marry her because she is such an "exception" to common humanity (pp. 198; 233). Gerty views Bart as an "idol," being awestruck by her "shining vision" (pp. 128–29).

Ironically, in the midst of this worship, Bart's troubles are partially caused by her superiority. She refuses to turn on her enemy-in-waiting, Bertha Dorset, from motives of "compassion" (p. 162), and Dorset hates Bart precisely because she fears her supremacy (p. 197). Bart's social world, like the world of her predecessor Isabel Archer's, shall make bad use of her.

Bart's troubles are partially caused in another way by her gifted nature. She revels in "her reflected sense of superiority" (pp. 27; 208–09), and this leads her into the typical snares for the Diana-type: pride and egoism. Bart is "not above a certain enjoyment in dazzling them by her fineness, in developing their puzzled perception of her superiorities," and she revels in "the gratifying consciousness of power" (p. 89). Bart admires in the mirror her slender, sylvan, and physical beauty (p. 12). Her egoism contributes to her bad judgement of her enemy, Bertha Dorset, too, for Dorset is far from the "poor shivering creature" whom Bart pleasingly imagines to need her "shelter." Dorset is in "full command" of a plan to "knife" Bart (pp. 160–62).

In another twist, however, Bart's egoism also serves to shore up her chaste nature, which is critical for her to endure her struggles. Her snowy pride aggravates her into "moral repulsion" from her society and its immoralities (p. 78). She recoils from the "vile" blackmail scheme of the Benedict's maid and of Rosedale, one that centers on Bertha Dorset's sexual corruption (pp. 82–84). Critically, her fastidiousness in society is correspondent to an inner "moral equivalent" (p. 66). In short, "Lily" is as white-natured and high-priced as the lilies-of-the-valley she admires (p. 27). She comes to "despise the world" which misguided and exiled her (p. 204), rejecting its "ideal" of "material achievement" (p. 223).

Bart was dangerously vulnerable to this world because of other traits inherent in a character who fits the pattern of a Diana-type. Like her predecessors Isabel Archer and Gwendolen Harleth, Bart is restless and she roves. She has no concept of domestic roots, of being "tied down" anywhere by the silken threads of affection (p. 12). In her youth, she and her mother wander from one foreign watering place to another (p. 29). Finally, Bart's lack of a home precipitates her fatal overdose:

> But there was something more miserable still—it was the clutch of solitude at her heart, the sense of being swept like a stray uprooted growth down the heedless current of the years.... the feeling of being something rootless and ephemeral, mere spindrift of the whirling surface of existence.... And as she looked back she saw that there had never been a time when she had any real relation to life. Her parents too had been rootless, blown hither and thither on every wind of fashion, without any personal existence to shelter them from its shifting gusts. She herself had grown up without any one spot of earth being dearer to her than another: there was no centre of early pieties, of grave endearing tradition, to which her heart could revert and from which it could draw strength for itself and tenderness for others (pp. 248).

In addition, Bart's natural energy, her enthusiasm for the thrill of hunting and in general for any "keen stimulant" (p. 226) combine with this lack of roots to make her as reckless a gambler as were Isabel Archer and Gwendolen Harleth. The first time we see Bart in society, "the gambling passion" has overrun her. She risks "higher stakes at each fresh venture" (p. 24), and the extent of her "gambling debts" is ominous (pp. 33; 61; 99).

This reckless attitude taints Bart's vision of life. She and Lawrence talk lightly of marriage between them as an of their "experiments," a tempting one because of the "great risk" it would involve (p. 58–59). When Trenor gives her the first four thousand, out of lewd motives, Bart's spirits are simply elated at this "stroke of luck," and she gladly believes her own "good fortune" causes this windfall (p. 73).

Ironically, the chaste Diana-hero Bart, though a gambler, is an honorable one, and this helps to lead to her material poverty and social isolation. She repulses Rosedale because he is at heart a sordid kind of gamer, and therefore suspects she may be, too. In their talk of a marriage deal, a kind of social game during which the two bat proposals between each other, he wants to hedge his bets by his blackmail scheme. This brings to Bart a minor revelation:

> Light comes in devious ways to the groping consciousness, and it came to her now through the disgusted perception that her would-be accomplice assumed, as a matter of course, the likelihood of her distrusting him and perhaps trying to

cheat him of his share of the spoils. This glimpse of his inner mind seemed to present the whole transaction in a new aspect, and she saw that the essential baseness of the act lay in its freedom from risk (p. 203).

Moreover, like her literary predecessors—Isabel Archer, Gwendolen Harleth, or Jane Eyre—Bart is an orphan, not only a rover but a solitary one. Bart has lost her father and her mother (pp. 20; 72). When Bart turns to the arms of Gerty Farish, she does so because she craves to pillow her head in the hollow of Gerty's arms, just as a lost child needs her mother's nest (p. 133). The Diana-hero is free-spirited, but also singular, and she is alone in a society which is in many ways so foreign to her nature. This casts her into the position of seeking solace from a young woman, of whom Diana was once the sure-footed protectress.

Another critical element in Bart's nature causes her initial inability to renounce her world. That is her love of luxury, the seeds of which lie in her identity as a Diana-hybrid. Like hybrid figures from Jane Eyre to Hester Prynne, the chaste Bart carries within her elements of Venus. This element inclines Bart to a life of ease and exacerbates her acquired habit of luxury, helping to sap her Dianesque vigor and chastity into a state of "moral lassitude" (pp. 184–85).

In appropriate symbolism, in the sexually corrupt realm of Mrs. Hatch, Bart finds herself sleeping in a magnificently worldly bed, replete with "ornamental excrescences on a vast concavity of pink damask and gilding, from which she rose like Venus from her shell" (p. 213). At this critical point, Wharton stresses Bart's dilemma as a mixture of "innocence" and of "experience," and these are literary, especially Blakean, ideas, ones that can correspond to the archetypal realms of the chaste Diana and of the earthly Venus (p. 213).

To resist this Venus within, Bart calls upon the steely chaste will of the Diana within, particulary that fiercely free and pure nature represented by the maiden goddess of the green chase. This is a difficult task, however, to which she rises with a struggle because her world has taught her to misapply her Dianesque powers, specially her hunting skills. Bart has been schooled thoroughly that marriage is her only possible "vocation" (p. 10), and to this end her mother has drilled Bart that she must use her beauty as her best "weapon" to achieve "conquest" over heirs (pp. 29–30).

The text clearly and importantly establishes Bart as an excellent huntress, a maiden of the chase, however misguided her gifts are in her social sphere. In the opening scene when she and Selden Lawrence meet, he freely converses with Bart because he knows that she would never waste her powers in the social chase on such "small game" as himself (p. 9). In the next scene, when Bart meets the heir Percy Gryce, she coolly studies "her prey," organizing her methods of "attack" and her means of "approach" (p. 17). She is "on the hunt for a rich husband" (p. 38).

Her skills, however misdirected, keep Bart from falling into certain snares. Rosedale perceives Bart is a great "dead game sport" (p. 200), moreso than any man or woman, and one who rejects his own base games. Her whole spirit is so fresh and radiant that it is itself like "a forgotten enemy that had lain in ambush and now sprang out on [Rosedale] unawares" (p. 226). Bart's fine instinct for "self-defence" not only stops her from uniting with Rosedale but with a still obtuse and hypocritical Lawrence (p. 217).

In a last irony, the Diana-hero ends saving her chaste self, but it is a self severely wounded. Bart feels deeply her "wounded vanity" when Trenor freely makes his "claim" on her (p. 68). As the crisis with Trenor worsens and his mood becomes "unmanageable," Bart's confidence in her "power of disarming" her opponent fails (pp. 101–03). Trenor inflicts a "wound" so deep that Bart rushes feverishly, and symbolically bleeding, to her friend Gerty Farish. The merciful Farish sees in Bart both the "siren" who can send her victims floating back "dead" to shore and the painfully wounded creature who craves Farish's arms and kind sleep (pp. 129–32).

These battles harden Bart's defenses. Lawrence, meeting Bart in the Mediterranean, sees that the youthful transparency of her beauty, one that revealed the fluctuations of her spirit, has undergone "a process of crystallization which had fused her whole being into one hard brilliant substance" (p. 149). He perceives that her newly acquired "bright security," which acts as her shield, also reveals her need for help. She must be engaged in a new and disturbing battle. Moments later, Bertha Dorset launches her attack on Bart and her society abandons her. This casts Bart toward the aid of Lawrence, who in the privacy of deserted

gardens sees "the struggling misery of her face" and senses the depth of
her "wound"'s (pp. 169–70).

Bart's fatal wound, however, shall derive from Lawrence's desertion
of her (p. 216). In her final stages, when her vitality ebbs to the point
where Bart is "so often unwell" (p. 232), she goes to Lawrence in a last
effort to save them both, and their love. She receives instead the
revelation that she has, for the moment, been shut out by her intended
Spouse. Then comes her "death-pang" (p. 239).

"An Interesting Study": The Diana-Hero in Gotham

Lily Bart has the fresh spirit and "smooth free gait" (p. 173) typical of
heroes modelled after the goddess of the green chase, and this trait
Wharton juxtaposes against her high society trappings and breeding:

> The attitude revealed the long slope of her slender sides, which gave a kind
> of wild-wood grace to her outline—as though she were a captured dryad subdued
> to the conventions of the drawing room; and Selden reflected that it was the same
> streak of sylvan freedom in her nature that lent such savour to her artificiality
> (p. 12).

Bart rues her fate in the gilt trap which is her social world: "Why must
a girl pay so dearly for her least escape from routine? Why could one
never do a natural thing without having to screen it behind a structure of
artifice?" (p. 15). Bart's society has thus shaped and caged her in its
trivial and artificial conventions, and having caged her, that society will
proceed to sully her beauty and grace. Lily Bart's radiant and gifted
figure is publicly gossiped about in her society's "dirty sheet" (p. 124).

In fact, Wharton states in her autobiography "a frivolous society can
acquire significance through what its frivolity destroys" (qtd. in Lewis, p.
ix), and the frivolous society of *The House of Mirth* betokens the death
of heroics, both female and male. Just as Henry James had Isabel Archer
sit, in a moment of helpless obtuseness, before the statute of the Dying
Gladiator, so ensconced in the home of Lily Bart is the Dying Gladiator,
one just as moribund in her social world (p. 77). This work of art should
inspire both Diana-heroes with heroic ideals, of their own, and of their
consorts, but those ideals are ignored and archaic in their shallow worlds,

and both Archer and Bart have been far too ill-educated and ill-prepared to begin to discern and judge these ideals through art.

Various details reinforce this theme. Like the literature possessed by Bart's predecessor Harleth, Bart's reading also seems to have consisted quite a bit of the "sentimental fiction" deemed appropriate for females by her milieu (p. 30), and her aunt's house contains a miniature of Beatrice Cenci whose artist, favored by Wharton's society, presents the tragic heroine with a "pink-eyed smirk." Bart has enough of natural taste that the miniature fills her with distaste (p. 135), but she seems to have no knowledge of the tragic story itself and its heroine.

Bart carries some literature as a token of 'correct' reading to impress herself and others, but this is her society's admired text, Fitzgerald's translation of Khayyam's *The Rubaiyat*, with its "emphasis on sensual pleasure and on living for the moment" (p. 53; 53 n.). Ironically, the one drama that shall affect Bart—Aesychlus' *Eumenides* with its Furies that shall come to pursue her—she had just "picked up" once while on a social visit (p. 117).

The beauty of jewels also wraps Bart's figure in irony. The sapphire, one gem of the heavenly moon goddess, signifies not only Bart's celestial beauty but her entrapment in this negative worldly milieu:

> As he watched her hand, polished as a bit of old ivory, with its slender pink nails, and the sapphire bracelet slipping over her wrist, he was struck with the irony of suggesting to her such a life as his cousin Gertrude Farish had chosen. She was so evidently the victim of the civilization which had produced her, that the links of her bracelet seemed like manacles chaining her to her fate (p. 8).

Bart perceives that she, as a woman, wears these jewelled chains while the men in world are free. Here we see Edith Wharton's unique tack on the Diana-hero's search for her own sacred space in the modern world. In essence, Bart's society is a prison to her. Every 'structure' that Bart inhabits is more and more unacceptable and oppressive. When she finally leaves the prison of her little world entirely, she discovers herself to be deserted, stranded, unprepared for, and even unwanted in the larger world. There is no sacred space for her.

Bart, who so fits the ideal of the goddess who was independent in her own free and green realm, cries out in envy at the free quarters enjoyed by Lawrence:

> How delicious to have a place like this all to one's self! What a miserable
> thing it is to be a woman (p. 8).

No woman in the novel has a room of her own, and in each one's
circumscribed role, she largely sees the other females as competitors or
conveniences in her social machinations for a husband and money. In this
atmosphere comes another irony for Bart, for the character fitting the
archetype of Diana, with her cortege of devoted maidens. Bart has
developed her own "utilitarian classification of her friends" (p. 34). She
tells Lawrence honestly, "And the other women—my best friends—well,
they use me or abuse me; but they don't care a straw what happens to
me" (p. 10). Most leave her to die alone in a shabby boarding room.

Overall, Bart's society allows for her no real freedom, substantive
education, honorable resource to earn her own living, or any role but that
of the "ornamental" (p. 232). Bart finds herself "stranded in a great waste
of disoccupation" (p. 235). The Diana-hero finally admits to her friend
Lawrence, "...I am a very useless person. I can hardly be said to have an
independent existence. I was just a screw or a cog in the great machine
I call life, and when I dropped out of it I found I was of no use anywhere
else" (p. 240).

Once dropped out of her social milieu, Bart perceives with newly-
acquired objectivity that her world and the situation of women in it can
be venal. The thought helps to send the first mortal chills through her:
"She was realizing for the first time that a woman's dignity may cost
more to keep up than her carriage; and that the maintenance of a moral
attribute should be dependent on dollars and cents, made the world appear
a more sordid place than she had conceived it" (p. 135).

The natural scruples of the Diana-hero Bart aid her rebellion against
this, but, sadly, her breeding—or rather her lack of true breeding—in her
civilization undercuts her fits of revolt:

> ...she had not lost her capacity for high flashes of indignation. But she could not
> breathe long on the heights; there had been nothing in her training to develop any
> continuity of moral strength (p. 251).

In the end, abandoned and betrayed by nearly everyone, Bart perceives
that she was "of no more account among them than an expensive toy in
the hands of a spoiled child" (p. 189).

Moreover, Bart's world demands that as a woman she be a very specific kind of toy. It would have her be ornamental so she will be more highly prized as a wife. No one person in this world seems to be any more enlightened on this subject than Bart. In fact, it is she alone who first broaches the subject of a different life for herself. When Bart initially rebels against the one accepted avenue for women—wifedom—and hints to Lawrence of her dislike of marriage to a boring heir, he flatly replies, "Isn't marriage your vocation? Isn't it what you're all brought up for?" (p. 10). She blandly agrees, for lack of alternatives, only to later fall into Trenor's money trap because she does not want to have to marry that boring heir, Percy Gryce. Bart admits, "I *can't* make that kind of marriage; it's impossible" (p. 67).

Even worse toils lie in the way of the fastidious Diana-hero. Gus Trenor, he of the "small dull eyes" and big sexual appetite, protests that a marriage of the superior Bart to Gryce would be a "desecration" (pp. 64–67). But he himself works hard to lure Bart into the "slough" with him (p. 134). He slurs his points about how he will invest her money so that he may lean closer and take her hands in his. In this way he tries to lay "claim" to her (p. 68).

From then on, he tends to "touch" Bart when overcome by "libations" (p. 72), and he blabs about his "relation" with Bart to other men. An ignoble gambler, he wagers that his money will have "put her in his power" (p. 90–91). In one of his many drunken states, he sets up a trap for her in his private house in New York City, while his wife is away at the estate in the country, and when Bart refuses to become his mistress, he calls her, in so many words, a whore.

One other so-called alternative for Bart, to socially redeem herself, is the pathetic George Dorset. He is stupidly "blind" to his wife's sexual corruption, which takes place under his own nose. Finally, he breaks down and spills his "wretchedness of his soul" to Bart in a flood of "self-contempt" (p. 158). When his wife viciously expels Bart from their yacht, he is "cowed" and allows Bart to be publicly humiliated (p. 169). Now, he confesses his "powerlessness" against his wife to Bart and begs her to set him free from his marriage, the self-inflicted "hell" in which he is a "prisoner" (pp. 190–91). In this society, marriage itself is typically a bore or an evil snare; the *hieros gamos* has degenerated into a prison in this culture.

Another alternative is Simon Rosedale, a man who entertains lurid ideas about her and Lawrence, ideas he blabs to Gus Trenor (pp. 13–17; 114). Together, he and Trenor are "hunting" Bart at sorties (pp. 75–76). Lily knows that Rosedale can, at moments, be "kind," but that he is, in total, a "gross, unscrupulous, rapacious...predatory creature" (p. 195).

In sum, Trenor and Rosedale are predatory creatures, seeking to prey on Bart at various times. And, Rosedale and Gryce are collectors, who would add her as an object in their expensive collections (p. 99). Dorset is a weak creature, the prey of any woman. Lily Bart, a type of the goddess of the chase, has come alive in a society where her natural sport has been perverted for social ends in the most sordid way, to hunt unworthy consorts, and to be perceived by those consorts as prey herself.

Throughout all this, quietly, Bart gravitates toward a pure and true love with Lawrence. From the opening scene, she is delighted when he comes to "rescue" her from the crowded scene and remove her to the haven of his lodgings (p. 6), and she continues to seek out his company, for she intuits that he offers her the vista of a better, freer world:

> It was rather that he had preserved a certain social detachment, a happy air of viewing the show objectively, of having points of contact outside the great gilt cage in which they were all huddled for the mob to gape at. How alluring the world outside the cage appeared to Lily, as she heard its door clang on her! In reality, as she knew, the door never clanged: it stood always open; but most of the captives were like flies in a bottle, and having once flown in, could never regain their freedom. It was Selden's distinction that he had never forgotten the way out (p. 45).

Lawrence's presence stirs in Bart those wonderful "germs of rebellion" (p. 47), and it aids her to persist in evading marriage to a society heir, which would clang that door shut. Carry Fisher discerns the deliberate nature of Bart's seemingly "flighty" rebellion. She tells Lawrence:

> That's Lily all over, you know: she works like a slave preparing the ground and sowing her seed; but the day she ought to be reaping the harvest she over-sleeps herself or goes off on a picnic.... I think it's just flightiness—and sometimes I think it's because, at heart, she despises the things she's trying for. And it's the difficulty of deciding that makes her such an interesting study (pp. 147–48).

Here, then, is Wharton's "interesting study": a Diana-hero despising the worldly milieu to which Wharton has consigned her.

Bart accurately identifies Wharton's consignment as "hateful," and she ponders modes of escape:

> It was a hateful fate—but how to escape from it? What choice had she? To be herself, or a Gerty Farish.... She knew that she hated dinginess as much as her mother had hated it, and to her last breath she meant to fight against it" (pp. 23; 33).

Nature is a powerful force, here, one stirring Bart's impulses to escape and one making Wharton's "interesting study" more complicated and absorbing. The Diana-hero's communion with the green realm nourishes her cravings for beauty that is not artificial and social but natural and ideal. At the Trenor mansion, Lily Bart has no haste to join "the circle about the tea table," for she prefers to remain amid the fragrant honeysuckles, the warm tints of the pale-gold maples and velvety firs, and the "river widened like a lake under the silver light of September" (p. 40).

In the open vistas of the natural world, Bart meets with true feeling her well-loved Lawrence, who has hastened behind her. For a magical moment they are united beneath the moon: "The soft isolation of the falling day enveloped them: they seemed lifted into a finer air. All the exquisite influences of the hour trembled in their veins.... across the valley a clear moon rose in the denser blue" (p. 59).

Significantly, Bart begins to discover not only nature, but through it her natural self:

> The landscape outspread below her seemed an enlargement of her present mood, and she found something of herself in its calmness, its breadth, its long free reaches. On the nearer slopes the sugar-maples wavered like pyres of light; lower down was a massing of grey orchards, and here and there the lingering green of an oak-grove.
> ...her quick-breathing silence seemed a part of the general hush and harmony of things.... But Lily, though her attitude was as calm as [Selden's], was throbbing inwardly with a rush of thoughts. There were in her at the moment two beings, one drawing deep breaths of freedom and exhilaration, the other gasping for air in a little black prison house of fears. But gradually the captive's gasps grew fainter, or the other paid less heed to them: the horizon expanded, the air grew stronger, and the free spirit quivered for flight (pp. 51–52).

As this Diana-hero discovers nature, and in it a moment of true unity with Lawrence and her invigorated self, she experiences the first luscious feelings of genuine fulfillment: "...her enjoyment proceeded more than she was aware from the physical stimulus of the excursion, the challenge of the crisp cold and hard exercise, the responsive thrill of her body to the influences of the winter woods. She returned to town in a glow of rejuvenation, conscious of a clearer colour in her cheeks, a fresh elasticity in her muscles" (p. 89).

Nature also stirs the romantic and the artist in Lily Bart: "The spot was charming, and Lily was not insensible to the charm, or to the fact that her presence enhanced it; but she was not accustomed to taste the joys of solitude except in company, and the combination of a handsome girl and a romantic scene struck her as too good to be wasted" (p. 49–50). Lawrence perceives that Bart is an "artist," that she is using his figure as a "bit of colour" in her scene (p. 53). His observation is true, both to her naturally creative eye and to her false upbringing, which has taught her to turn her gifts into social plastic.

Nonetheless, her affinity with the natural world and its harmony progressively continues to enhance Bart's creativity, and this eventually brings about a revelation to her groom. In the Brys's *tableaux vivants*, Bart artfully arranges for her dress to be simple white drapery against a "background of foliage." The design accentuates her "long dryad-like curves" to reveal "the touch of poetry in her beauty" (p. 106). Her poetic image lifts the veil obscuring the ideal world for Lawrence:

> ...for the first time he seemed to see before him the real Lily Bart, divested of the trivialities of her little world, and catching for a moment a note of that eternal harmony of which her beauty was a part....
> ...It was as though her beauty, thus detached from all that cheapened and vulgarized it, had held out suppliant hands to him from the world in which he and she had once met for a moment, and where he felt an overmastering longing to be with her again" (pp. 106–07).

After the *tableaux vivants*, Bart and Lawrence move away from the artificial glare of the supper-room to "the fragrant hush of a garden" and "the transparent dimness of a midsummer night." There, they discover their true and natural love: "Hanging lights made emerald caves in the depths of foliage, and whitened the spray of a fountain falling among lilies. The magic place was deserted: there was no sound but the splash of the water on the lily-pads, and a distinct drift of music that might have been blown across a sleeping lake.... her face turned to him with the soft motion of a flower.... and their lips touched" (pp. 108–09).

The moment is innocent, precious—and singular. As Bart's social situation worsens, she and Selden once again find themselves in gardens, but now they have become "deserted" ones (p. 170). The magic of the night and lilies has been dispelled, more and more, by the glaring realities of their worldly milieu. Ultimately, when Bart's ends by taking doses of laudanum in the dingy boarding house, Wharton attributes her fate to the antithetical forces of nature and society, between her true self and her artificial world:

> She had been fashioned to adorn and delight; to what other end does nature round the rose-leaf and paint the hummingbird's breast? And was it her fault that the purely decorative mission is less easily and harmoniously fulfilled among social beings than in the world of nature? That it is apt to be hampered by material necessities or complicated by moral scruples?
>
> These last were the two antagonistic forces which fought out their battle in her breast during the long watches of the night; (p. 235).

On the night of her overdose, Bart draws from her trunk the simple costume of the *tableaux vivant*. Holding the white robes, Bart knows again that moment when she rebelled against this fate:

> ...the long flexible folds, as she shook them out, gave forth an odour of violets which came to her like a breath from the flower-edged fountain where she had stood with Lawrence Selden and disowned her fate (p. 247).

The Wedding and the Apocalypse

The Poetry of the Ideal Bride. As the Diana-Bride, Bart possesses that ideal soul, the one that shall join in creative power with her true lover's. In fact, Bart's crises occur because her "real self" rises up to thwart any worldly marriage that her social self has been working toward. When she goes to Lawrence at the end of the novel, near her death, she does so to leave a part of this real "self" with him and to keep it alive within her: "that self must indeed live on in his presence, but it must still continue to be hers" (p. 241). Having preserved her spirit and given Lawrence a part of that spirit, Lily Bart obtains a final "victory for her real self," and "she goes home with it to die" (Lewis, p. xv).

Her tragedy thus contains a certain element of comedy: she saves her real self and shares a part of it, forever, with her lover. Lawrence once told Bart of the "republic of the spirit" and added that her "genius" lay in converting "impulses into intentions." Bart replied that "any final test of genius" would lay in "success," and that "I certainly haven't succeeded" (p. 54). The statement is ironic. Bart has not "succeeded" in their social world because her "genius"—for ensuring the victory of her true self—will succeed, by unmaking every material marriage her social self has made. In a further irony, Bart is the one who will depart this world for the republic of the spirit, leaving behind Lawrence, who wavered at the critical moment. Bart accomplishes more, on this level, than anyone else in her world.[2]

Throughout the novel, Bart continues to dream of that "ideal state of existence" of which Lawrence told her, imagining that she will have the luxury to indulge with him in spirited discussions (p. 70). Wharton states that Bart is an "idealist" trapped by "vulgar necessities" (p. 197), and, privately, Bart follows her ideal to the end. On the verge of her destitution, she destroys in the fire Bertha Dorset's incriminating love letters, she refuses Rosedale's offer of a monetary loan, she rebukes George Dorset's offer of a tainted union, and she uses her entire inheritance to pay her debt to Trenor. All of this leaves Bart facing "unmitigated poverty." She has deliberately dispatched the "danger" of material ease so that it may never again tempt her into compromises that are intolerable to her spirit (pp. 230–31).

In short, she destroys her old life and old social self to make way for the ideal self within. As an apocalyptic Diana-hero, one capable of making and re-making selves and worlds, Bart possesses that power of poesis. Even Bart's social self intuits that her "beauty is only the raw material of conquest, and that to convert it into success other arts are required." The "art" here is perilously close to "art"ifice, but Wharton qualifies even this social desire of Bart: "Her ambitions were not as crude as Mrs Bart's." Mrs. Bart considered her husband's evenings "reading poetry" a total waste, but Lily felt sympathy with her father's longings for "romantic charm" and admiration of beauty (pp. 30; 152). She seeks to "convert" her life in this context.

Her best match, Lawrence, recognizes this poetic element in Bart. He perceives that her nature as an "artist" inspires her to shape the scene of the *tableaux vivants* or to paint, in her mind, a landscape with as Lawrence as "colour" (p. 53). Bart naturally experiences "poetic enjoyment" of the opera and of her unequalled beauty that is "the bodily counterpart of genius" (p. 91). Her "vivid plastic sense," whose only opportunities for expression so far have been "dress-making and upholstery," starts to shine when a genuine artist, Morpeth, guides her (p. 103).

One reason that Lawrence is Bart's true spouse is that he himself possesses a "vision-building faculty." He alone perceives at the Brys's *tableaux vivant* that Bart's beauty is "a note of that eternal harmony." He alone understands that she has gifted him with a revelation that night, that her enchanted scene offers to him "magic glimpses of the boundary world between fact and imagination" (pp. 105–06).[3] At that moment, the poetic spirits of Bart and Lawrence meet each other in human sympathy and love, and they exchange their first kiss (p. 109).

This ideal moment cannot survive in their world. Her friends will turn on her precisely because she refuses to "sacrifice herself" and her ideals for socially expedient ends. Wharton stresses this idea over and over. Rosedale states the case clearly: "...you've simply been sacrificed to their laziness and selfishness" (p. 201). George Dorset repeats it: "You were singled out as a sacrifice" (p. 190). Mrs. Gormer reinforces the idea when she, too, makes Bart "the first sacrifice to this new ideal" of hers, her friendship with Bertha Dorset and consequent entry into Dorset's corrupt milieu. The Diana-hero, fitting so neatly the idea of the goddess who rescued maidens like Iphigenia, finds herself the proffered sacrifice in the modern world.

But her sacrifice is also her own decision. When Dorset offers himself to her, he offers her "Revenge and rehabilitation" in one swift stroke, a prospect "dazzling" in its opportunity for Bart to vanquish her enemy Bertha Dorset and to secure for herself "great golden vistas of peace and safety." Bart abhors the offer. She chooses to endure her difficult state. She chooses to conquer her "past weaknesses" toward worldly temptations

(p. 191). When Dorset returns to tempt her once again, Bart informs him, "You sacrifice us both" (p. 194).

Bart also refuses to acquiesce in Rosedale's scheme of blackmail and marriage, knowing that this act of renunciation constitutes a far deeper sacrifice of her own, and it does so in a milieu that will never appreciate her chaste decision. She makes the sacrifice for her ideal of "honour" and nothing else:

> In fending off the offer he was so plainly ready to renew, had she not sacrificed to one of those abstract notions of honour that might be called the conventionalities of the moral life? What debt did she owe to a social order which had condemned and banished her without a trial? (p. 234).

Lily Bart achieves honorable victory for herself, and in the end her sacrifices and her suffering soften her crystal shell. She has undergone a humanizing process. She has engaged in the poetic process of realizing her best self, and in this lies one key to her redemption, for in this lies her coming attainment of human fellowship and love.

The Drama of the Bride. The first man Bart encounters in *The House of Mirth* is Selden Lawrence, the first woman she encounters is Bertha Dorset, and both characters are equally catalytic in the drama of her life.

Bertha Dorset is Bart's nemesis. She is an active agent in destroying Bart's old self, pursuing Bart as fiercely as the Furies. The imagery surrounding Bertha Dorset is that associated with the mytheme of the Furies. She is wrapped in "sinuous draperies"—a serpentine allusion (p. 21). She wears "serpentine spangles" as she lures a male victim into the dark shadows of a nook (p. 22). She is, by the final pages, the "anaconda" of the text (p. 196).

Serpents are the heraldic animals of Diana precisely because they shed the old skin for the new, thus renewing themselves as rhythmically as the moon, and into this symbolic pattern fits the serpentine and mortifying figure of Bertha Dorset. Even more, this pattern fits the literary tradition of Diana-heroes. Isabel Archer in her Palazzo "Crescentini" is haunted by the old moon figure, Madame Merle, and inherits her lover, Gilbert Osmond. Jane Eyre is haunted by the dark moon figure, Bertha Mason, and inherits her lover, Rochester. Lily Bart, who in her youth and freshness is like the crescent phase of the moon, is haunted by Bertha Dorset, and inherits her lover, Selden Lawrence.

This pattern is a persistent one for many of the Diana-heroes that form the kaleidescope in Western literature. In Poe's "Ligeia," the dark Ligeia, modelled on and gifted with the powers of the waning moon goddess, haunts and subsumes the fair and young Rowena, the new bride and personification of the waxing crescent. Wharton undertakes two other interesting experiments with such a paradigm elsewhere in her writing. She constructs the pattern in *Ethan Frome*, where Mattie Silver enjoys a brief and radiant love with the hero, only to have the dark and Hekatish figure of Zeena reclaim her husband and domain. In this text, Ethan remains forever frozen in Zeena's hellish realm.

In *The Age of Innocence*, however, Newland Archer cannot break free from his social prison, which is his marriage to the young and cool Diana-hero, May Welland, and successfully enter the realm of the more mature and bewitching Countess Ellen Olenska. Therein lies his individual tragedy. Over and again the characters in each text desire fresh life, and over and again the author's unique experiment with this paradigm opens another consideration of the comedic and tragic possibilities of our life.

More details point to this paradigm and its complexity in *The House of Mirth*. Dorset emerges as a type who personifies the occult powers of the waning moon, a type opposed to Lily Bart who personifies the regenerative powers of the new crescent. Dorset has a "visionary gaze" in her "dark exaggerated eyes," and she is like "a disembodied spirit," the latter conjuring an image of the realm of Hekate (pp. 21–22). Like a true Hekate-type, Dorset traps her husband in "hell" (p. 191), where he berates himself with "his furies of denunciation and wild reactions of self-contempt" (p. 158).

This context further places Dorset, like her first name, within the literary tradition of "Bertha" Mason, who also creates a fiery hell for her husband, Lord Rochester.[4] Bertha Dorset flares with the same fires of lunacy as Bertha Mason does, for she, too, is a "madwoman" who is "dangerous," and she, too, has many an unchaste "fall" (pp. 37; 60; 187).

The "Bertha"s of Edith Wharton and Charlotte Bronte bear similar last names, too. "Mason" is the name of those who work with stones, and "Dorset" is the name for those who dwell among stones. In myth, stones, hard and everlasting substances, have always been connected with sacred rites. In the mytheme of the moon goddess, sacrifices were made on sacred stones for the rain-making ceremonies, ones intended to invite the moon goddess's waters of rebirth and life. Both Mason and Dorset make, or try to make, sacrifices of the youthful heroes, and in both cases the result, however qualified, is the spiritual rebirth of the intended victims.

Further, stones are not only everlasting from their hardness, but they are also barren from this, and "Mason" and "Dorset" are barren and deadly figures, ones contrasting to the types of the moon goddess in her stage of rebirth, to types of the new moon embodied in Jane "Eyre," the heir of Bronte's novel, and in Lily "Bart," which denotes those who live among overgrown bushes—not stones.[5] Together, the Diana-types of the waning moon enact with the Diana-types of the crescent moon a drama of mortification and regeneration.

Like the Furies, Dorset smiles victoriously when she is able to "flay" her victim Lily Bart (p. 87). To Bart's mind "...the pursuing furies seem to take the shape of Bertha Dorset" (p. 231). And, Bertha Dorset's fury is no less murderous than the fury of Bertha Mason, or the Greek Furies, for Bertha Dorset wields the "knife" of treachery against Bart. Bart, in serpentine imagery that intertwines with Dorset's, recoils from her, having a "fatalistic sense" of her "enemy" (pp. 101; 162; 170).

In general, the Furies are not only alluded to throughout *The House of Mirth*, but many allusions tie them to the archetype of the moon goddess. Wharton's Furies are hunters, seeking their own special type of prey. On the night of Trenor's bitter attack on Bart, at his private house in the City, Bart becomes flooded with "moral shame" (p. 116). She awakens to the Furies' presence and her coming "ordeal" to find that she will, equally to Orestes, be hunted and purged by them:

> She had once picked up, in a house where she was staying, a translation of the *Eumenides*, and her imagination had been seized by the high terror of the scene where Orestes, in the cave of the oracle, finds his implacable huntresses asleep, and snatches an hour's repose. Yes, the Furies might sometimes sleep, but they were there, always there in the dark corners, and now they were awake and the iron clang of their wings was in her brain.... —and she was alone in a place of darkness and pollution (p. 117).

With her fresh "wound," Bart flees to the shelter of Gerty Farish. She confesses for the first time her sins, along with her moral shame and her new acquaintance with "the furies...you know the noise of their wings—alone, at night, in the dark?" (p. 131). These Furies will pursue Bart relentlessly to her death. When Mrs. Peniston refuses to give Bart the funds needed to free her from Trenor's debt, Bart shuts herself in with her "dishonour" and her terror: "She was trembling with fear and anger—the rush of the furies' wings was in her ears" (p. 137).

The Furies pursue Bart to the point that they fill her being. Their "dangerous" nature gives a singularly nervous edge to her voice and makes her eyes shine with "a peculiar sleepless lustre." By the end, there is no rest for this hero, visited every night by the "perfect horrors" of the Furies (p. 207). Bart's flurried fingers reveal her "feverish" state, and her cry that she is "sick to death" of her world reveals that her mortification is nearly complete (p. 207–08).

In the final pages, this action rises to the level of Greek drama. Dorset, the mortal embodiment of the Furies, is Bart's "antagonist," one who becomes triumphant for the moment (pp. 49; 170). Bart endures a fierce struggle between "two antagonistic forces," her better, fairer self and her dark side, the one tempted to re-enter the realm of Bertha Dorset by using the latter's letters of sexual corruption against her. During long watches of the night, the Furies visit Bart with their perfect horrors (p. 235). However, she preserves that fairer self, and with it she is able, as her final act, to create the "word" with her intended Spouse.

The Sacred Wedding. The *hieros gamos* is the ephemeral goal of *The House of Mirth*, one for which two characters struggle so hardly until the final pages. The reason for Lawrence's prolonged failure is hinted at from the first pages. He has elements of a type like Gilbert Osmond, a collector (p. 11), like Ralph Touchett, a cool spectator, one interested in watching persons like experiments, and even like Chillingworth, a cool alchemist (p. 56). When Lily Bart asks him why he came after her to Bellomont, he replies in the spirit a detached observer: "Because you're such a wonderful spectacle" (p. 53). Further, he lives in the Benedick, the "Bachelor" (p. 15), a name pointing toward his detached stance from society. Ironically, the Spouse in Wharton's sterile modern world has arrived at an isolated condition.

Overall, Lawrence possesses a superior nature that, eventually, comes to embrace Bart (p. 53). If he initially follows her for the sport of "admiring spectatorship," her first small cry for help nonetheless draws him into a "dawning intimacy" with her (p. 55). He tries to resist judging her, and at moments he extends the limited help he can (pp. 166; 217).

Moreover, like Bart, Lawrence has that touch of poesis. He sees that material wealth has value largely because it can be transformed into a more wonderful product. Gold can be turned into "something else" more beautiful. He is an alchemist seeking to transmute the dross of this world into a more glorious one (p. 56). With this sense of ideal—not material—ends, Lawrence is capable of receiving a critical revelation from Bart. She perceives "victory" in the shining faces of Nettie Struther and her gurgling baby, which is her own revelation that the love of a man and a woman is the central truth of life (p. 245). She visits Lawrence with this knowledge, and, when it penetrates him fully, he sets out to meet her.

It is, literally and figuratively, a day too late. Both have too long been "cowards" in their inability to throw off their social world (pp. 59; 255). On this level, each is equally a "victim" of their "environment" (p. 120). Nevertheless, their love for each other proves truer than all else. Each had the imagination to "vividly conceive of a love which should broaden and deepen till it became the central fact of life" (p. 121). Lawrence dreams that their love shall, like Bart's wax seal, carry both away: "...a grey seal with *Beyond!* beneath a flying ship. Ah, he would take her beyond, beyond the ugliness, the pettiness, the attrition and corrosion of the soul—" (pp. 122; 125). As with Jane Eyre, the Diana-hero Lily Bart is surrounded by nautical imagery, indicative on her desires, her quests, her frustrations.[6]

In Bart's sad final days, to think of Lawrence and their frustrated love is "pure pain" (p. 230). In the few natural dreams she has left, untainted by the Furies or narcotics, Lawrence appears to her in his old guise of "fellowship and tenderness" (p. 230). Their love, ultimately, belongs to this visionary realm, to this dream world, not their real and sordid one.

Lawrence realizes how much he loved her and how much "the conditions of life had conspired to keep them apart." He admits to himself that he had been influenced by his material culture to the extent that he did not know how "to live and love uncritically." His one consolation is that "he *had* loved her," and that one moment of their love has "been saved whole out of the ruin of their lives" (p. 255).

That moment of love is their fleeting victory of the novel; that ephemeral moment is their sacred union—all that they can know of it in their secular and material world.

Lawrence, once, speaks lightly, but prophetically, to Bart:

Ah—but will he find you in the end? That's the only test of success (p. 50).

They do find each other "in the end," so theirs is a success, and it is a hardly tested one that lasts so momently.

Other moments in the text hint at and hold out this promise of momentary bliss. Only near Lawrence does Bart enjoy rare moments of peace from the turmoil of her spirit (p. 216). She feels, too, the "stir of the pulses" and the "quicker beat" of fresh life and joy (pp. 74; 108). And through Bart's spirit Lawrence experiences visions of a better life. On the night of the *tableaux vivants*, he sees:

This was the world she lived in, these were the standards by which she was fated to be measured! Does one go to Caliban for a judgment on Miranda?

In the long moment before the curtain fell, he had time to feel the whole tragedy of her life. It was as though her beauty, thus detached from all that cheapened and vulgarized it, had held out suppliant hands to him from the world in which he and she had once met for a moment, and where he felt an overmastering longing to be with her again (p. 107).

Their moments alone are enchanted ones. They wander in the moon-soaked "transparent dimness of a midsummer night" in a "fragrant hush of a garden," one filled with fountains, emerald caverns, lilies, and magic (p. 108). It is an "illumined moment" (p. 212).

But, true to the idea of a Diana-type, a goddess who offers to mortals like Acteon a glimpse of immortal beauty, Bart can only *promise* this bliss to a creature in the real world. In her "white robed slimness," she charms, then flees, Lawrence's human grasp: "...and before he could speak she had turned and slipped through the arch of boughs, disappearing in the brightness of the room beyond" (p. 109). Just as Lawrence arrives a day too late to Bart's side, so the vision is fleeting in this scene, too, for it is the of the ideal, not intended for the world of vulgar realities—into which, in the height of irony, the Diana-type has fled.

The cycle of the novel also links the theme of the sacred wedding to the death and rebirth of the Diana-hero. The story begins and ends on a September day when Bart and Lawrence meet, September being the month of the Virgin, as it was in Joyce's *Ulysses*. The last time they meet, Bart goes to visit Lawrence because her feelings for him are a "throbbing brood of the only spring her heart had ever known" (p. 237). She discovers that he still lacks the "determining impulse" for an outrush of feeling, and this destroys the "secret hope" Bart has carried with her to his home, a hope "revealed" to her in the painful clarity of "its death-pang" (p. 239).

But when something dies, something better is been born in Bart, and though she does not know it yet, this shall also touch a fresh spring in Lawrence:

> Something in truth lay dead between them—the love she had killed in him and could no longer call to life. But something lived between them also, and leaped up in her like an imperishable flame: it was the love his love had kindled, the passion of her soul for his.
>
> In its light everything else dwindled and fell away from her... (p. 241).

Basking in this "light" of revelation, Bart now knows first hand "the central truth of existence," that life should move toward the wedding, its future life and its nest, built by both bride and groom, "the man's faith as well as the woman's courage" (p. 248). She has succeeded as much as possible with her quest for an ideal love in her sordid world, for on the next morning Lawrence sets out to join his faith to her courage.

Aided by her courage, he finally "passed beyond all...conventional observances.... —he had found the word he meant to say to her" (p. 252). Indeed, the two have already joined in Bart's dream world. She has in her narcotized visions of the night met Lawrence and desired to speak the "word" to him (p. 251). As he strolls to her home that morning, he remembers how her "real self had lain warm on his heart but a few hours earlier" (p. 252–53). Thus, her ideal dreams, in many senses, prefigure and precipitate their real union, however brief, in this world.

Now he can see "deep into the hidden things of love" (p. 253). Lawrence kneels reconciled by her side (p. 256), and if the "word" which passes between them remains unspoken and, to us, unrevealed, that is the greater testament to the mystery of their love.

The Apocalypse. Apocalyptic imagery—the lifting of veils, the glittering of gems—pervades *The House of Mirth*. Gems imbue the figure of Lily Bart with glimmers of apocalypse as much as they do other Diana-heroes. The one good stone that Jane Eyre bears on her quest is the pearl, emblem of the moon and its powers. Hester Prynne intends symbolic meanings in the name of her offspring Pearl, who shall lead her mother into the New Jerusalem. The tragic Harleth feels her first mortification when Lydia Glasher sends her the cursed diamonds, which allow the Furies to enter Harleth's life. Or, Isabel Archer catapults herself into tragedy when she makes the fatal error of unlocking her inner "cabinet of jewels" to Madame Merle and offering the "spiritual gems" therein to her (p. 163).

Gems figure significantly throughout The Book of Revelation, but they particularly signify the ideal, for in the new heaven the holy city is made of the purest gems.[7] This imagery has, like much imagery from The Book of Revelation, come to pervade a lot of Western literature. At the wedding of Jack Stepney and Miss Van Osburgh, Bart is spellbound by the unearthly beauty and symbolism of

> the bride's jewels...the milky gleam of perfectly matched pearls, the flash of rubies relieved against contrasting velvet, the intense blue rays of sapphires kindled into light by surrounding diamonds:... The glow of the stones warmed Lily's veins like wine. More completely than any other expression of wealth they symbolized the life she longed to lead, the life of fastidious aloofness and refinement in which every detail should have the finish of a jewel, and the whole form a harmonious setting to her own jewel-like rareness (pp. 71–72).

In this passage, the gems signify the ideal in *The House of Mirth*, be it beauty, wedded bliss, or Bart's being, and this makes the sordid barter that takes places around Bart and throughout her social world all the more ironic and damning. Bart herself wears the sparkling sapphires of the moon goddess (p. 8). More significantly, Bart dazzles humans with her own jewel-like radiance. Her cousin comments on Bart's triumph at the *tableaux vivants*: "Talk of jewels—what's a woman want with jewels when she's got herself to show?" (p. 109). This is why Rosedale wants to marry Bart:

> ...some women looked buried under their jewelry. What I want is a woman who'll hold her head higher the more diamonds I put on it. And when I looked at you the other night at the Brys', in that plain white dress, looking as if you had a crown on, I said to myself: "By gad, if she had one she'd wear it as if it grew on her" (p. 140).

As her trial progresses, Bart's gem-like beauty undergoes a process of "crystallization" (p. 149). Lawrence observes that her face takes on "the sharpness of a tragic mask," one illuminated by a "glare" from a "jeweller's window" (p. 167). That is a precise image of Bart's jewel-like rareness suffering in the glare of her world and its harsh realities. Bart is "sick to death" of the "artificial brightness" of that false world and her life in it (p. 208). Thus, the apocalyptic imagery of gems is, in *The House of Mirth*, significant of mortal versus immortal realms.

Moreover, the novel's title clearly points toward biblical ideas as well as Greek, for the "house of mirth" is itself a biblical allusion to spiritual discovery. The Bible urges one to gain wisdom and understanding of human life in the "house of sorrow" instead of the foolish "house of mirth." Wharton reinforces this central idea with repeated biblical references to discovering a new, a higher, life, one divorced from this foolish and materialistic world. When Bart asks Lawrence if she may join his "republic of the spirit," he cautions her: "But you will marry someone very rich, and it's as hard for rich people to get into as the kingdom of heaven" (p. 55–56).

Bart enters the house of sorrow when she comes to her "bare unmitigated poverty" in the final pages (p. 255). In this context, her tragedy can further be read simultaneously as biblical and Greek, for both dramas lead to the most profound wisdom known to the Western world, knowledge of the joy but tragedy of human life, "the central truth" of human existence that Bart comes to perceive (p. 248). It is her personal apocalypse.

In fact, the schemata of biblical and Greek tragedies smoothly blend in *The House of Mirth*.[8] For instance, Bart uses Mrs. Peniston's legacy to pay her sordid debt to Gus Trenor (pp. 175; 249). Since the legacy and debt are equal amounts, Bart's earthly inheritance is exactly the amount

needed to cancel her earthly debt. This makes her a "suppliant" in that
"house where she had so long commanded" (p. 179). The images of the
house of mirth and of suppliants have biblical significance, but in a text
replete with images of Greek tragedy, the term "suppliant" also calls to
mind *The Suppliants* of Aesychlus, the famously tragic maidens who cry
to Diana for salvation from worldly forces. In total, Bart undergoes an
"ordeal" that she, as the hero, biblical or Greek, typically must pass
(p. 179).

Bart's high tragedy can be read as Romantic, too.[9] After leaving the
flat of the poor but joyous Nettie Struther, Bart returns to her own dingy
flat. She knows that she still wants "happiness," but that her world still
offers "baser possibilities" and leaves her only with "the emptiness of
renunciation." The veils are lifted to show Bart her empty life in her
world:

> She was appalled by the intense clearness of the vision; she seemed to have
> broken through the merciful veil which intervenes between intention and action,
> and to see exactly what she would do in all the long days to come (p. 249).

In the "terror" of her vision, one that equals the terror and the cold
sickness of Keats when he sees beneath the lifted veil (p. 251), Bart
chooses to leave behind her empty world, taking with her only that
memory of love with her intended Spouse: "If only life could end
now—end on this tragic yet sweet vision of lost possibilities, which gave
her a sense of kinship with all the loving and foregoing in the world!"
(p. 249).

Bart is "at the heart" of humanity now (p. 238). She goes to Lawrence
to share with him the knowledge that "she had saved herself whole from
the seeming ruin of her life" (p. 239). She thanks him for the help he
offered her, and he answers with a truth: "...nothing I have said has really
made the difference. The difference is in yourself—it will always be
there" (p. 239). Lawrence recognizes that real heroism lies within his
intended bride.

In this moment of truth between them, Bart treads "the buoyant ether
which emanates from the high moments of life" (p. 242). Her soaring so
high, even momently, points to the exultation as well as the sorrow of a
spiritual apocalypse. And, she is comforted by her awareness of real love.

When Bart next kisses her lover and takes his hand, he receives
intimations of her coming death, of his own tragic lifting of the veil:

> Selden had retained her hand, and continued to scrutinize her with a strange
> sense of foreboding. The external aspect of the situation had vanished for him as
> completely as for her: he felt it only as one of those rare moments which lift the
> veil from their faces as they pass (p. 241).

Together, their eyes meet in "an illumined look" (p. 241).

Bart leaves him "still groping for the word to break the spell" (p. 241),
the "word" he will find on the morrow and create with her.

Bart returns home to her narcotized dreams, but these dreams have
changed. No longer do the Furies pursue Lily Bart. She is comforted by
the warmth of Nettie Struther's infant whom she cradles close to her
heart. Here is the crux in the trial of Edith Wharton's Diana-hero. She
cannot acheive the birth of a heroic self in the modern world. She can
only midwife her self, her new self of whom the loving and loved infant
is an emblem, in her dreams. This new life she carries with her as she
crosses into the other world of death and immortality that next morning.

On that day, the "sunlight" slants "joyously down on Lily's street" to
coincide "with the inner mood" and "intoxication" of the lovers' breath (p.
251). True to his name, which signifies the laurel crown, Lawrence is for
one moment   victorious. He is like a Greek hero touched by the
sun—though that moment is completely effervescent. In this moment,
Lawrence is Bart's fitting if flitting Groom.

Upon reaching her room, the two find all that their "heart craved."
Their love has kept alive their "faith," and that is a hard-won "victory"
over themselves and their world. In the midst of their troubled world, the
two discover a precious "moment of love.... draining [it] to its lees; and
in the silence there passed between them the word which made all clear"
(pp. 255–56).

❧ CONCLUSION

Where is the Antique glory now become,
 That whilome wont in women to appeare?
 Where be the braue atchieuements doen by some?
 Where be the battels, where the shield and speare,
 And all the conquests, which them high did reare,
 That matter made for famous Poets verse,
 And boastfull men so oft abasht to heare?
                                    —*The Faerie Qveene*, Edmund Spenser (III: iiii, 1)

The Diana-heroes analyzed in this study are six representatives of a great number throughout English literature. What is to be made of all this? Modern authors desired and created a dynamic woman who answered their need to create a new hero for the New Worlds envisioned in their texts. Leaving behind the stale image of Diana as merely a maiden of the moon, modern authors forged a variety of Diana-heroes who, relentlessly, engaged in the task of self-realization. They gave her a liberatory quest. They gave her the full inheritance that comes with being derived from the image of the Queen Moon. Her powers of rhythmic death and renewal, of midwifery, of an invincible spirit and englorying light, bring immensely comedic—or tragic—possibilities to our modern world.

In so creating this woman in their fiction, these authors gave birth to a new myth, that of the modern Diana-hero. Each author elected a highly individual metaphoric line of development for his or her individual Diana-type, and the result was an inspiring and kaleidoscopic pattern throughout our literature of a new kind of female hero, one constantly visioned and re-visioned. The pervasiveness of the Diana-hero itself reveals the strong need of modern authors to create new women for the New World.

Why has this new myth not been reified before? Esther Labovitz has pointed out in her ground-breaking work, *The Myth of the Heroine: The Female Bildungsroman in the Twentieth Century*, that the exclusion of the heroic female in our literary considerations was a "historical, social, and cultural fact" which resulted not from "the evil conspiracies of men, in general, or male novelists, in particular" but from works, such as the *Bildungsroman*, being "considered only in male-centered terms" (p. 245).

When one opens her or his eyes to perceive the existence of many female characters derived from high models such as Diana, Saint Theresa, Aphrodite, Saint Ursula, Juno, and many more, the same issue re-arises. Where has been the attention and body of criticism that these figures merited?

One of the great moments of challenge in this book came when I was reading Northrop Frye's *Anatomy of Criticism*, a work so ground-breaking in its time. In searching to arrive at an idea of "genuine poetics," Frye postulated that fiction may "be classified, not morally, but by the hero's power of action" (pp. 8; 33). He proceeded to offer a model of the hero: the divine male being Dionysus. Labelling a series of mythical male heroes "Dionysiac," Frye elaborated on the high elegiasm and tragedy inherent in the figures of Hercules, Orpheus, Balder, Beowulf, Christ, Roland, and more (pp. 35-36). But what of divine female beings? Ones whose powers are equally elegiac, tragic, or comedic? Why define a hero as "Dionysiac"? Why not define a hero as "Dianistic?" And so I launched this study.

The ideas and perspectives offered by the advances in literary theories, especially feminist theory, have demanded that we ask fresh questions about our literature. The answers are yielding exciting discoveries. Bringing gender to the center of literary explorations has revealed that many texts, especially modern ones, are not so "male" as previously considered and "established."

Not only does this work reveal that modern female authors were engaged in a relentless quest to forge new women for their worlds, but it demonstrates that in doing so they re-wrote and re-claimed the goddesses, Greek and otherwise, from the domain of male writers. They revived the ancient concepts of a powerful Queen Moon, and they re-endowed this Myriad-Named Triformis with all of her old powers, plus some new ones. In so revising and correcting history, they revised our myths. The result was a new empowerment of themselves and other females through their configuration of the New Woman. Theirs was an inspiriting act.

This study reveals that many male authors turned to the feminine for the heroic, too. In the cases of Nathaniel Hawthorne, who feels his heart burn as he presses Hester Prynne's scarlet letter to his chest, or of James Joyce, who borrows the loom of the moon to weave his tapestry of words, poetic inspiration comes from genuine identification with the creative feminine principle.

Modern authors, male and female, so placed the female consciousness at the crux of their texts and their artistry. The result was a revolutionary shift, from past visions of a male-centered Old World to current visions of a female-centered New World.

This occurrence also empowered anew the novel itself. Shelly Ekhtiar, a specialist in 18th century British literature, with emphasis on the roots of the novel as a genre, has commented on this study that the novel was always a subversive mode. It began by scaling down to real life its human figures, an act that was in opposition to the Renaissance's predilection for larger-than-life heroes. The novel's more human protagonists could then be observed within their social context and interpersonal relations. Many 18th century characters, therefore, had their roots in the "empirically based nonfiction" of the time.

Early female protagonists, such as Moll Flanders, Pamela, or Clarissa, "are strong mainly in that they merely survive against great odds or prevail through persistence or through the effects of their virtue. They are not heroic in an active sense, nor do they *create* themselves in a modern way." The new mythological connections, made by 19th century novelists, not only changed the nature of female protagonists radically, but it also allowed for "these new female types to connect" with one of the grandest veins in Western literary tradition.

I discovered that the multitude of Diana-heroes they shaped was impossible to cover in one study. However, a brief but representative sampling of some is warranted to show her existence in a variety of other modern texts, to illustrate the myriad forms she can take in these texts, and to consequently open up a fresh interpretation of these texts. The process of identification and analysis of Diana-heroes that I conducted in this study will reveal much on the true nature of those below, and of the multitude elsewhere, when applied with care.

In many 19th century novels, the figure of the Diana-hero retains that pagan coldness but brilliance. Charles Dickens, in *Dombey and Son*, models the figure of the cold, proud, and independent Edith Dombey after the coolly chaste, and potentially deadly Diana, the huntress of the chase. Discovering herself in the prison of a monetary marriage to an arrogant merchant, Edith Dombey's pride and desire for vengeance catapult her into flight—a flight both necessary and unhappy.

In Elizabeth Gaskell's *Wives and Daughters*, the narrative tension evolves partially from the meeting of the gentle and passive Christian Mary-type, Molly Gibson, and her stepsister, the active and colorful but chilly Diana-type Cynthia Kirkpatrick. This "sisterhood" between the Greek and the Christian goddesses of the moon surfaces throughout English fiction. In a more benign instance, of the two innocent and young maids in L.M. Montgomery's *Anne of Green Gables*, Anne is the heroic Christian maid and her best friend is the sweet and fresh Diana.

The huntress Diana-type's malignancy, however, is central to William Thackeray's *The History of Henry Esmond*. One of the hero's main conflicts arises from making his choice between Beatrix Esmond, a chilly and classical Diana-type, and her mother Rachel, a warm and loving Christian heroine. And in Oscar Wilde's "Salome," a drama enacted under the white moonlight, the princess Salome is a complex Diana-type, one caught between the pagan world represented by Herod and his court and the Christian world represented by St. John.

This configuration persists in literature today. In F. Scott Fitzgerald's *The Great Gatsby*, both Daisy Buchanan and Jordan Baker are surrounded by nymph imagery associated with the goddess Diana and her woodland train, though the manifestation of such sylphs in Fitzgerald's affluent class is that of hollow and cool social huntresses. An exemplum of a truly deadly Artemis arises in Diana der Hovanessian's "Game," wherein the goddess is imaged with perfection as the fatal huntress.

In another image in the kaleidoscope, oftentimes the Diana-hero's green freshness and silvery music are imprisoned, rebellious, or sadly faded in our grey and staccato modern world. E.L. Doctorow, in *Ragtime*, launches his novel with Evelyn Nesbit serving as the model for Saint Gaudens's famous statute of Diana, and the integral symbolism between the character and the goddess continues to be interwoven throughout as a source of the spirited Nesbit's potential regeneration in a bleak society. Likewise in Kurt Vonnegut's *The Sirens of Titan*, Beatrice Rumford is a Diana-type who passes from the white and virginal stage of the maiden to the prophetic stage of the old woman, enacting a full cycle of the moon, as she ends generating reams of writing to shape her ideas of her life and her world. D. H. Lawrence creates the marvellous Diana-hero

Ursula Brangwen, the touchstone of heroism, of the forging of a new self stone, is a Diana-hybrid who leaves conventionality behind to fulfill her destiny of song and music.

On a more sorrowful note, John Cheever in "Artemis, the Honest Well Digger" creates a male Diana-hero, Artemis, who, like the Hippolytus of Euripides' drama, is a follower of Diana. He futilely seeks revivification of some sort in our banal modern world. In many of T.S. Eliot's poems, the females are linked imagistically with Diana. In poems such as "Rhapsody on a Windy Night," "Ash-Wednesday," and "The Fire Sermon" the link serves as a reminder of the tragic lose of purity, love, and poetry in our 20th century world. Similarly, Lawrence Durrell in *Justine* molds the image of the dancer Melissa Artemis on the goddess Diana, and her fate is a tragic one. In *Gravity's Rainbow* Thomas Pynchon creates a host of colorful Diana-types, enveloped in the imagery of the moon and its goddess, and more than one meets a dubious, if not horrific, fate.

Authors frequently experiment with the opalescent and beguiling Diana-type in more than one novel. Sinclair Lewis in *Arrowsmith* creates one of his few truly sympathetic female characters, Leonora Arrowsmith, who, as her name indicates, is modelled after the best in the fresh and natural figure of Diana as goddess of the green chase. In *Dodsworth*, however, he creates Fran Dodsworth, a negative portrait through which he condemns the icily cold version of the huntress Diana. George Meredith in *The Egoist* creates Clara Middleton as a refreshing, natural, and liberating female modelled after Diana, an idea so appealing to him that he created a more complex configuration of this hero in the well-known Diana Merion of *Diana of the Crossways*. In Kenneth Rexroth's "Iphigenia at Aulis," as in Aesychlus' drama whence it derives, the heroic Iphigenia harbors the powers of ritual death and rebirth, of transformation, and in Rexroth's "Phaedra," the overwhelming force of an Aesychlean Diana-type propels the tragedy in the clash with a lustful antoganist.

Especially, the authors in this study explored the complex archetype of Diana over and again, each time revealing another color in this myriad-hued figure. Edith Wharton uses the Diana-figure everywhere; not only does she surface as Lily Bart in *The House of Mirth*, but she surfaces as May Welland in *The Age of Innocence*, Mattie Silver in *Ethan Frome*, as Susy Branch in *Glimpses of the Moon*, and as many other intriguing figures in Wharton's other novels. Henry James uses the Diana-type not only for Isabel Archer in *The Portrait of a Lady*, but in *The Golden Bowl*, a central clash occurs between the naive and Christian Mary-type, Maggie Verver, and the striking social huntress, Charlotte Stant. In *The Bostonians*, the chaste and independent Diana has temporarily devolved, in James's ironic view of the new world and its trapped women, into the cold and egocentric social huntress, Adeline Luna.

As a final point, the new Diana-hero arises in literature everywhere. Categories, such as "English literature," are classifications we make artificially to tackle the wonderful flood of art and literature throughout our world and study it. We discover that the limits of our own chosen categories are frustrating, and that the boundaries of our categories, so suited to our own conveniences, can distance us from other works we value. The moment we briefly escape from our literary category to study the work of another realm, we are rejuvenated by the unique genius there. I discovered awesome creations of the Diana-hero each time I delved into the literatures of other cultures.

Typical instances are Isak Dinesen's "Ehrengard," wherein the author creates a tall, strong, and virginal Diana-hero Ehrengard, with the artist Herr Cazotte serving as her Acteon. In *Eva Luna*, Isabel Allende has any music, moonlight, and poetry that are still possible in her fictional worlds derive from the main character and Diana-type, Eva Luna, and her tribe, the Children of the Moon. Johann Wolfgang von Goethe, in *Iphigenia in Tauris*, presents a German romantic interpretation, one highly sublime, of the idea of Diana in the maiden Iphigenia. In Australian literature, a typical example would be Elizabeth Jolley's *Miss Peabody's Inheritance*, whose myriad heroines are modelled after the most puissant Diana.[1]

In short, a multitude of Diana-heroes exists in an ever-living and ever-shifting *Gestalt* throughout our literature. Her first radiant manifestations in Western literature came in medieval times, with those such as Dante's Beatrice, and this heroic type continued through Renaissance literature, with such figures as Ariosto's knight Bradamante and Spenser's questing Britomart. Then, the host of Romantic Diana-types arose, not only in the poetry of Keats, Browning, Coleridge, Byron, and others, but in Romantic novels and stories. She is the vibrant Die Vernon of Sir Walter Scott's *Rob Roy*, the virginal Elizabeth Temple of James Fenimore Cooper's *The Pioneers*, the dark and powerful Ligeia of Edgar Allan Poe's short story, and many more.

Not only is a survey of such literary works far too extensive to undertake here, but the Diana-type surfaces in other modes of literature, too. Her figure has entered and permeated the realm of popular literature. Diana's moonlight and mystery, for instance, make her types particularly well-suited to that genre. She is the enigmatic Dian de Momerie in Dorothy Sayers's *Murder Must Advertise*, and she is the embodiment of medieval mystery and the glimmering moon goddess in Margery Allingham's *The Gyrth Chalice Mystery*. The Queen Moon is also the symbol of light, beauty and poetry in Martha Grimes's *The Five Bells and Bladebone* and *I Am the Only Running Footman*, whose 20th century worlds are ridden with crime and bloodshed. On another variation, in quite a few of Agatha Christie's stories, such as "The Idol House of Astarte," the narrative drama derives from the tension between the dark pagan myth of Diana and the enlightened Christian myth of Mary. This list could go on extensively.

Modern novelists shattered the old construct of Diana, the stereotypical image of a pretty and youthful maiden of the moon, and re-visioned Diana Triformis in all her heterogeneous powers and manifestations. Here was an image for an unconventional New Woman who struggles toward an ideal as she resists the rigid forms of a stagnant old world around her.

As these authors de-structured the old idea of the male hero, to make way for the new, they presented a singular challenge for readers and critics to de-code their new hero, and the nebula of symbols and images, surrounding her figure. There came a radical new hero into our literature, and she persists today. The persistence of the Diana-hero indicates that modern authors still need and desire to create heroic women to meet the demands and to cross the new frontiers opened by our on-going social revolutions. This challenged and challenging hero continues to struggle in her quest to be Diana Victrix.

೪ NOTES

INTRODUCTION

1. Diana's figure was prolific in Romantic art, too. Blake's *Hecate* is illustrative, a fabulous chiaroscuro of the triple-faced moon goddess in her waning aspect, magical with her darkest powers. The drawing contains an ass and other items significant of Blake's homage to Apuleius, whose *The Golden Ass* pays extensive homage to Isis, the Egyptian configuration of the moon goddess, and whose work wielded a clear influence on Romantic poetry. In *The Creation of Eve*, Blake's Eve rises in a "misty, crepuscular light" that flows from the crescent moon above her; it is a new moon, representative of the "feminine principle in nature," incarnated in the human Eve (Essick, pp. 120–21).

2. Lacan analyzes this quest, the creative seeking of Diana: "...he cannot stop until he reaches the grottoes in which the chthonian Diana in the damp shade, which makes them appear as the emblematic seat of truth, offers to his thirst, with the smooth surface of death, the quasimystical limit of the most rational discourse in the world, so that we might recognize the place in which the symbol is substituted for death in order to take possession of the first swelling of life" (p. 124). The field is rich and open for a Lacanian analysis of Diana-heroes and their worshippers now that this work has established her existence and clarified her configurations.

ONE. JANE EYRE

1. All quotations from *Jane Eyre* are taken from the Norton Critical Edition, which, under the editorship of Richard J. Dunn, uses the 1848 third edition text, the last that Charlotte Bronte corrected. Further page references to the works under study will be given in the text.

2. One can make a reasonable argument that Bronte intended this. Rochester labels Eyre "a disguised deity" (p. 120), and this term, with similar ones, suggest a conscious typing on Bronte's part. Continually, Eyre is identified as an immortal; she is "no transitory blossom" like most mortals but rather she is "the radiant resemblance of one, cut in an indestructible gem" (p. 276).

    The profuse imagery, allusions, and references to the moon and its deity, not only in *Jane Eyre* but in Bronte's juvenilia and *Villette*, reinforce the suggestion of a strong authorial intention.

3. This image also has roots in the blood-red moon that heralds the apocalypse in St. John's The Book of Revelation, a text whose importance to *Jane Eyre* I discuss further on.

4. Lacan notes that the "mirror stage" is critically formative in the function of the "I" and

explains the "symbolic efficacity" of the mirror-image: it is a threshold, of the visible world, hallucinations, dreams...appearances of our *doubles*, and such images "in which psychical realities, however heterogeneous, are manifested" (p. 1–3). This reinforces my theory that, however different the ghastly image in the mirror may appear to be from the child Eyre, it is her psychical reality, a double of her inner self.

5.   Bronte repeats this image in *Villette* with France's moon-soaked midsummer festival, to which Lucy Snowe wanders at the moon's bidding (pp. 431–442). The French name of the midsummer festival makes clear its origins: in Limousin, the fest is "La Lunade," or at Vallon de la Suille it is "Bois de la Lune," and they begin not at sunrise but at moonrise (Briffault, III, 72). Again, this idea in *Villette*, coupled with the plethora of images of the moon in *Jane Eyre* and Bronte's juvenalia, would point to a certain level of authorial intention.

   In general this image is a fairly traditional one in literature, an example being Shakespeare's *A Midsummer Night's Dream*, a drama in green forests over which shines the bright midsummer moon, emblem of Queen Titania, whose name is a variation of Diana and who, with her lover, rules the woods and their magic. References in the novel connect Jane Eyre with this tradition. Rochester, for instance, uses the epithet, "Is this my pale, little elf? Is this my mustarseed?" Mustardseed, of course, is one of the fairies in *A Midsummer Night's Dream* (p. 226, n.).

6.   Bronte repeats similar details on prophecy and witchery throughout the novel. On meeting Jane Eyre, Rochester says that she had "rather the look of another world" and wonders if she "bewitched" his horse (p. 107). During the initial bed-burning scene at Thornfield, Rochester springs awake and cries to Jane Eyre, "What have you done with me, witch, sorceress?" (p. 131). He later says her love is a "witchery beyond any triumph *I* can win" (p. 229). The servants say that Rochester is "bewitched" by Eyre, and her power is soon linked to that of Bertha Mason, the "witch" who spellbound Rochester in his naive youth (p. 376). Bronte also links the powers of bewitching to prophecy in scenes such as that with the sibyl in the fortune-telling episode at Thornfield. This sibyl is labelled a "real sorceress" and a "genuine witch" (pp. 169–170).

7.   With beauty and force many artists have depicted this motif. The Metropolitan Museum of New York City's tapestries of *Lady and the UNICORN: Touching* show the immensely fertile powers that chastity must harness. The Lady holds in her left hand a banner emblazoned with white crescents and under her right hand is a unicorn, another symbol of virginity. The entire background is laden with images of fecundity—fruit-bearing trees, flowers in full blossom, and lively animals.

   Rubens especially painted Diana in this type of glorious virginity. In *Diana and her Nymphs Departing for the Hunt*, a magnificently regal and bare-breasted Diana, clad in a tiger's skin and red drapery, strides in chaste sensuality through a shiningly green earth. In a variation, *Diana's Return from the Hunt*, her arms are laden with prey, hinting at her as *potnia theron*, and she is accompanied by nymphs and fauns whose arms are laden with fruit.

Other fantastic illustrations abound. Raphael was the first to celebrate this idea of Diana as *potnia theron* at her ancient temple at Ephesus, an idea then glorified by Romano Guilio, the Elder Heemskerck, Rubens, and scores more. Heemskerck's *An Allegory of Nature* came to be the model for this idea of Diana as the multimammia of the teeming wilds. Below her waist are fierce animal heads, and below her feet are heaps of fruits. This idea persisted for centuries, and in Robert Home's *John Hunter*, the founder of the Hunterian Museum sits before a portico with a woodcut of this Ephesian Diana. Ultimately, from this well-known tradition, statutes of Diana came to grace teeming gardens from Italy to England.

8. In this vein, Queen Elizabeth's "virginity" indicated that she could never be subjected, possessed, or conquered (Warner, p. 48). The condition of chastity for heroism surfaces throughout the poetry of the period, too, as in Spenser's prologue to Book III of *The Faerie Queene*, where he praises Palladine:

> But she, or such as she, that is so chaste a wight....
> Her well beseemes that Quest (quoth *Satyrane*).... (VII, 52–53)

9. Bronte makes this theme central to "Apostasy," a poem in which the Virgin Mary represents an unnatural ideal for mortal woman, literally a "statute" like the lifeless Mary Ingram:

> This last denial of my faith,
>   Thou, solemn Priest, has heard;
> And, though upon my bed of death,
>   I call not back a word.
> Point not to thy Madonna, Priest,—
>   Thy sightless saint of stone;
> She cannot, from this burning breast,
>   Wring one repentant moan.
>
> Thou say'st that, when a sinless child,
>   I duly bent the knee,
> And prayed to what in marble smiled
>   Cold, lifeless, mute on me.
> I did. But listen! Children spring
>   Full soon to riper youth;
> And, for Love's vow and Wedlock's ring,
>   I sold my early truth.... (*Complete Poems*, pp. 58–59)

10. This idea is not unique to *Jane Eyre*. Miss West was Bronte's new type of heroine by 1838. She is a female who shares the capacity of Mary for a submissive manner and of Zenobia for intellectual power (Tayler, p. 143).

11. Jane Austen creates a perfect picture of a Diana-type mired in this modern situation in *Sandition*, a story that opens with the scene of an overturned rushing carriage. Diana Parker is, literally, a hyperactive and over talkative hypochondriac, as preoccupied and urgent about trifles as the chaotic modern world in which she roams. At root, however, she is energetic, good-hearted, and an eager actor and mover. Diana Parker is suffering from a complete want of expression for her powers in her social sphere.

12. In Bronte's *Villette*, such imagery resonates with Dantean overtones. Dante, upon reaching the sphere of the moon, exhorts his readers to consider whether they are prepared to follow his ship, steered through the heavens by Beatrice, his guide (p. 315). The only other living man who completed the journey to paradise previous to Dante's quest was St. Paul (p. 315). In the last chapter of *Villette*, images of a journeying Paul, of a chaste heroine, and of nautical voyages culminate not in medieval visions of paradise but in modern disaster. The heroine Lucy Snow loses forever her bridegroom, Paul Emmanuel, in an earthly tempest which wrecks his ship, the "Virginie." That chapter opens with Snow's modern cry, "Man cannot prophecy" (pp. 471–474) any longer.

    The persistence of this motif in Bronte's writing, be it *Villette* or *Jane Eyre*, hints, if one is interested in conducting such a study, of Bronte's clear intentions in this matter.

13. See Irene Tayler's *Holy Ghosts* for an excellent analysis of the manner in which the simultaneous rise to prominence of females as authors and as subjects of art led to "an unsettling new consideration of ways genders are assigned or assumed in our concepts of creativity and creation" (pp. 16–17), particularly in   the artist, and particularly for Charlotte and Emily Bronte.

    Beyond a sterling examination of this theme, Tayler offers many instances of a range of Charlotte Bronte's characters as illustration, and one, Shirley, especially forms a pattern with Jane Eyre. Though Bronte's portrait of Shirley is not the paradigm of female power that Bronte achieves in *Jane Eyre* and *Villette*, nonetheless Bronte stresses Shirley's "originality," she longs for "virgin freedom," and she is like a lion, leopard, and panther (p. 191), which, I would add, are the main heraldic animals of Diana as *potnia theron*, the free and commanding mistress of the green chase.

14. In Keats's *Endymion*, the hero is also likened to a blind Orion being guided by Diana (II, l. 198). Artists have used this tale, too, Jacques Bellange's *The Hunter Orion Carrying Diane on His Shoulders* being one example.

15. These are the exact words from *The New King James Bible* (22:21). Of all the Bibles consulted, most had either this quote or an abbreviated version, "Amen. Come, Lord Jesus."

16. Rochester, Eyre's real bridegroom, is a figure as hybrid as she. He is sometimes surrounded by sun imagery, but he is also allied, like Eyre, to this earth. At these times, the allusions to his figure frequently point to "Vulcan" (p. 389) or the flesh. He is said

to have, for instance, an "athletic" build, one sharply in contrast to the ethereally elegant lines of an "Apollo," (p. 123, n.), and the purer "Apollo" of the text is clearly identified as the celestially chill St. John Rivers (p. 389).

17. In the symbolic novels of the Victorians, characters typed after mythical beings, or mixtures of mythical beings, are rife. For a sterling explication of this phenomenon, see Felicia Bonaparte's *The Triptych and the Cross*, which establishes *Romola* as the first symbolic novel in English, plus *Will and Destiny* and *"Middlemarch*: The Genesis of Myth in the English Novel." In the latter, Bonaparte discusses many characters in this vein. A typical instance would be the manner in which Eliot's "Rosamond" Vincy is the Rose of the World, with strong elements of Ariadne and the sirens of Odysseus interwoven (pp. 125–27; 135).

18. I happily borrow here Wordsworth's proclamation that all poets are each to each connected in a mighty scheme of truth.

19. Bronte seems to be enacting to a certain extent the "poetic incarnation" delineated by Harold Bloom in *A Map of Misreading*. Her work, when anchored in its meaningful relationship to other texts, evidences both her inheritance and her revision of the ideas of the greatest authors of the past.

20. Tayler admirably expounds on this theme of redemptive love in Bronte's texts. She elaborates the way in which the Old Testament journey for the Promised Land and the New Testament's journey for salvation were, for Bronte, types of women's struggle to free herself from a devotion that is a fatal bondage and find, instead, a love that redeems and revives her (p. 190). Not only does the symbolism surrounding Jane Eyre and Rochester's union point toward meanings on this level, shaping it as a *hieros gamos*, but Tayler provides other instances of metaphorical marriages in Bronte's texts. The marriage of Frances and William in *The Professor* is a marriage that embodies, for Bronte, the critical union of certain male and female elements within herself as an artist, or the "bridal hour of Genius and Humanity," the climax of the story of Eva, as a mystical union that is an analogue to the sacred weddings of Christianity, including the lamb and the Bride in The Book of Revelation (pp. 168; 198). The Book of Revelation also happens to be one of Eyre's favorite texts, along with several other books of the Bible (Bronte, p. 28).

21. The royal name "Georgiana" for a Diana-type stems from a phenomenon of the 17th and 18th century. The goddess Diana, of the green chase, was cast in the role of protectress of the grounds of the aristocracy, where they conducted the favorite sport of the goddess Diana—hunting.

The tradition began with Francois I (1515–47), whose Italian painters La Primatrice and Il Rosso decorated his chateau at Fontainebleau with images of the classical Diana as Huntress. The theme exploded with Francois I's successor, Henri II (1547–59) because his mistress, Diane de Poitiers, nourished the myth to extraordinary lengths.

It soon spread to English shores. Thackeray, in *Henry Esmond*, mocks this tradition through the art of the day and the character of the vain Beatrix Esmond. She is named after the Restoration Queen, and directly associated with Charles and this tradition through the portrait of the decrepit aristocrat, the Viscount Dowager:

> Harry laughed at recognizing in the parlour the well-remembered old piece of Sir Peter Lely, wherein his father's widow was represented as a virgin huntress, armed with gilt bow and arrow, and encumbered only with that small quantity of drapery which it would seem the virgins in King Charles's day were accustomed to wear (p. 142).

Other female characters fitting this model are Lady Adeline, the "perfect Diana" of Byron's *Don Juan*, or the vain Adeline Luna of Henry James's *The Bostonians*. Other examples would be too numerous to list here. The point is that Bronte's Georgiana Reed has much company in literature, both precedent and antecedent to her.

This famous legacy of Diane de Poitiers persisted well into the 20th century. D.H. Lawrence refers to Diane de Poitiers as the archetype of sex appeal in "Sex versus Loveliness" (*Selected Essays*, p. 17). When William Randolph Hearst built *La Cuesta Encantada* in the 1920s, with its huge grounds being the largest private zoo of elk, leopards, lions, bears, and more, he ordered three statues of Diana to grace the mansion's front gates.

As the excerpt from Thackeray hints, this concept of Diana was rife in art. Depictions like "Diana in the Chase," "Diana with Hounds," or "Diana Huntress" are by far the most frequent of the goddess. Some of this most famous are *Diana Huntress* by Jean Antoine Houdon, *Diane de Versailles* in the Louvre, the *Diana* of Augustus Saint–Gaudens, and the *Diana* of Anne Hyatt Huntington.

22. "Ingram" may also allude to Blanche's partaking of the underworld realm, for it means "Angel-Raven." The black raven functions as the bird of dying moon, hell, and Hekate. Bronte elsewhere makes associations between birds and the moon, as in "The Fairies' Farewell":

> And to the moon the desert-bird
> Shall make her thrilling moan.

Bronte very likely was conscious of the name's meaning, for she makes a turn on it for the malevolent goddess of *Villette*, Madame Walravens. Ingram as "Angel-Raven," therefore, is another strong indication that Bronte was associating her Diana-types with the three realms of the Triformis.

23. See Susan Finkel Smith's *Diana and the Renaissance Allegory of Love* for an excellent analysis of the manner in which the figures of a black-haired and black-eyed Endymion and Diana came to stand, in English poetry, as figures of the black-haired and black-eyed Bride and Groom of the Canticles. See especially pp. 161–62; 108–81; 268.

24. Jane Eyre, a "spectre" at the threshold of death in the Whitcross episode, also enters this state of a "lost and starving dog" and a "masterless and stray dog" (pp. 288; 297). From this deathly condition, she will be re-born and make herself anew.

25. The theme of evolution from pagan to Christian values informs some of Bronte's earliest poetry, such as "Pilate's Wife's Dream":

> The world advances; Greek or Roman rite
> Suffices not the inquiring mind to stay;
> The searching soul demands a purer light
> To guide it on its upward, onward way.

Eyre not only flees from John Reed, with his disposition of a Roman tyrant, but she also flees from the unreformed Rochester, and the name "Rochester" also has Roman roots. It likely derives from "Hrofoecoestre," a compound of "hrofoe" for *roof* and "coestre" for *Roman fort*, derived from the Latin "castra."

The presents interesting psychological interpretations on the theme of pagan versus Christian values. The unredeemed Rochester is trapped in his own torrid past, and with a hard-willed force he tries to dupe Eyre first into a false marriage, then into being his mistress. He would subsume her life into his afflicted one. Further, a potential false bride in Rochester's past, Blanche Ingram, hails from a family whose Dowager has "Roman features," ones reminiscent of the cold and harsh Mrs. Reed's (p. 151).

If one turns to Lacan one finds explanation, for Rochester's name is an apt sign of his own structure—that of a fortified work of almost obsessional neurosis (p. 5). It is good, then, on this level, that Rochester's mansion and his body, his 'fortified work,' is burned down; he is now free of his past and its neurosis. He can be "retransformed" (p. 123).

Allusions in the text develop this theme more. Rochester seeks to free himself from Bertha Mason, whom he dubs, in disgust, an "Indian Messalina," the debauched wife of the Roman Emperor Claudius (p. 274; 274, n.). He seeks redemption in a marriage to Jane Eyre, whom he dubs his "Queen Boadicea," the Iceni ruler who led a revolt against the Romans (p. 215; 215, n.).

26. The figure of Bertha Mason reinforces this theme, too, for it alludes to the historical fact of yet another fallen empire besides the old Roman one. Mason is one of the "mad Creole heiresses in the early nineteenth century...products of an inbred, decadent, and expatriate society" (Wyndham, p. 12). On this level, Mason's figure expands the theme of fallen empires. Her figure links the idea of the fallen Roman Empire with the fallen British one, with its spiritual nightmare and forced exploitation that constituted its rule in the Caribbean colonies. The idea is a catalytic one for Jean Rhys's *Wide Sargasso Sea*. Eyre comes dangerously close to inheriting this legacy on the brink of her false marriage to Rochester. Rochester did inherit it upon his marriage; he had hoped, evidently, to reap the profits of the Empire in his marriage to the rich Mason, but he received a fuller dowry, a disturbed woman who is the emblem and culmination of the generations of exploitation and decadence in the Colonies.

27. Thornfield, and Bertha Mason, specifically constitute a Shakespearean nightmare at key moments. Jane Eyre uses the epithet, "after life's fitful fever they sleep well" from *Macbeth* to comment on Mrs. Fairfax's observation that the race of Rochesters, though a violent one, rests tranquilly in their graves (p. 93, n.). During bleak times at Thornfield, Eyre echoes the opening lines of the witches of *Macbeth*: "I know not whether the day was fair or foul" (p. 253).

Rochester explains his "destiny" which presides over Thornfield:

She stood there, by that beech-trunk—a hag like one of those who appeared to "Macbeth" on the heath at Forres (p. 125).

The "fearful hag" is embodied in Bertha Mason (p. 264). The beech tree, then, of Shakespearean hags and witches, is one like the Lacanian "tree of Diana," the tree which "traces our destiny for us" (p. 155).

28. Images of an infant and changeling trouble Jane Eyre throughout the novel, a fact in accord with the mytheme of the moon goddess, for Hekate, as goddess of the underworld, has demonic charge of changelings.

Moreover, Eyre dreams of one infant "for seven successive nights" and is profoundly disturbed by "this iteration of one idea—this recurrence of one image." It is "from companionship with this baby phantom" that Eyre is roused by Mason's first horrific cry. The link between this "baby phantom" and the moon goddess and her underworld is repeated when, on the day after the seven nights' dream, Eyre receives word her cousin John Reed is dead and his mother on the verge of death (p. 193–95).

Eyre herself was even a "changeling" at Gateshead, the cold hell in which she's first entrapped, and she remains the "changeling" of Rochester at the end, one who's preserved her best, unique self (pp. 241; 386). The identity is perfectly in accord with a nature rooted in the idea of the Triple Dian.

29. The epithet, from Keats's "Ode to a Nightingale," refers to the spell cast over the poet in the night reigned by the "Queen Moon" on her throne. One can assume that a craftswoman like Charlotte Bronte is using the quote by design, not chance.

30. Examples are "Rosamond" Oliver and Blanche Ingram, who is titled a "golden rose" and appears at Thornfield wearing an "amber-coloured flower" (p. 139). As the bride in the charade, Ingram wears "a wreath of roses round her brow" (p. 160).

31. The scene echoes the actual conception of Aeneas, for in myth Venus usually appears to Anchises, Aeneas's father, as an earthly huntress of Diana's train.

The garb of Diana seems to be one of Venus's favorite disguises. In Drayton's "Muses of Elizium," Venus assumes this guise so that she can wreak mischief among the nymphs of Diana. In George Sandys's *Ovid's Metamorphosis...*, Venus woos Adonis:

Now like *Diana* she her self attires;
And trips o'er hills and rocks, through brakes and
    briers:
Hollowes the hound; pursuing beasts of chace,
Bucks, high-hornd Harts, and hares, who fly apace: (X, ll. 526-64)

In Spenser's *The Faerie Queene*, not only Venus but also her son Cupid delights in assuming the garb of Diana's train to go among her nymphs and create mischief. When Venus comes one day to search among Diana's company for her son, she says:

And tell me, if that ye my sonne haue heard,
To lurke amongst your Nymphes in secret wize;
Or keepe their cabines: much I am affeard,
Least he like one of them him self disguize,
And turne his arrowes to their exercize:
So may he long himself full easie hide:
For he is faire and fresh in face and guize,
As any Nymph (let not it be enuyed.)
So saying euery Nymph full narrowly she eyde.   (III, vi, 23)

Evidently, authors throughout the ages have delighted in experimenting with the two goddesses, sharing love, and clothes, with a twist.

32. This idea permeates Shakespeare's *A Midsummer Night's Dream*. King Theseus directs Hermia:

You can endure the livery of a nun,
For aye to be in shady cloister mewed,
To live a barren sister all your life,
Chanting faint hymns to the cold fruitless moon,
Thrice-blessed they that master so their blood,
To undergo such maiden pilgrimage;
But earthlier happy is the rose distilled,
Than that which, withering on the virgin thorn,
Grows, lives, and dies in single blessedness.   (1.1, ll. 70-78)

When the characters finally achieve "the concord of this discord" (5.1, l. 60), they have reconciled the elements of Diana and Venus, of cold chastity o'er heated passion:

Dian's bud o'er Cupid's flower
Hath such force and blessed power.   (4.1, l. 76-77)

33. Once the mystery is revealed, the suprahuman laughter proves to belong to Eyre's nemesis, Bertha Mason, the dark and hidden member of the triangle.

34. Moon imagery surrounds Helen Burns. She is all "radiance," her eyes have "liquid lustre," and the light of an "unclouded summer moon" guides Jane Eyre to her deathbed (pp. 63; 70). Jane Eyre describes Miss Scatcherd's inability to appreciate Helen's true nature through the image of a glowing planet:

> Such is the imperfect nature of man! such spots are there on the disc of the clearest planet; and eyes like Miss Scatcherd's can only see those minute defects, and are blind to the full brightness of the orb (p. 59).

35. Bronte experimented with the concept of trinities from the time of her early poems. The structure of "LXXII" consists of a trinity of martyrs of faith, patriotism, and philosophy (p. 193).

36. Robert B. Heilman notes that the moon is an aesthetic staple, one forming an intriguing pattern of lunar imagery, throughout Charlotte Bronte's four novels in "Charlotte Bronte, Reason, and the Moon." He examines the manner in which her Moon always evokes lunar superstition, particularly in moments of crisis, and he discovers and examines the amazingly close structural parallels in scenes where the Moon is present, both within specific novels of Bronte's and within her entire works. He concludes that Bronte's visions of the moon always partake of the revelatory, suggesting a transcendental force at work, one going beyond an individual character's inner light to point toward some universal illumination; therefore, her Moon must be an aesthetic objectification echoing some great myth (pp. 283–302).

37. Irene Tayler keenly observes that "Eyre" is also an alternate spelling of Hiere or Eire, i.e. Ireland, and this places Jane Eyre in the context of Bronte's heroic females such as "Miss West" (p. 143). Indeed, the creative meanings opened by Tayler's theory are intriguing. Jane "Eyre," on her journey from old Rome to New Rome, is indeed an "heir" to Western civilization in a grand way, specially its legacy of the idea of paradise regained.

Other meanings have been posited. Adele, who is French, pronounces the name "Aire," which in her language has not only "particular geological and mathematical uses," but indicates a "threshing ground," "nest for a bird of prey," and "area or space'" (Dunn, p. 89n). This French "aire" is evocative in the text, given the imagery of birds surrounding Eyre and her constant search for autonomous space. She leaves one confining prison of a structure after another, seeking a sphere in which her spirit can soar. One can best conclude that the opalescent nature of Bronte's names, and symbols, are a powerful source of meaning in her text.

38. Apuleius so describes the marvelous statue of Diana in the wise and chaste Byrrhaena's house (*The Golden Ass*, p. 53).

TWO. HESTER PRYNNE

1. The debate around the honored text for *The Scarlet Letter* is one of the most interesting, and it is still on-going. Perkins *et al*, eds., use the text of the first edition (March 1850), with Hawthorne's brief preface to the second edition prefixed. For a capsule of the debate, see Perkins *et al* (p. 1668 n.)—and the host of evidence and reasons offered everywhere by devoted and painstaking Hawthorne scholars. All page references refer to the Perkins edition unless I specify that they refer to one of the excellent annotations in the Norton Critical Edition of Seymour Gross *et al*. Both editions, of Perkins and Gross, share the editorship of Richard Croom Beatty, Sculley Bradley, and E. Hudson Long.

2. Many critics have documented the use of myths, Greek and otherwise, in Hawthorne's texts. One of the most concise studies is Hugh McPherson's *Hawthorne as Myth-Maker: A Study in Imagination*. McPherson completes a thorough investigation of Hawthorne's character types, of his image patterns, of his main source of Greek myth and tales, Anthon, and of his narrative configurations, including an analysis of "types" from Adam, Adonis, and Aegeus to Ulysses, Venus, and Vulcan.

3. Studying the *Elixir of Life Manuscripts*, Swann explores the manner in which the Puritan Septimus's quest, to interpret secret words and their mystery, becomes in Hawthorne's hands a unique way to mix the concerns of the American Puritans and the problems of the Romantic poet. It is an original linkage of Puritan mysticism and Romantic fervor. In general, Hawthorne stressed the analogy between the struggle of the artist to construct his work and the alchemist's search for the golden elixir of immortality. Both he and his hero Septimus, for example, in *The Elixir of Life* are engaged in "a genuine and persevering search" for the truth (pp. 376–81; 383).

4. McPherson also observed that Hawthorne seems to have had a "fully developed idea of the significance of moonlight," that the moon was "at once productive and destructive," and this intriguing fact gave rise to the presence of extensive and complex moon images in Hawthorne's text (pp. 124–25).

5. The text is laced with other alchemical images pointing to this idea and its corollaries. The alchemist Chillingworth concocts an "Elixir of Life," a golden liquid sought by medieval alchemists (p. 83). It is golden because the male figures are linked with the golden sun god in alchemy and the females with the silvery moon.

The marriage of the two is an emblem of alchemy's concern with the *coniunctio* of opposites, the progression from dualism to unity, and the traditional opposites of alchemy are those of *The Scarlet Letter*. There is (1) manifestum versus occultum [the hidden "A" of Dimmesdale versus the open "A" of Prynne]; (2) oriens versus occidens [the "Oriental" nature of womanly Prynne (p. 59) versus the Western law of the Puritan fathers]; (3) Sol versus Luna [Dimmesdale in the sunlit community versus Hester/Hibbins in the moonlit woods]; (4) superiora versus inferiora [Dimmesdale's and Hester's struggle from the depths of their sin to celestial heights of triumph and the New Jerusalem], and others (Jung, p. 3).

Lastly, the alchemist's elixir is frequently seen as the "golden" liquid that will be like the water of the fountain of youth. Chillingworth's insistence on marrying the young Hester further places him in the context of alchemy, as the evil old man seeking after youth.

6.   Hawthorne's sketches of tales from Greek mythology, *A Wonder-Book for Boys and Girls* and *Tanglewood Tales*, indicate his familiarity with Hekate as the goddess of night and darkness. Hawthorne's Hekate is the mistress of unrelieved blackness, the symbol of all darkness (McPherson, pp. 102; 117).

7.   Cf. Jung's *MC*, Chapter III, Part 4, "Luna" pp. 129–183, and Part IV, "Rex and Regina" (Sol and Luna) pp. 258–381.

8.   "Arthur" types are widespread in the literature of this era. Bonaparte succinctly states the case for the "vigorous revival" of the Arthurian legend in nineteenth century novels when she explores the works of George Eliot, an originator of this symbolic motif. Eliot "appropriates Camelot because in it she too sees for England a mythological past in which a spiritual brotherhood sought through temporal deeds of valor to fulfill a mysterious destiny in a quest not for personal glory but for the good of the commonweal" (*Will and Destiny*, p. 138). That is a description well fitting the mission of the Puritans in New England, too. In typical modern irony, the Arthur type of Hawthorne is, like Eliot's are, notably unequal to his name.

9.   McPherson conducts a smooth analysis of the way in which moon and sun imagery, and these "types," are complementary in most of Hawthorne's work. A male hero's quest may usually begin in the daylight world, of the sun and empiricism, but this hero must enter the moon's realm, of dreams and imagination, to discover his full creative powers (15). When Dimmesdale, a sun-type, undergoes his initiation in the dark and moonlit realm, which belongs in the main to the feminine in *The Scarlet Letter*, to the maternal forest, Hester, Pearl, and Mistress Hibbins, Dimmesdale could be considered, while in this phase, a moon-hero. Indeed, McPherson documents that there are some specific moon-heroes in Hawthorne's works, such as Quicksilver, Pluto, and Theseus (p. 255), just as there are sun-heroines, such as Phoebe Pyncheon (p. 216).

10.   Vivan notes there is an intermediate state of *viriditas*, green, in alchemy, which Pearl and her green letter fulfill (p. 78).

11.   This "airy" nature strengthens Pearl's identity to the Triple Dian in another sense, too. Hekate is the witch who flies through the night air and has trysts with the "Black Man," who is known, in *The Scarlet Letter*, as the "Prince of the Air" (p. 164). The "weird" witch of the novel, Mistress Hibbins, invites the airy Pearl to "ride" with her through

"some fine night" to see her father (p. 164).

Hawthorne's allusions to Pearl's airy and seemingly demonic nature is evidence that he envisions Pearl as a creative moon-child, for as McPherson writes on Hawthorne's characters:

> Wizards are moon people whose creative power appears evil to rationalists; and, if their magic is denied, they may use it vengefully. In Puritan terms they are associated indiscriminately with demons or witches; but as the Rev. Mr. Wilson and Arthur Dimmesdale correctly recognized, the "demon child" Pearl is really like "one of those fairies or elfs" that they had known in England.... Hawthorne's intention in this imagery, it would seem, is to suggest that his moon people are "nature spirits"; their magic seems demonic only when they are repressed, or when their real gifts are misunderstood, as they are by the Puritans (pp. 230-31).

12. Critically, the heiress and "living hieroglyphic" of *The Scarlet Letter* is not the traditional male savior of Christianity, but Pearl. Interestingly, her birth parallels Christ's, on the level of a mortal mother and no father but an "heavenly" one (p. 49).

Alchemical images in the text further make Pearl a feminine parallel of Christ. The goal of alchemy is the synthesis of opposites which come to resolution in the production of the *lapis philosophorum*. This *lapis* is an emblem of Christ because it is symbol of psychic totality (Jung v-vi; xv; p. 16). Pearl alone has this totality; she is this "one united substance" in *The Scarlet Letter*.

As this priceless stone, Pearl must also be fatherless, or the "orphan" of alchemy, because she is meant to be unique (pp. 17; 37). Hawthorne's knowledge of the *lapis philosophrom* is documented in Swann's "Alchemy and Hawthorne's *Elixir of Life Manuscripts*" (p. 371) and Vivan's "An Eye into the Occult of Hawthorne's Text: The Scar in the Letter." The latter notes especially that "the philosopher's stone of alchemic search" is the treasure of Hawthorne's novel (p. 80)—and that treasure is the singular and precious "Pearl."

Further, when Prynne casts her scarlet letter aside in the forest, Pearl bids her mother, "Come thou and take it up"—recalling Christ's command to "take up" one's cross and follow Him in Matthew xvi:24 (Perkins, *SL*, p. 1778n). These words form another parallel between the figures of Christ and Pearl.

13. Dorena Allen Wright in "The Meeting at the Brook-Side" conducts a detailed exegesis of Pearl as a figure who guides one to the otherworld in the tradition of Dante's Beatrice in the *Divine Comedy* and the Pearl maiden in the medieval *Pearl*.

14. Prynne's name may, to a certain extent, link her with Queen Elizabeth. "Hester" or "Esther" means "Star," and a variant of this is "Astrea," the epithet bestowed on Queen Elizabeth in her aspect as a type of the heroic and virgin goddess Diana. This idea was well-known enough throughout literature and art to make this hypothesis feasible. Ben Jonson likened Queen Elizabeth to Diana, his "Goddesse, excellently bright" ("Hymn to Diana," Wilbur, p. 145) as did Spenser with his Britomart. Particularly, Cynthia and Delia,

birthplace epithets of Artemis or Diana, were 16th century favorites. Spenser, as Colin Clout, and Ben Jonson, in "Cynthia's Revels," both give the name to Queen Elizabeth (Long, p. 93). In painting a typical example is Floris de Vriendt's celebrated *Diana with a Hound: The So-Called Portrait of Queen Elizabeth as Diana*, in which a figure assumed to be Elizabeth wears a lion's pelt and a gauze veil billows behind her like a full moon. She also bears a white crescent and pearls, emblems of Diana, along with the goddess's quiver.

15. The description of Queen Elizabeth as "man-like" raises the issue of androgynous heroic women in the text. Carolyn Heilbrun has extensively and perceptively explored this idea in *Toward A Recognition of Androgyny*. Her analysis, so brilliantly comprehensive, looks at some of the female characters under analysis in this study. She discusses the "tremendous sources of androgynous energy" in Hester Prynne (pp. 63-67), the "revolutionary demands" made by Jane Eyre as this kind of heroic woman (pp. 58-59), and the birth of the "Woman as Hero" with Isabel Archer, also an androgynous figure (pp. 86; 95).

16. The mythical idea of the moon goddess as a creative spinner Briffault documents in "The Moon as Spinstress and Patroness of Feminine Occupations." Feminine duties such as spinning and weaving were from time immemorial assigned to the moon (II, pp. 624-28). The task of spinning, combined with the moon as a measure of time, created the myth of the moon goddess as the undying "spinster" of the heavens. She wove an ever-unfinished web of time and destiny.

Thus, nearly every configuration of a moon goddess—Artemis, Athene, Minerva, the Nymphs, the Triple Fates—is a weaver and spinner (II, 625-28). The idea is catholic, and it is a main symbol of the moon goddess's power of poesis. She weaves new patterns, and she does so eternally.

17. Cf. Dorena Allen Wright's "The Meeting at the Brook-Side: Beatrice, the Pearl-Maiden, and Pearl Prynne" for an analysis of the myriad and clear connections between the medieval Pearl and Hawthorne's.

18. The theme of heraldic illusions and symbols marks *The Scarlet Letter* throughout, demonstrating the importance of this imagery surrounding Hester Prynne, its main bearer. In the climax of the novel, for instance, Hester stands in solitude as the main bearer of a "mystic symbol," the scarlet letter that encloses her in a "magic circle" (pp. 1789; 1795). She is in the midst of a public procession, a "body of soldiery" that is "ironically compared with the College of Arms or Heralds' College, which since about 1460 has been custodian of the genealogies and armorial bearings of persons entitled to them, and with the Knights Templars, a scandalous order of twelfth-century crusaders suppressed by Papal authority in 1312" (Gross *et al*, p. 160 n.).

THREE. MOLLY BLOOM.

1. The edition used is "The Corrected Text," edited by Hans Walter Gabler, with Wolfhard Steppe and Claus Melchior.

2. This mythical imagery woven into the cloth of James Joyce's text is so obvious that it is like an outfit with the seams showing. Joyce's profuse notes demonstrate the care with which he wove this conspicuous pattern, not only in *Ulysses* but in *Finnegans Wake* and elsewhere. Joyce was writing for a 20th century audience, a community of readers whose education, indeed whose entire Western world, had moved further away from religious and mythic archetypes than the world of eighteenth or nineteenth century readers. The mythic typing and imagery of his text needed to be more evidently manifest. One consequence of this is that there is little arguing with Joyce's intentions to type his characters and scenes.

3. Robert Graves gives detailed analysis of Hippolytus' tale and its relation to the worship of Artemis in *The Greek Myths*.

4. Bonnie Kime Scott astutely observes that in *Finnegans Wake* images of the goddess Artemis include mirrors, magic, moons, woods, witchcraft, and maidenhood, the heroic Tuatha de Danaan women of Ireland, and more (pp. 10; 128; 186; 190; 196). Vickery also noted that Diana is directly linked with the hunt in that text (p. 414).

5. Briffault believed that Penelope was a configuration of Diana, for Penelope was originally a priestess of Dionysus, who was the son of the mother-moon Artemis (III, p. 128). In further examining Penelope's roots as a Diana, especially as a *potnia theron*, he notes that she is also the mother of the woodland Pan (III, p. 141).

6. Most of these varying configurations of the moon goddess in different cultures are conflated in *Ulysses*. Mary is "Our Lady of Loreto" (p. 290), and that latter world is strikingly similar—in an epic full of word play—to the last name of Molly's mother, Lunita Laredo.

One configuration deserving special mention in Joyce's host of moon goddesses is the Egyptian Isis and her spouse Osiris. Many critics have documented the importance of that archetype in *Ulysses* and *Finnegans Wake*. "Moonface the Murderer," as one instance, is a composite of the myth and ritual of human sacrifices for the moon, centered on Isis (Vickery, pp. 415-16). On this theme John Richards elaborates in "Isis on Sandymount" and so does Gerber in "More on Isis in 'Nausicca'." And, importantly, Scott notes and explores the importance of Isis and her sister Nephthys in *Finnegans Wake*, too, especially as "Issy" derives her name from that goddess (pp. 197-98).

7. In *Ulysses as a Comic Novel*, Zack Bowen documents clearly the importance of this progression from celestial chastity to earthly sexuality (p. 127), and Richard Ellman's criticism aligns with Bowen's. Ellman concludes that Joyce "corrects" Dante (and Plato)

by placing sexual love above all others kinds, purposely, so that the Blooms can fertilize a terrestrial paradise (p. 111).

8.   In poetry dedicated to the "Triformis," images of "nine" abound. In "To Lunacie," Drayton claims he has been in a state of poetic inspiration for "nine yeeres," and in "Endimion and Phoebe" he celebrates the hero's poetic ascension to "this sacred number nyne" (ll. 884–900).

9.   Scott documents the manner in which female sovereignty over the realm of words and creation is a theme in *Finnegans Wake*. Issy helps to write the book. She gives the author advice on at least two occasions, and she suggests modifications in his rendition of the Quinet motif (p. 194). Issy is a writer of letters, and no other Joycean character can surpass her in wordplay. Being "chary" with the "word" is also witchery, and in this Issy's group of girls could resemble a coven of witches, whose secret words work magic. In the "Lessons," Issy provides a reference to "Llong and Shortts Primer of Black and White Wenchcraft" (Scott, p. 192).

At the end of "Mime," "Geamatron" or the earth goddess, shows the children "coneyfarm leppers" (Cuneiform letters), which makes for another female knowledgeable in ancient letters. Issy is also provided with the Greek letter gamma in the image of the celebrated and "inbourne" "gramma's grammar" of the "Lessons" chapter (p. 193).

10. Bloom in this passage refers to Molly as a passive object, but Molly, in her soliloquy, soon refers to herself as an active agent, marking Bloom as the passive—she is going to create books using her husband as a model. Thus, active and passive turn out to be terms relative to the narrative mind of the moment.

11. This image Molly might angrily deprecate as coming from a "nonsensical book," especially as she represents *nature* as art, but it is this image she retains as an important memory of the moment which led her to choose Leopold.

12. Unkeless reports that Joyce wrote of Molly Bloom, "Ich bin der [sic] Fleisch der stets bejaht." That transforms Goethe's line in *Faust I* from "I am the spirit that always denies" into "I am the flesh that always affirms!" This is a re-stating of Goethe's affirmative and female-centered coda (p. 158).

FOUR. ISABEL ARCHER

1.   Many critics have documented that of the writers of the Italian Renaissance, Ariosto was third, coming after Dante and Petrarch, in influencing English authors. Henry James's novel is not directly modelled on Ariosto's epic, and this study on Diana-heroes unfortunately obviates a study of James's intentions, but Ariosto's work, its quests, its heroes, its ideals, were well known, from Spenser to James.

2. The text used is that of the Norton Critical Edition, which, under the editorship of Robert D. Bamberg, employs the New York Edition (1908), revised by Henry James, with extensive textual notes detailing comparisons to the first edition of 1880-81.

3. Archer's entrapment on the decayed Continent indicates the grave extent to which the theme of imprisonment versus freedom has procceeded on a tragic bend in Henry James's text. In *The Portrait of a Lady*, Isabel Archer is snared in Gilbert Osmond's Farnese Palace, its name implying a fortress (p. 307 n.). In Charlotte Bronte's *Jane Eyre*, Jane Eyre weds a morally redeemed Rochester. As discussed in that chapter, the "roman fort" of his neurosis is burned down; he is finally freed from his past, albeit at a great price, and Jane Eyre can wed him in bliss..

4. A similarly troubled fate befalls another grand and virginal hero, Clarissa, when she receives a worldly inheritance, her grandfather's dairy, in Samuel Richardson's novel. Thus, the "virgin" type enters the empirical world, becoming subject to its trials, a somber motif in English literature.

5. Thus, as Jane Eyre carries a "green Eden" in her mind, and Molly Bloom strives to envision a terrestrial paradise, so does Isabel Archer enjoy an Edenic spirit.

6. Brownstein notes that the ending of the novel is not merely inconclusive, but elaborately that, so that it is conspicuously a rewriting of romance (p. 248). Where shall the heroic female go in the new, modern world? Especially, where shall the heroic female, of mythic proportions, go?

7. Henry James opens up the question of Madame Merle as a Niobe when he has the Countess comment to Isabel Archer on Merle's former marriage, "If she had ever had children—which I'm not sure of—she had lost them" (p. 452). Such statements open up evocative questions and raise subtle but powerfully resonating suggestions in a text, doubly so when the statements allude to mythical identities.

8. In this sense, the old moon has "mothered" the new, another piece fitting Merle's identification as a type of Juno or Niobe, mother goddesses.

9. Anne Humpherys observed to me that this points to Henry James's individual assessment of the paradox of the fortunate fall. The Dian of Keats's *Endymion*, for instance, was fortunate in her fall. It bestowed upon her human warmth and happiness. But James's Diana-hero is not so fortunate. She gains wisdom, but a wisdom tainted with sadness, not joy. Thus, Isabel Archer's fall is closer in nature to the fall of Hester Prynne, a character who acknowledges that the future herald of the apocalypse must be a woman made wise through the ethereal medium of bliss, not sorrow. The unqualified Romantic bliss of Dian's fall has evaporated in modern prose. The women become heroic, but infinitely touched with sadness, a return closer to the original condition of Adam and Eve,

a condition without Romantic idealism and ebullience.

10. Henry James opens up the question of Archer's childbirthing as much as Madame Merle's. When Madame Merle asks if Archer will have children of her own, Ned Rosier comments: "She may have yet. She had a poor little boy, who died two years ago, six months after his birth. Others therefore may come" (p. 305). The suggestion is as passing but evocative as when the Countess alludes to Merle's possibly having lost children.

11. Brownstein has also examined the manner in which Archer's "revision" of her former beliefs, through reconsidering images of her life, makes her poetic. Isabel, "reputed to be a writer...learns to reread" the heroine's story she had pictured for herself. Her triumph is "a clarified, completed vision of the truth," and that is James's own goal as a writer. In Chapter 42, when Archer sets herself to revise her portrait of her marriage to Osmond, particularly after a pose of Osmond and Merle sets off in her mind a "gallery of images," she comes to see her life's "true meaning" as she sits alone "by a dying fire, calling for candles to illuminate her private, internal re-viewing." In this pose she actually "pre-figures the Master preparing his works for the New York edition, seeing the true images come clearer." Archer is engaged is precisely the same act as James—drawing, with revelatory accuracy, her own "portrait" (pp. 244; 246; 250; 252; 259).

FIVE. GWENDOLEN HARLETH

1. Three of the authors in this study, George Eliot, Henry James, and Edith Wharton, particularly engaged in reading and revision of each other's ideas and characters. The interesting twists arise in the different assessment by each author toward their own creation. As Anne Humpherys has pointed out to me, George Eliot problematizes the figure of Gwendolen Harleth more than Henry James problematized his archetype of the Diana-hero, for the presence of Daniel Deronda pushes Gwendolen Harleth off center stage. This reveals quite a difference in George Eliot's attitude toward her creation, a less sympathetic view on her part than Henry James has of Isabel Archer. Especially, I would add that Harleth begins to mature under Deronda's tutelage, an indication that Harleth improves when she moves out of the ancient Greek realm and into the modern Christian one.

2. All page references and quotations refer to the World's Classics edition of Oxford University Press, which uses the text of Graham Handley's Clarendon edition, based on the novel's first published form.

3. Gwendolen Harleth has both the high spirit of horses that James Joyce associates with Molly Bloom and the aristocratic love of horses and hunting that Charlotte Bronte associates with Blanche Ingram and Georgiana Reed.

4. Herein lies one key to her last name, "Harleth." Bonaparte has shown that the names

of characters are "Thematically significant" even in Eliot's "earliest fiction." They become "increasingly important as symbolic keys to the symbolic narratives. In her Berg and Folger Notebooks, Eliot was, in fact, often concerned with the allegorical meaning of names" ("*Middlemarch*," p. 150).

For *Daniel Deronda*, Brownstein has shrewdly observed that "Harleth" sounds much like "harlot" and conveys the same meaning that it does in Clarissa, that of a hard and cold virgin, one who indulges in the love of self, one for whom the life of passion has thus begun negatively (*Becoming*, pp. 215–26).

This theory not only fits Gwendolen's nature as a type of chilly Diana, but if one examines the roots of "harlot," even more is revealed about Gwendolen as a tragic Diana-type. Originally a word applied to men who performed acts of knavery, the term only later came to be applied to women who also performed disreputable acts. A "harlot" indicated a female juggler, a dancing girl, a ballet dancer, an actress, *or* a strumpet, women who share performances, the perfection of false appearances for success in their craft. All are painted women (cf. *Oxford English Dictionary*). The egoistic and icy virgin Gwendolen certainly does seek public homage by striking poses and literally acting at Offendene.

Indeed, not only does Eliot make "Harleth" an actress, but she likens her to Rachel (p. 84), a real actress whose figure wielded a strong influence on the minds of the Victorians. For an analysis of that power, potentially malign, that Rachel embodied for the Victorians, see Brownstein's "Representing the Self: Arnold and Bronte on Rachel."

5. That Harleth is a "dowerless beauty" and not an heiress, unlike comedic Diana-hybrids from Una to Jane Eyre, points toward her tragic role. Eliot shaped her comedic heroines, such as Dorothea Brooke, as heiresses. Brooke is an "heiress...because she has inherited the religious truth of theology" (Bonaparte, "*Middlemarch*," p. 115), but Gwendolen has a legacy so small that it is remarked upon in the book. On this theme, the tragic Isabel Archer is also an heiress, one who misappropriates her legacy in an egoistic desire to collect a fine specimen for a husband (cf. Brownstein, *Becoming*, pp. 259–60).

6. The idea is a persistent one for Eliot. Bonaparte explores the manner in which Eliot makes Dorothea Brooke a symbol of what is amiss in the modern world, too. Dorothea, a hybrid of such blessed women and grand moral pioneers as St. Theresa, the Virgin Mary, Ariadne, and Antigone, has no avenue to express her own gifts. As Bonaparte concludes, "The ache of modernism is precisely that Dorothea can never again address us directly. In a secular age, religion must forever 'run' 'underground'." As the narrator concludes in the Finale, Dorothea remained a "river" that had to "spend itself in channels" which have "no great name on the earth" ("*Middlemarch*," pp. 108; 110; 133; 148). Gwendolen, too, though a rank egoist compared to Dorothea, is a young woman with sadly misspent energies and frustrated ambitions.

7. In his lengthy treatise, Fagles documents that Artemis precipitates the action of Aesychlus' drama because she is the goddess of childbirth and therefore desires to avenge

the Grecian child-murderers of Iphigenia (p. 25). The mother of the murdered child, Clytemnestra, welcomes her husband in a nightmarish parody of homecoming so that she can slay him in the name of Artemis and the Furies (p. 29). Through her ominous words and tapestries, Clytemnestra transforms her husband's murder into a grand sacrifice (p. 34). In effect, when she enacts the trapping and killing of the king, she impersonates Artemis the Huntress (p. 40).

In sum, the more murderous Clytemnestra becomes, the more mother, human, and vulnerable she also becomes. In her act of destruction lies her creativity, that of "the Great Mother within the Terrible Mother" (p. 41). Clytemnestra first generates destiny in the person of her son, then she confirms it in her union with Aegisthus. The combination of her son and her deliberate union with Aegisthus secures her deadly fate and her son's subsequent trials. Thus, with majesty Clytemnestra "...embraces her fate. From that union [with Aegisthus] comes her death, from her death the liberation of her race. The play is named for Agamemnon, but the tragic hero is the queen" (p. 46).

8. The progress of civilization is a critical theme in Eliot's works. For a thorough analysis, see Bonaparte's *"Middlemarch."*

SIX. LILY BART

1. The text used here is the Norton Critical Edition, which reprints the original 1905 edition of Charles Scribner's Sons, under the editorship of Elizabeth Ammons.

2. Bart and Lawrence, perceiving their small world is a gilt cage and seeking to convert their lives into something better, are the text's alchemists. Lawrence talks with her: "The real alchemy consists in being able to turn gold back again into something else;" (p. 56). Bart is attracted by material marriages so that she may have the means to live a life of refinement and beauty, to turn all that gold into poetry, but the base realities of such a marriage continually repulse her. She and Lawrence finally succeed in discovering the golden word of love, but they do so at an enormous price and in a highly qualified fashion. In this way they are like Nathaniel Hawthorne's protagonists in *The Scarlet Letter*. Bart is as gifted and struggling as the fallen Hester Prynne, and Lawrence is a conflated Chillingworth and Dimmesdale, for he fluctuates between being a cold spectator and an impassioned but cowardly lover, both of whom were seeking transformation and treasures.

3. As a goddess-type who rules over boundaries, Lily Bart is like Nathaniel Hawthorne's Diana-maiden Pearl, who flits across the boundaries of all kinds of natural and supernatural spheres in *The Scarlet Letter*; like Charlotte Bronte's Jane Eyre, who encompasses the spirit of the fairy realm and the human one in herself; and like James Joyce's Molly Bloom, who reigns over the liminal points in *Ulysses*.

4. The care and intricacy with which Edith Wharton chose the names of her characters, and the derivation of those names from the myth of the moon goddess, has been studied by Carole Shaffer-Koros in relation to *The Glimpses of the Moon*. Shaffer-Koros documents that Wharton is re-telling the story of the great moon-mother goddess, Isis, of the Egyptians, with the main characters modelled on and acting out the annual quests of Isis, Osiris, and Seth. In that text, the hotel "Noveau Lux" is an allusion to Luxor, one of the Egyptian seats of the worship of Isis, "Lansing" is a reference to a famous archeologist of Egypt at that time, and the initials "N.L." [Nick Lansing] are meant to be, in essence, "Nile." His young wife Susy Branch is also linked imagistically to the moon.

Shaffer-Koros also delves into the general imagery of the novel, with the "red crown" being a symbol of Egyptian worship of Isis, or the "mongoose," the pet of the child Clarissa, being the animal sacred to Isis. Interestingly, the "drugged" states of the characters, on their boat journeys, Shaffer-Koros correlates to the rhythmic death and renewal of the moon. In *The House of Mirth*, Bart, too, undertakes such a significant journey, on the Dorset's yacht, from which she emerges further mortified after Bertha's expulsion of her from the yacht. This is prelude to her completely drugged state, on laudanum, and her final mortal death in the novel, but it is a death that finally frees her soul, and Selden Lawrence's, to true love.

5. The name is not unsimilar to that of another heroic young female, Susy "Branch," of Wharton's *The Glimpses of the Moon*. The title indicates the centrality of the mytheme of the moon goddess to that novel. Susy "Branch" fares better than "Bart," perhaps, because *The Glimpses of the Moon* is essentially a comic novel whereas *The House of Mirth* is a tragic one.

6. Edith Wharton experiments on this theme in *The Glimpses of the Moon* also, a text replete with images of boats, water, "drugged" states, and separations and re-unions around Susy Branch, who is clearly typed after the moon goddess Isis (Shaffer-Koros).

7. The ideal beauty of gems figures throughout The Book of Revelation, but the description of the holy city in the new heaven is the most significant:

> And the building of the wall of it was *of* jasper: and the city *was* pure gold, like unto clear glass.
>
> And the foundations of the wall of the city were garnished with all manner of precious stones. The first foundation *was* jasper; the second, sapphire; the third, a chalcedony; the fourth, an emerald:
>
> The fifth, sardonyx; the sixth, sardius; the seventh, chrysolite; the eighth, beryl; the ninth, a topaz; the tenth, a chrysoprasus; the eleventh, a jacinth; the twelfth, an amethyst.
>
> And the twelve gates *were* twelve pearls, every several gate was of one pearl: and the street of the city *was* pure gold, as it were transparent glass (*The Holy Bible*, 21:18-21).

8. The point here is not Wharton's intentions but the blend itself of Greek and Hebraic themes. This idea has gripped Western thought, especially modern Western thought. In literature, for instance, there is James Joyce's blend of "Jewgreek is greek jew" in *Ulysses*, in social criticism there is Matthew Arnold's analysis of Hebraism and Hellenism as the two points of influence which move our world in *Culture and Anarchy*, and in philosophy we have Derrida's exploration of this motif in *Writing and Difference* (pp. 79; 153).

9. One reason is that Romantic tragedy is itself so infused with Biblical and Greek elements.

CONCLUSION

1. See Dorothy Jones's "The Goddess, the Artist, and the Spinster" for an intricate analysis of this phenomenon [cf. *Westerly* (1984), 29:77-88].

❧ WORKS CITED

Abbott, Sally. "Artemis: The Pre-Homeric Source of Marion Tweedy Bloom." *James Joyce Quarterly* (1986), 23:497-500.

Abrams, M.H. *The Mirror and the Lamp: Romantic Theory and the Critical Tradition.* New York: Oxford University Press, 1953.

Apuleius, Lucius. *The Golden Ass: Being the Metamorphoses of Lucius Apuleius.* Ed. Rev. S. Gaselee. Trans. William Adlington. New York: G.P. Putnam's Sons, 1935.

Ariosto, Ludovico. *Orlando Furioso.* Trans. Barbara Reynolds. New York: Penguin English Library, 1981.

Bellange, Jacques. *The Hunter Orion Carrying Diana on His Shoulders.* Frick Art Reference Library, New York.

Blake, William. *Hecate.* Frick Art Reference Library, New York.

Boccaccio, Giovanni. *Nymphs of Fiesole.* Trans. Joseph Tusiani. Rutherford, N.J.: Fairleigh Dickinson University Press, 1971.

Bonaparte, Felicia. "*Middlemarch*: The Genesis of Myth in the English Novel: The Relationship Between Literary Form and the Modern Predicament." *Notre Dame English Journal: A Journal of Religion in Literature* (1981), 8:107-54.

———. *The Triptych and the Cross: The Central Myths of George Eliot's Poetic Imagination.* New York: New York University Press, 1979.

———. *Will and Destiny.* New York: New York University Press, 1975.

Bowen, Zack. *Ulysses as a Comic Novel.* Syracuse, New York: Syracuse University Press, 1989.

Briffault, Robert. *The Mothers: A Study of the Origins of Sentiments and Institutions.* 3 vols. 1927 1st ed. New York: MacMillan Co., 1969 rpt.

Bronte, Charlotte. *The Complete Poems of Charlotte Bronte.* Ed. Clement Shorter. New York: George H. Doran, Co., 1971.

———. *Jane Eyre.* Ed. Richard J. Dunn. 2d ed. New York: W. W. Norton & Co., Inc., 1987.

———. *Villette.* New York: Bantam Books, 1986.

Brownstein, Rachel. *Becoming a Heroine: Reading About Women In Novels.* New York: Viking Press, 1982.

———. "Representing the Self: Arnold and Bronte on Rachel." *Browning Institute Studies: An Annual of Victorian Literary and Cultural History* (1985), 13:1-24.

Ciardi, John. "How To Read Dante." In John Ciardi, ed., *The Purgatorio*, pp. 339-50. New York: New American Library, 1961.

Colacurcio, Michael J. "'The Woman's Own Choice': Sex, Metaphor, and the Puritan 'Sources' of *The Scarlet Letter.*" *New Essays on* The Scarlet Letter. Ed. Michael J. Colacurcio. Cambridge: Cambridge University Press, 1985.

Comparetti, Domenico. *Virgil in the Middles Ages.* New York: Macmillan & Co., 1895.

Dante, Alighieri. *The Inferno.* Trans. John Ciardi. New York: Mentor Books, 1982.

———. *Paradiso.* Trans. Allen Mandelbaum. New York: Bantam Library, 1986.

———. *The Purgatorio.* Trans. John Ciardi. New York: New American Library, 1961.

Day, Robert. "Dante, Ibsen, Joyce, Epiphanies, and the Art of Memory." *James Joyce Quarterly* (1988), 25:357–62.

Derrick, Scott. "Prometheus Ashamed: The Scarlet Letter and the Masculinity of Art." In Harold Bloom, ed., *Nathaniel Hawthorne's* The Scarlet Letter. New York: Chelsea, 1986.

Derrida, Jacques. *Writing and Difference*. Chicago: The University of Chicago Press, 1978.

Diane de Versailles, Louvre, Paris. Frick Art Reference Library, New York.

Dunn, Richard J., ed. *Jane Eyre*. By Charlotte Bronte. New York: W.W. Norton & Co., 1987.

Eagleton, Terry. "Jane Eyre's Power Struggles." In Richard J. Dunn, ed., *Jane Eyre*, 2d ed. New York: W. W. Norton & Co., 1987.

Ekhtiar, Shelly. Professional Correspondence. The State University of New York at Oswego, 26 June 1995.

Eliot, George. *Daniel Deronda*. Ed. Graham Handley. New York: Oxford University Press, 1991.

Ellman, Richard. "Why Molly Bloom Menstruates." *Joyce: A Collection of Critical Essays*. Ed. William M. Chace. Englewood-Cliffs, NJ: Prentice Hall, Inc. 1974.

Emerson, Ralph Waldo. "Self-Reliance." In George Perkins *et al*, eds., *The American Tradition in Literature*, vol. one, pp. 1134–1150. New York: McGraw-Hill Pub. Co., 1990.

Essick, Robert N., ed. *William Blake at the Huntington: An Introduction to the William Blake Collection in the Henry E. Huntington Library and Art Gallery*. San Murno, Calif: Harry N. Abrams Inc., Pubs. with the Henry E. Huntington Library and Art Gallery, 1994.

Fagles, Robert and W.B. Stanford. "The Serpent and the Eagle." In Robert Fagles, trans., *The Oresteia*, pp. 13–97. New York: Penguin English Library, 1988.

Floris de Vriendt, Frans I. *Diana with a Hound* (so-called "Portrait of Queen Elizabeth as Diana"). Frick Art Reference Library, New York.

Frye, Northrop. *Anatomy of Criticism: Four Essays*. Princeton: Princeton University Press, 1957.

———. *A Natural Perspective*. New York: Columbia University Press, 1965.

Gerber, Richard J. "More on Isis in 'Nausicaa'." *James Joyce Quarterly* (1988). 25:519–20.

Graves, Robert. *The Greek Myths*. 2 vols. New York: Penguin Books Ltd., 1984.

———. *The White Goddess*. New York: Farrar, Straus and Giroux, 1948.

Gross, Seymour, *et al*, eds. *The Scarlet Letter*. 3rd ed. New York: W. W. Norton & Co., 1988.

Gustafson, Fred. *The Black Madonna*. Boston: Sigo Press, 1990.

Hairston, Maxine. "Diversity, Ideology, and Teaching Writing." *College Composition and Communication* (May 1992), vol. 43, no. 2.

Hardy, Barbara. "Notes." In Barbara Hardy, ed., *Daniel Deronda*, pp. 885–903. New York: Penguin English Library, 1967.

"Harlot." *The Oxford English Dictionary*, 2d ed. Oxford: Clarendon Press, 1989.

Hawthorne, Nathaniel. *The Scarlet Letter: A Romance*. In George Perkins *et al*, eds., *The American Tradition in Literature*, vol. one, pp. 1688-1804. 7th ed. New York: McGraw-Hill Pub. Co., 1990.

Heemskerck (the Elder), M.J. van. *Allegory of Nature*. Frick Art Reference Library, New York.

Heilbrun, Carolyn G. *Toward A Recognition of Androgyny: A Search into Myth and Literature To Trace Manifestations of Androgyny and To Assess Their Implications for Today*. New York: W. W. Norton & Co., 1973.

Heilman, Robert B. "Charlotte Bronte, Reason, and the Moon." *Nineteenth-Century Fiction* (1960), 14:283–302.

The Holy Bible. Authorized King James Version. Canada: World Bible Publishers, [n.d.].

Home, Robert. *John Hunter*. Frick Art Reference Library, New York.

Houdon, Jean Antoine. *Diana Huntress*. Frick Art Reference Library, New York.

Humpherys, Anne. Professional Correspondence. The Graduate Center of The City University of New York, May 1993.

———. "Locating the Popular Text." *Victorian Literature and Culture* (1991), 19:351–59.

Huntington, Anne Hyatt. *Diana*. Frick Art Reference Library, New York.

Hutchinson, Earl R., Sr. "Antiquity in *The Scarlet Letter*: The Primary Sources." *Studies in Literature* (1981), 13:99–110.

James, Henry. *The Portrait of a Lady*. Ed. Robert D. Bamberg. New York: W. W. Norton & Co., 1975.

Johnston, Sarah Iles. *The Development of Hekate's Archaic and Classical roles in the Chaldean Oracles and Related Mystic Literature*. Diss. Cornell University, 1987.

Joyce, James. *Ulysses*. Ed. Hans Walter Gabler with Wolfhard Steppe and Claus Melchor. New York: Random House, 1986.

Jung, Carl G. *Mysterium Coniunctionis*. Ed. Sir Herbert Read *et al*. Bolligen Series XX:14. Princeton: Princeton University Press, 1963.

Kerenyi, Karl. *Goddesses of the Sun and Moon*. Trans. Murray Stein. Dallas: Spring Publications, Inc., 1979.

Labovitz, Esther. *The Myth of the Heroine: The Female Bildungsroman in the Twentieth Century: Dorothy Richardson, Simone de Beauvoir, Doris Lessing, Christa Wolf*. 2d ed. New York: Peter Lang, 1988.

Lacan, Jacques. *Ecrits: A Selection*. Trans. Alan Sheridan. New York: W.W. Norton & Co., 1977.

Lady and the UNICORN: Touching. The Metropolitan Museum of Art, New York.

Lawrence, D.H. *Selected Essays*. Middlesex: Penguin Books in Association with William Heinemann, 1960.

Lewis, R.W.B. "Introduction." In *The House of Mirth*, pp. vii-xvi. New York: Bantam Books, 1986.

Long, Harry Alfred. *Personal and Family Names*. London: Hamilton, Adams, & Co., 1883.

MacAllister, Archibald T. "Introduction." In John Ciardi, trans., *The Inferno*, pp. xiii–xxvi. New York: Mentor Books, 1982.

MacCurdy, Raymond R. "The Bathing Nude in Golden Age Drama." *Romance Notes* (1959), 1:36–39.

——. "The Bathing Nude Revisited in Golden Age Poetry." *Res Publica Litterarum* (1982), 2:159–67.

McPherson, Hugo. *Hawthorne as Myth-Maker: A Study in Imagination.* Toronto: University of Toronto Press, 1971.

Mandelbaum, Allen. "Introduction." In *Paradiso*, pp. iix–xxii. New York: Bantam Books, 1986.

Male, Roy. *Hawthorne's Tragic Vision.* New York: W.W. Norton, 1957.

Martin, Luther. "The Scarlet Letter: A Is for Alchemy." *American Transcendental Quarterly* (1985), 58:31–42.

Milton, John. *Paradise Lost.* In Maynard Mack, ed., *Milton*, 2d ed., pp. 102–286. Englewood Cliffs, N.J.: Prentice-Hall, Inc., 1961.

Moglen, Helene. *Charlotte Bronte: The Self Conceived.* New York: W.W. Norton & Co., Inc., 1976.

Neumann, Erich. "On the Moon and Matriarchal Consciousness." In Patricia Berry, ed., *Fathers and Mothers*, 2d ed., pp. 210–230. Dallas, Texas: Spring Publications, Inc., 1991.

The New King James Bible. New Testament. New York: Thomas Nelson Pub., 1979.

Oldcorn, Anthony and Daniel Feldman, with Guiseppe Di Scipio. "Notes." In *Paradiso*, pp. 310–429. New York: Bantam Books, 1984.

Perkins, George, *et al* eds. *The Scarlet Letter.* In *The American Tradition in Literature*, vol. one, pp. 1668–1804. 7th ed. New York: McGraw-Hill Publishing Co., 1990.

Plato. *Theaetetus.* Trans. John McDowell. Oxford: Clarendon Press, 1973.

Plutarch. *De Iside et Osiride.* Trans. J. Gwyn Griffiths. University of Wales Press, 1970.

——. *Moralia.* 15 vols. Trans. Benedict Einarson and Phillip H. De Lacy. Cambridge: Harvard University Press, 1957.

Rickard, John S. "Isis on Sandymount." *James Joyce Quarterly* (1983), 20:356–58.

Ringe, Donald A. "Hawthorne's Psychology of the Head and Heart." *Critics on Hawthorne.* Ed. Thomas J. Roundtree. Coral Gables, FL: University of Miami Press, 1972.

Rubens, P.P. *Diana and Her Nymphs Departing for the Hunt.* Frick Art Reference Library, New York.

——. *Diana's Return from the Hunt.* Frick Art Reference Library, New York.

Saint-Gaudens, Augustus. *Diana.* Frick Art Reference Library, New York.

Sandys, George. *Ovid's Metamorphosis Englished, Mythologized, and Represented in Figures.* Eds. Karl K. Hulley and Stanley T. Vandersall. Lincoln: University of Nebraska Press, 1970.

Scott, Bonnie Kime. *James Joyce.* Atlantic Highlands, NJ: Humanities Press International, 1987.

——. *Joyce and Feminism.* Bloomington: Indiana University Press, 1984.

Scott, Sir Walter. *Rob Roy*. London: J.M. Dent & Sons, Ltd. 1962.

Shaffer-Koros, Carole. "Egyptian Mythology and *The Glimpses of the Moon*." Lecture, Modern Language Association Convention, San Diego, 29 December 1994.

Sidney, Sir Philip. *Arcadia*. Ed. Maurice Evans. New York: Penguin English Library, 1977.

Smith, Susan Finkel. *Diana and the Renaissance Allegory of Love*. Diss. Princeton University, 1979.

Spenser, Edmund. *The Faerie Qveene*. Ed. J.C. Smith and E. de Selincourt. London: Oxford University Press, 1970.

Swann, Charles. "Alchemy and Hawthorne's Elixir of Life Manuscripts." *Journal of American Studies* (1988), 22:371–387.

Tayler, Irene. *Holy Ghosts: The Male Muses of Emily and Charlotte Bronte*. New York: Columbia University Press, 1990.

Thackeray, William Makepeace. *The History of Henry Esmond*. New York: Penguin English Library, 1985.

Titian. *Diana and Acteon*. Frick Art Reference Library, New York.

——. *Diana and Callisto*. Frick Art Reference Library, New York.

——. *Titian's Daughter, Lavinia, as Diana, Goddess of the Chase*. Frick Art Reference Library, New York.

Tolomeo, Diane. "The Final Octagon of *Ulysses*." *James Joyce Quarterly* (1973), 10:439–54.

Trachey, Carole Law. *The Mythology of Artemis and Her Role in Greek Popular Religion*. Diss. Florida State University, 1977.

Unkeless, Elaine. "The Conventional Molly Bloom." *Women in Joyce*. Ed. Suzette Henke & Elaine Unkeless. Chicago: University of Illinois Press, 1982.

Vickery, John B. *The Literary Impact of The Golden Bough*. Princeton: Princeton University Press, 1973.

Virgil. *The Aeneid*. Trans. Allen Mandelbaum. New York: Bantam Books, 1981.

Vivan, Itala. "An Eye into the Occult of Hawthorne's Text: The Scar in the Letter." *Quaderni di lingue e letterature* (1983), 8:71–107.

Wharton, Edith. "Artemis to Actaeon." *Artemis to Actaeon and Other Verse*. New York: Charles Scribner's Sons, 1909.

——. *The House of Mirth*. Ed. Elizabeth Ammons. New York: W. W. Norton & Co., 1990.

Wilbur, Richard, ed. *Jonson, Ben*. New York: Dell Publishing Co., 1961.

Wright, Dorena Allen. "The Meeting at the Brook-Side: Beatrice, the Pearl-Maiden, and Pearl Prynne." *Emerson Society Quarterly: A Journal of the American Renaissance* (1982), 28:112–120.

↬ INDEX

Gil Haroian-Guerin received her Ph.D. in English Literature from The Graduate Center of The City University of New York. She has published widely in scholarly and literary journals. Her fiction has won the Jerome Lowell DeJur Award and a Goodman Fund Grant.

Writing About Women
Feminist Literary Studies

This is a literary series devoted to feminist studies on past and contemporary women authors, exploring social, psychological, political, economic, and historical insights directed toward an interdisciplinary approach.

The series is dedicated to the memory of Simone de Beauvoir, an early pioneer in feminist literary theory.

Persons wishing to have a manuscript considered for inclusion in the series should submit a letter of inquiry, including the title and a one-page abstract of the manuscript to the general editor:

Professor Esther K. Labovitz
Department of English
Pace University
Pace Plaza
New York, NY 10038
(212) 488-1416

DATE DUE

MAY 2 1 1996			
APR 3 0 2004			
AUG 2 9 2005			